Agriculture in World History

Civilization from its origins has depended on the food, fiber, and other commodities produced by farmers. In this unique exploration of the world history of agriculture, Mark B. Tauger looks at farmers, farming, and their relationships to non-farmers from the classical societies of the Mediterranean and China through to the twenty-first century.

Viewing farmers as the most important human interface between civilization and the natural world, *Agriculture in World History* examines the ways that urban societies have both exploited and supported farmers, and together have endured the environmental changes and crises that threatened food production.

Accessibly written and following a chronological structure, *Agriculture in World History* illuminates these topics through studies of farmers in numerous countries all over the world from antiquity to the contemporary period. Key themes addressed include the impact of global warming, the role of political and social transformations, and the development of agricultural technology. In particular, the book highlights the complexities of recent decades: increased food production, declining numbers of farmers, and environmental, economic, and political challenges to increasing food production against the demands of a growing population. This wide-ranging survey will be an indispensable text for students of world history, and for anyone interested in the historical development of the present agricultural and food crises.

Mark B. Tauger is an associate professor of history at West Virginia University. He has published extensively on famines and agriculture in the USSR and India. His work has won the Eric Wolf Prize of the *Journal of Peasant Studies* and the Wayne D. Rasmussen Award of the Agricultural History Society.

Themes in World History

Series editor: Peter N. Stearns

The Themes in World History series offers focused treatment of a range of human experiences and institutions in the world history context. The purpose is to provide serious, if brief, discussions of important topics as additions to textbook coverage and document collections. The treatments will allow students to probe particular facets of the human story in greater depth than textbook coverage allows, and to gain a fuller sense of historians' analytical methods and debates in the process. Each topic is handled over time – allowing discussions of changes and continuities. Each topic is assessed in terms of a range of different societies and religions – allowing comparisons of relevant similarities and differences. Each book in the series helps readers deal with world history in action, evaluating global contexts as they work through some of the key components of human society and human life.

Gender in World History
Peter N. Stearns

Consumerism in World History:
the global transformation of desire
Peter N. Stearns

Warfare in World History
Michael S. Neiberg

Disease and Medicine in World History
Sheldon Watts

Western Civilization in World History
Peter N. Stearns

The Indian Ocean in World History
Milo Kearney

Asian Democracy in World History
Alan T. Wood

Revolutions in World History
Michael D. Richards

Migration in World History
Patrick Manning

Sports in World History
David G. McComb

The United States in World History
Edward J. Davies, II

Agriculture in World History

Mark B. Tauger

Routledge
Taylor & Francis Group

LONDON AND NEW YORK

First published 2011
by Routledge
2 Park Square, Milton Park, Abingdon, Oxon OX14 4RN

Simultaneously published in the USA and Canada
by Routledge
711 Third Avenue, New York, NY 10017

Routledge is an imprint of the Taylor & Francis Group, an informa business

© 2011 Mark B. Tauger
The right of Mark B. Tauger to be identified as author of this work has been
asserted by him in accordance with sections 77 and 78 of the Copyright,
Designs and Patents Act 1988.

Typeset in Times New Roman by Taylor & Francis Books

British Library Cataloguing in Publication Data
A catalogue record for this book is available from the British Library

Library of Congress Cataloging in Publication Data
Tauger, Mark B.
Agriculture in world history / Mark B. Tauger. -- 1st ed.
p. cm. -- (Themes in world history)
ISBN 978-0-415-77386-7 (hardback) -- ISBN 978-0-415-77387-4
(pbk.) -- ISBN 978-0-203-84748-0 (ebook) 1. Agriculture--History. I. Title.
II. Series: Themes in world history.
S419.T38 2010
630.9--dc22
2010027391

ISBN13: 978-0-415-77386-7 (hbk)
ISBN13: 978-0-415-77387-4 (pbk)
ISBN13: 978-0-203-84748-0 (ebk)

I dedicate this book to the memory of my father,
Herbert Tauger

Contents

Acknowledgements

I would like to thank all the people who helped me in researching and writing this book, but especially:

Gary Halvorson, Senior Archivist of the State of Oregon, for providing me with a full-size digital version of the cover photo from the state's archives;

My wife, Attorney Eva Segert-Tauger, Ph.D., for discussions, editing, and encouragement;

James Scott for inviting me to speak at one of his seminars at Yale University, and for his seminar syllabus which was an inspiration for my work;

Peter Stearns, Emily Kindleysides, Victoria Peters, and an anonymous reader for valuable assistance and patience in the completion of this project;

My colleagues at the WVU History Department for its open-minded encouragement of my research, publication, and teaching in new fields, the WVU Library staff for providing rapid access to publications by purchase or ILL, and Professor William Bryan of the WVU Davis College of Agriculture for valuable discussions and opportunities to contribute to the WVU Organic Farm Project;

The Agricultural History Society, and Tom Brass and *The Journal of Peasant Studies* for their recognition of my work and the model they have provided of multidisciplinary studies of agrarian history.

Introduction

The place of agriculture and farmers in world history

This book is pa[rt] ... [th]emes in
World History," ... [fo]r use in
undergraduate wo... [un]iversities
in the U.S. and o... [course]s in this
growing series are... [t]he topic
of agriculture has...

While all of th[e] ... [civiliz]ation or
important produc... [th]at made
civilization possi[ble] ... [c]onstruct
large permanent s... [abl]e-bodied
members to specialize ... [to] societies
must have had systems o... [were] not in a
position to form governme[nt] ... [sc]ale trade
and markets, sophisticated writing and education systems, and other elements
of a full-scale civilization. A civilization with those elements required the
production of a reliable and substantial surplus of food before anything else.
That surplus would free a significant group of people from food production,
allowing them to develop the specializations necessary for a civilization. The
anthropologist Robert Redfield in the 1950s contrasted civilization's advanced
culture, what he called the "great tradition," with the peasants' folkways or
"little tradition." Yet that great tradition utterly depended on that little
tradition for its survival.

Agriculture was thus prior to and a prerequisite for civilization. Farmers
supported civilization by producing crops and livestock, work which placed
farmers in continual interaction with the natural environment. Farmers thus
served as the interface between civilization and the environment. The
problem that is the main focus of this book, however, is that civilizations did
not simply rely on farmers, but most of the time dominated and exploited
them. The relationships between farmers and urban civilization, and between
farmers and their environment, were highly complex, but in general, in
both relationships, the farmers were subordinate: a pattern I call the dual
subordination.

[Handwritten note:]
Ag made civilization possible
Civilization — surplus or food
Farmers supported by
producing crops / livestock
(middlemans)
Subordinate farmers

This book examines these relationships between farmers, environment, and the civilizations that depended on farmers. It describes and analyzes the changes in these relationships in the main world civilizations. In particular it focuses on the actions of the small but important groups of reformers, from politicians to scientists to groups of farmers, who tried to reduce farmers' subordination and improve their lives. Such groups had limited success at first, but in more recent times they increasingly won their case, so that by the modern period the status of most farmers improved greatly.

Yet this improvement was qualified, even ironic, because as reforms eliminated most of the old oppressions, though not completely and not everywhere, new and greater problems emerged. These problems, such as global warming, declining oil production, environmental pollution, debt, and the declining numbers of farmers, are issues of great importance for both farmers and those who depend on them. This book seeks to provide a long-term historical perspective on many of these issues. This long perspective provides a moderate optimism that people have survived a quite difficult, even disastrous, agrarian crises, and at least have the potential to overcome the present ones.

My approach here is chronological, because farming systems had a history of conflict and development over time. This approach also makes this book more compatible with survey courses. The nature of agrarian history and its sources, however, required certain compromises. Despite the importance of South Asia in the modern period, there is so little evidence about South Asian farming before the Mughal period that it is not discussed until Chapter 4. Certain processes have their most important part in one period but their roots in an earlier one, and it would fragment the story too much to discuss that beginning in one chapter and the sequel in the next. So the discussion of Chinese collectivization in Chapter 7 begins with the late nineteenth century and reviews the early twentieth century, topics that might have been included in Chapters 5 and 6. For the most part, however, the chapters are chronologically cohesive and discrete.

This book relied on many sources, both primary and secondary. I have listed the main sources, mostly books and a few of the articles, in the suggested readings. These readings and their bibliographical sources will lead interested readers to additional sources. Agrarian history is a growth field, with important new publications and findings appearing regularly. Certainly new research can qualify or challenge some of the information and views presented here. I present this book as an introduction for students, a possible overall interpretation for scholars, and as an encouragement for discussion and further work for all interested readers.

Chapter 1

The origins of agriculture and the dual subordination

The origins of agriculture are visible to us today only from archaeological digs and studies of foraging societies and groups that survived into the twentieth century. Western ideas about agricultural origins began when Europeans encountered "primitive" peoples, who were often foragers and knew little or nothing about farming. Other investigations showed that humans and their societies and technologies had evolved during long evolutionary periods that came to be called Paleolithic and Neolithic, that crop plants and domesticated animals of the world's agricultural systems had definite geographical and temporal origins.

These findings led by the 1930s to the idea that early humans had developed agriculture in a "Neolithic Revolution" approximately 10,000 years ago, in response to a drying climate after the end of the last Ice Age. This shift to agriculture led to the development of cities and civilization some 5,000 years later. In this view, farming first developed in the "fertile crescent" of Mesopotamia, where the local flora and fauna included the wild progenitors of the main domesticated food crops and animals.

New archaeological research has qualified this conception of the first "agricultural revolution." Several scholars argued that the shift to farming was so rapid that it must have been preceded by "protoagriculture" for thousands of years before the Neolithic period. A cool and dry period about 11,000 years ago, the Younger Dryas, was followed by a warmer period favorable for the spread of plants and animals in the Near East. New research and rethinking of the evidence have shown that some of the presumed centers of agricultural development actually acquired the idea and techniques of farming from one or more of the smaller number of earlier centers. Studies of human remains from the periods before and after the shift to farming, and of modern surviving pre-agricultural peoples, have led to more complex and uncertain explanations for the shift to agriculture and evaluations of its nutritional, social, and political consequences.

The Earth's changing climate, especially its history of ice ages, served as the background for these developments. The last expansion of the ice sheets peaked about 20,000 years ago and then receded. By 14,000 BCE the planet *[handwritten margin note:]* "Pleistocene Extinctions" = disappearance of large Animals after the Ice Age b/c of overhunting by Man.

round 11,000 BCE a brief resurgence d glaciers for several centuries. By ent period or Holocene began.

d until by about 5000 BCE they may now. Climate in the equatorial and hid; much of the Sahara desert until wth. These were ideal conditions for world.

e first farmers

estors foraged and hunted for their eriodically settled in certain places the Paleolithic era human remains include mainly bones of relatively larger animals. Starting about 50,000 years ago, however, the proportion of large animal remains declines, while that of birds, fish, and other small animals increases. Sites in the Near East show that beginning at least 23,000 years ago people began to gather increasing amounts of a wide range of plants, in   that would later be domesticated. This shift, the "Br   lution," resulted from increasing human populations in   nd also from the "Pleistocene Extinctions," the disappea   nals after the Ice Age, which many scholars attribute to   y man.

Remains from the last millennia of   n Period suggest that people engaged in protoagricultur   removing unde- sirable plants from stands of desirable   d food, burning fields and then returning to them to gat   sowing gathered seeds. The Qadan sites in the upper N   appeared there about 13,000 BCE, and used grinding   for cutting and grinding wild crops. After 11,000 BCE,   red, the people returned to a more primitive level of fo   doned the sites because of the drying and cooling e   r Dryas. Their remains also include people killed by a   weapons, so the abandonment could have resulted from   gn invasions.

Studies in Central America, Asia, a   ve found many sites with evidence of semi-agricultural   the remains of an increasing variety of animals, in use a thousands of years before the Neolithic developments. The Broad Spectrum Revolution overlapped with the experiments of protoagriculture. The crucial step was domestication.

People began to raise domesticated crops and livestock in several different regions of the world at different times. The archaeological evidence is uncertain on many points but agriculture probably developed in the Near East earlier and more fully than elsewhere. Evidence exists for domestication of plants in other regions at about the same time, but in these other areas (including China and South America) the agricultural systems developed into towns and historical states much later.

Archaeological remains from farmers differ from those found earlier. Remains of domesticated animals show that they generally had smaller bones than their wild ancestors, and include many more bones of young animals and diseased animals because human herding of them helped communicable diseases to spread among them. Domesticated grains, including wheat, barley, millet, and rice, differ from their wild counterparts in more subtle ways. Grains, like other grass seeds, take the form of spikelets that contain a small seed with a heavy protective husk or glume, and attach to the stem of the plant by a small stem called a rachis. In wild grains, evolution favors plants with a weak or brittle rachis that allows the mature seeds to scatter easily, and with a glume that protects the seed long enough for it to sprout the following season. Domesticated grains, as a result of selection by early farmers, developed larger seeds with a lighter or smaller glume and a tough rachis that holds the grains much more securely in the plant.

The archaeological record shows that human settlements at various sites in the eastern Mediterranean littoral, ranging from the low mountain ranges in what is now southern Turkey, the Levant (present-day Israel, Lebanon, and Syria), and upper Mesopotamia had domesticated wheat, rye, sheep, goats, and pigs, and to a lesser extent cattle, by 9000–8500 BCE. This region was unusually rich in the "raw materials" for agriculture. It had many large wild animal species, like sheep and goats, that were social "herd" animals, amenable to domestication. It had numerous wild varieties of grains, legumes, and other plants, capable of rapid genetic variation in response to environmental changes, including human-generated ones. After the Younger Dryas the region had a stable climate, which allowed changes that enabled domestication to take hold.

As these people became more agricultural, they began living in larger settlements, villages of ten to sixteen hectares, almost the size of a small town. Their buildings were larger and remains include religious symbols, from sculptures of voluptuous women, which most scholars consider to have been goddess-figures, to rooms or buildings that appear to have been monuments or shrines, because of their wall paintings and separation from other structures. The settlements have special rooms or even buildings filled with human remains buried in a ritualized way or manipulated, such as skulls coated with plaster and with cowrie shells inserted in the eye sockets. Some argue that the beginnings of religion preceded and supported agricultural development by changing people's attitudes toward nature. After 7000 BCE many of the settlements shrank or were abandoned, but many new agricultural villages were founded in neighboring regions as people moved from the earlier centers of domestication.

Farming spread from about 8000 BCE around the Mediterranean. In the Balkans, Greece, and Italy, farming villages appear from 7500 BCE. After

7000 BCE farming villages emerge in northern Europe, with remains of cattle and pigs, more suited to northern regions than the sheep and goats of the Mediterranean environment. These villagers cleared thousands of farms in the European forests by 6000 BCE. They did not reach the North Sea and England until some time later.

Despite the size and significance of the later historical Egyptian farming system, Egypt did not have the wild wheat or other crops of Southwest Asia. The early Egyptians during the Ice Age hunted, fished, and foraged. The protoagriculture of the Younger Dryas period had disappeared by the time of the earliest archaeological evidence of farming in the Nile, from 5500 BCE, which already had the complex of plants and animals of the farming settlements of Southwest Asia. The remains of sites such as Fayum, an agricultural region near the Nile delta, have characteristic Egyptian artifacts but clearly Southwest Asian farming, which was the basis for the great development of the Egyptian state around 4000 BCE.

The settlements that became the Mesopotamian city-states are located in the southeast end of the valley of the Tigris and Euphrates rivers. These regions were rich with wildlife, and hunting and fishing remained important food sources. Farmers here used the Southwest Asian complex as the Egyptians did, but had to learn to adapt it to the flood cycle of the rivers. Regulating this process and organizing people to deal with it gave rise to city-states and eventually the imperial states of the Ancient Near East.

The pattern of the development of agriculture in these core regions followed by dissemination to neighboring regions recurred in China and America. The new region often had its own domesticated food sources. In most cases, however, once the core region's farming complex was introduced, it became dominant.

China

China was less affected by the Ice Ages and as a result has ancient, deep and rich soils as well as plant species, like the gingko, that are "living fossils" dating back before large-scale glaciations. In particular, north-central China, where its people first began farming, had loess or aeolian soils, formed from wind-blown sediments, which are fertile and easily worked. China is also relatively flat and traversed by several major rivers that provided water sources and transport.

Sites in central China near the Yangtze River show that people were gathering wild rice and millet by at least 12,000 BCE. Early villages during the seventh millennium BCE in north-central China and south of the Yangtze have remains of domesticated rice and millet. While both crops were found in both regions, the evidence indicates that millet remained the main crop in the north, while rice came to dominate around and especially south of the Yangtze.

Wild millet was native to China, and by 5000 BCE a substantial population of Chinese farmers cultivated millet extensively in many settlements, consuming it as boiled whole grain and ground into flour. They lived in villages of five hectares or larger, with sunken houses and storage pits that in one site could hold 100 tons of grain. Early Chinese written sources indicate that millet was more important than rice through the first millennium BCE. The ancient Book of Odes emphasizes the importance of millet and has few references to rice. The ancestor of the ruling clan of the Chou dynasty, the longest-lived before the emergence of the Chinese Empire, was named "lord of millet" (Hou Chi).

At the same time many settlements south of the Yangtze grew rice. Remains at Hemudu, located on the central coast of China, include, in addition to tools and artifacts, rice husks and other evidence of more than 120 tons of rice. At this phase, Chinese farmers grew rice as either a dry field crop or in swamps or wetlands, both of which gave low yields but required relatively little work. The earliest evidence of wet-rice cultivation and transplanting (to be discussed more below) dates back only approximately to CE 100.

The Chinese also grew barley and wheat. These crops came much later and represented special, even luxury, foods. Chinese farmers also domesticated a legume later than the Near Eastern farmers, but one with an enormous future: soybeans. Sources from the Chou dynasty indicate that people were cultivating soy by 1000 BCE. By the eighth century BCE conquered peoples gave the Chou ruler soybeans as tribute, and by the fourth century BCE the two main Chinese crops were millet and soybeans. Farmers recognized that soy cultivation improved the soil, and may have suspected the reason, because the Chinese character for soybeans refers to the nodules on the roots of the plant, which were later shown to contain nitrogen-fixing bacteria.

China did not have the wild herd animals of the Near East and Europe. They domesticated pigs as their primary farm animal. The earliest sites had remains of pigs, as well as dogs, which were domesticated earlier and that in many parts of Asia were a food source as well. Some sites have remains of cattle, water buffalo, and goats, but pig remains are more widespread and numerous. The Chinese also appear to have independently domesticated chickens, the earliest remains of which were found in sites dating to 5400 BCE.

Southeast Asia

This region consists of two main parts: mainland Southeast Asia, including the present-day states of Myanmar, Thailand, Laos, Cambodia, Vietnam, and part of Malaysia, and island Southeast Asia that stretches from Taiwan through the Philippines, Indonesia, and the island chains in the south and central Pacific Ocean. These regions acquired agriculture relatively late, some only in the modern period.

Mainland Southeast Asia resembles southern China with many rivers, good soils, and monsoon rainfall patterns. Nonetheless, archaeologists have found evidence for food production in the region only from 3500 BCE. Agricultural production moved into the region slowly, some scholars argue, because foragers resisted the introduction of farming. When farming did begin in the region, its methods derived first from China to the north. Taiwan's first evidence of rice and millet cultivation dates back to 3500 BCE, but many sites have been found from slightly later periods. Rice cultivation spread from Taiwan to the Philippines and Indonesia.

Farming spread much more slowly through the island societies of Southeast Asia. These societies did not need agriculture urgently; these regions are generally quite rich in a wide variety of plant and animal food sources. Archaeological sites have vast remains of nuts, fruits, roots, and seeds, as well as wild birds and animals. Yet even in this region, highland New Guinea may have been an independent locale of domestication, as from 5000 BCE its inhabitants began domesticating taro, yams, and certain other crops, growing them in gardens.

South Asia

The prehistoric agriculture of South Asia, from present-day Afghanistan to Pakistan, India, and Bangladesh, combined indigenous components, such as humped cattle, with agricultural complexes from the Near East, Africa, and East Asia. The first clear evidence of agriculture in the subcontinent was found at Mehrgarh, west of the Indus River, and dates back to 7000 BCE. Remains at the region indicate the existence of a near-complete Near Eastern complex with wheat and barley, as well as the characteristic sheep, goats, and cattle. The Mehrgarh remains also contain the rectangular houses and female figurines similar to those found at the Near Eastern Neolithic sites.

This agricultural complex supported the Harappan or Indus valley civilization that began in the third millennium BCE. By the last phases of this civilization, 2600–1900 BCE, archaeologists found rice and millets from Asia, and sorghum and pearl millet from Africa. The Indus people apparently obtained these crops by trade, the African crops through Sumerian intermediaries and the rice via Southeast Asia and central India. By this time the Indus civilization had developed large and complex cities with elaborate but still untranslated symbols and language. Other regions of the subcontinent have remains of early farming that date back at most to the time of the late Harappan cultures. Their farming complexes include a similar blend of Asian rice, Near Eastern wheat and animals, and local South Asian plants and cattle.

Sub-Saharan Africa

Sub-Saharan Africa, a very large and diverse region, has limited remains from the Neolithic period. After the Ice Age, the Sahara was smaller and less arid, and the Sahel region of grasslands and savannah extended hundreds of miles further north than it does now. The region had a rainy season that formed lakes, and people lived there hunting wild cattle and other animals, and gathering grasses including wild sorghums and millets. These favorable conditions began to change by about 4000 BCE, and by 2000 BCE the Sub-Saharan environment resembled present-day conditions.

The most definite evidence for domestication of cattle dates back only to 3000 BCE. Plant domestication and farming came much later, 2000 BCE at the earliest, and in many parts of Sub-Saharan Africa much later. The staple plants in the region differed from those of the Near East: African rice in the west, several varieties of sorghum, pearl millet in the Sahel, teff (an Ethiopian small grain) and finger millet in Ethiopia, oil palms, cowpeas, and groundnuts. Africans domesticated both sorghum and millet in the Sahel region by 2000 BCE.

By that time, the Sahel region had a mixed-farming economy of crops and livestock. The Bantu migrations that began approximately 1500 BCE carried with them the farming methods of the innovators of the Sahel to the rest of Southern Africa. These techniques reached the Kalahari by the seventeenth century. During this expansion Africans also domesticated a native strain of rice, which originated in the western Sahel.

The Americas

People crossed the exposed land bridge at the Bering Straits at the latest by 11,500 BCE, and by 10,000 BCE had reached nearly the southern tip of South America. With very few exceptions, all of these now American peoples were hunter-foragers until about 3000 BCE. The two continents had few herd animals or wild grasses like those of the Near East. The development of agriculture in the Americas thus began later than in the Near East and much more rapidly, required a more dramatic transformation of wild plants into domesticates, and lacked most of the livestock component found in the old world. The early Americans produced two main staple crops in this period: maize and potatoes. Maize originated in central Mexico, potatoes in the foothills of the Andes in present-day Peru and Ecuador.

The earliest evidence of domesticated maize from caves in the Tehuacán valley of south-central Mexico dates back to 2700 BCE. While the wild grain teosinte was the genetic ancestor of maize, it remains a mystery just how, where, and when early Mexicans transformed this small wild plant into maize, with much larger kernels and ears, by its earliest appearance around 2000 BCE. From this time, maize cultivation spread widely through Central America and into South and North America.

The domesticated potato likewise seems to date back to 3000–2000 BCE, although some investigations have found remains of wild tubers dating back to 10,000 BCE. The potato is only one of several types of tubers that people in the Andes domesticated and continue to grow; others include the root crops oca, ullucu, mashua, and bitter potatoes. In this period Andean peoples domesticated the llama, the alpaca, and the guinea pig. Other domesticates of local significance in the Americas include the grain quinoa in the Andean region, and certain seed plants in eastern North America.

Interpretations of the origins of agriculture

The arguments for protoagriculture and the limited but highly suggestive evidence for it, and the long period over which different societies developed or adopted farming, challenge the old concept of a Neolithic agricultural revolution. Everywhere the shift to farming was gradual and ambivalent. Before people began to farm, they had established a pattern of settling for seasons or years at a time. They expanded their foraging and hunting, apparently driving some larger species of animals into extinction. People continued to hunt and forage even while they settled and raised crops and livestock.

Recently archaeologists have argued that humans and certain plant and animal species changed together in a process of co-evolution. The plants and animals that people used became more productive and more amenable to domestication with human use. Adaptation also made people in turn more dependent on their crop plants and domesticated animals. Research also shows that as people shifted from hunter-gathering to broad spectrum foraging and then to farming, their physical condition generally deteriorated. Farmers in particular were physically smaller than foragers and more subject to disease.

These findings and arguments suggest broader interpretations of the human shift to agriculture. The economist Colin Tudge argued from the concept of protoagriculture that basic farming skills gave farmers advantages over neighboring non-farmers. Farmers could survive temporary declines in foraging and hunting food sources, which may have encouraged them to hunt more intensively, and might explain the Pleistocene extinctions of large animals; the hunters may have calculated they could fall back on raising plants if the animals disappeared.

This fall-back plan, in Tudge's view, turned out to be a trap. Farming increased food production and enabled more children to survive, which in turn obliged people to rely on farming to support the growing population. He notes that early writings such as Genesis in the Bible as well as archaeological findings emphasize how strenuous and difficult farming was and how people hated it. Some ancient myths, from the Epic of Gilgamesh to the Biblical conflict between Jacob and Esau, contrast the free but animal-like (e.g., hairy) hunter with the more civilized farmer, and in both stories show the farmer tricking the hunter into giving up his freedom for the attractions of civilized life.

An extreme version of the view that agriculture and civilization were a trap is Jared Diamond's essay that calls agriculture "The Worst Mistake in the History of the Human Race." Based on the evidence of the decline in physical condition from hunter-gatherers to farmers, Diamond argues that the expansion of agriculture spread epidemic disease, malnutrition, and famine. He then connects the emergence of agricultural societies to the development of social stratification, in which the farmers are always the lowest class or caste, and women the lowest status among farmers. Further, because farmers could produce more food and thereby support more people, farming societies could field large armies that pushed the remaining hunter-gatherers off their lands and destroyed them, or forcibly assimilated them to the farmers' state. He claims that agriculture's promise of abundance has never been realized.

These pessimistic views seek to challenge a common view of agriculture as progress, a great human discovery that made possible art, science, technology, urban life, and the other accomplishments of civilization. Among other factors, such pessimistic views have inspired much research into pre- or non-agricultural human societies. Some scholars even argue that people should return to a hunter-gatherer lifestyle as more natural and harmonious. Yet such views are as one-sided as the views they criticize.

The shift to farming did not logically require, for example, subordination of women or enslavement of the main laboring groups. There are agricultural societies where men, women, or both perform the main or most difficult jobs, and farming societies that were based on free labor. Studies of pre-agricultural societies have shown that many of them had or have social divisions without agriculture; some of them subordinated women or other groups. Such considerations undermine an exclusive connection between agriculture and social hierarchy and oppression. It seems unfair to blame agriculture for the decisions of leaders and social groups at different times and places to oppress or emancipate lower-status people.

The pessimistic interpretation overlooks the problem that agriculture solved. According to current views, people moved from ordinary foraging to the broad spectrum revolution because population growth had made the previous level of foraging impossible, and even then their physical condition worsened. This implies that successful foraging societies are likely to grow in population, deplete their main food sources, intensify foraging, and then either migrate in search of new sources or develop some sort of food production if they are to survive. Archaeology has documented all of these results, and the only one that has any long-term prospects is food production. It seems at least paradoxical for Diamond and others to criticize agriculture when in the long run agriculture was what made their lives and their culture possible.

The pessimistic interpretation also leaves out the exchanges of crops and livestock in certain key periods and places, which had both short- and long-term results of massively increasingly the quantity and quality of food produced worldwide. The Muslim transfer of Asian crops to Europe in the late Middle Ages, the Columbian exchange that began in the sixteenth century, and the global distribution of high-yielding varieties in the twentieth century, among others, all present a much more positive image of agriculture's potential than that of the critics of agriculture.

Perhaps most important, the pessimistic views raise many questions that call for further investigation. If agriculture was a trap and its development a mistake, then why did it happen at all? Did the few elites who benefited from agriculture force the much larger numbers of poor people to farm? How could that happen? And is that all that happened? After thousands of years of foraging, protoagriculture, domestication, and farming, villages and cultures, in the late-fourth- to third-millennium civilizations, emerge with clear social hierarchies in which farmers have an ambivalent position. They are clearly the economic basis of the society and the majority of the population, they were poor yet their history is considerably more complicated than a trap and a mistake. How can we explain this ambivalence?

The dual subordination

An analytical framework that I call the "dual subordination" can reveal much about the varied relationships between farmers and their natural and social environments. Farmers are dependent on the natural environment: the changing circumstances of water, soil, and weather, and the actions of animals, plants, and other life forms that can threaten farm production. In response to such threats, farmers have changed their farming methods or intensity, introduced new crops, or migrated in search of better lands and conditions. On the other hand, farmers through most of history have been subject to the rule of agencies outside their villages, usually urban authorities such as kings, armies, tax collectors, banks, and markets. In some cases farmers under extreme duress have risen up against towns and overthrown empires, or at least played an important role in a complex circumstance of regime change.

These two components of the dual subordination, environmental variation and political control, were usually self-limiting and contradictory. Governments and other authorities, such as noble landlords, maintained farmers in a low, subordinate status, as peasants, serfs, or slaves, keeping farmers politically weak to make sure that they work and pay their taxes and dues. Yet towns, governments, and other authorities are also dependent on farmers for their subsistence. Environmental crises that destroyed harvests, oppression, and neglect of farmers threatened the survival of groups outside the villages as well as those within them. This prospect sooner or later has led almost every government to introduce policies to improve farm production and alleviate the oppression of farmers through emancipation, reduced taxes or dues, subsidies for prices, credits for farm purchases, government investments in irrigation, power generation, and education.

The dual subordination implies an agrarian-centered – or farmer's eye view – of history. The human discovery of agriculture made civilization possible. Once people became civilized, in Sumer, Egypt, India, China, the Americas and beyond, agriculture remained at the base of civilizations in three key ways. First, civilizations – towns and cities, urban people, armies and leaders – all needed agriculture to survive. Second, the farmers worked at the interface between the natural world and human society, and served as a kind of "buffer" – natural disasters usually struck the farmers first and they were the people who had to deal with it most urgently. Third, farmers were the lowest or next-to-lowest social group, and were the largest occupational group by far in most of history.

In this sense, civilization acquires a different and less positive meaning than ordinarily assumed, although not quite as negative as Diamond's view. Most definitions of civilization emphasize its complexity, sophistication, development, and the opportunities civilization allowed for growth and change. From the farmers' perspective, however, civilization looks more like the dominion of the town over the village, of the townsman over the peasant. Civilization depends on what scholars who study Africa have termed a "captured" peasantry. This capture has taken a variety of forms, some indifferent or hostile to the farmers and some considerate and solicitous of the farmer. Famines historically have reflected these relationships as well. In some cases townspeople have extorted food from villages in crises or wars; in other cases the towns have rescued rural populations from natural or economic disasters. Social groups outside agriculture have played a variety of roles in farmers' dual subordination. In relatively few societies were farmers in power or allotted equal rights, or at least granted a significant degree of autonomy and protected from oppression.

The development and character of farmers and agriculture, and their relationship to groups outside the villages, are crucially important for our understanding of both the past and the contemporary world. The history of farmers and agriculture has great diversity but also key common themes, and includes some of the most dramatic aspects of human experience. This book focuses mainly on agricultural, economic, and social aspects of this history. In the broadest sense, it describes the chronic environmental crises that plagued agriculture, and the formation of servile agrarian systems in most world regions. It then outlines the rapid and accelerating processes of emancipation and modern technological developments that eliminated many traditional aspects of the dual subordination. These developments benefitted almost all farmers, but also changed the millennia-old patterns of farm–town interaction. In some places towns and farms have almost merged, with farmers living in towns and farming as a part-time occupation.

Yet this history has not ended. Modern societies have made great progress, but still have not resolved many of the problems that date back to the beginning of this history. Most farmers in the world are still subject to an unpredictable nature, and the demands of the townspeople, whether businesses, governments, or armies, appear today as persistent as ever.

Further reading

To find more information on many of these topics, see especially Colin Tudge, *Neanderthals, Bandits, and Farmers* (New Haven, CT: Yale University Press, 1998); Michael Balter, *The Goddess and the Bull* (New York: Free Press, 2005); Peter Bellwood, *First Farmers* (Oxford: Blackwell Publishers, 2005); Bruce Smith, *The Emergence of Agriculture* (New York: Scientific American Library, 1994); Ping-Ti Ho, *Cradle of the East* (Chicago: University of Chicago Press, 1975). Jared Diamond's essay is available at several internet sites.

Chapter 2

Agriculture in antiquity

The first great conflicts over land and freedom

Introduction

The earliest written text sources in history date back to the late fourth and early third millennium. These sources show that societies already had elaborate social hierarchies, both urban – with rulers, priests, soldiers, officials, traders – and rural – with landowners, farmers, and laborers. Many of these farmers and laborers were slaves. At one time scholars proposed that governments needed to force masses of people to work to manage water systems, or that the ancient world was based on a "slave mode of production." Very few scholars today accept either of these views.

Most farmers began as small-scale producers owing obligations such as taxes or labor to the government, whether city-state or empire. While sources on the earliest civilizations (Mesopotamia, Egypt, and South Asia) are too limited to document subsequent developments in any detail, in Greece, Rome, and China eventually a group of large landowners emerged, either members of a ruling elite or farmers who acquired more land at the expense of other farmers. These large landowners threatened to subordinate the small farmers to a degree that would transform the nature of the government. Some of the first social reformers in history attempted to reverse or at least slow down this transformation, with very limited success at best.

Greece

Ancient Greece, especially Athens, contributed central innovations and values to world civilization: political democracy, philosophy (including the "Socratic method"), and achievements in the arts. The basis for these was a crucial reform in the sixth century BCE by the Athenian ruler Solon, a reform that enabled Athens to escape the typical pattern of most of the other Greek *poleis* (city-states). To understand these circumstances we begin with Greece's Mediterranean environment and farming.

Greece, on the eve of civilization, was a highly forested region with rocky soils and a Mediterranean climate: hot and dry in summers and rainy and cool in the fall–winter period. The forests held the soil in place against rain and runoff. Most of the soils were thin, but the province of Messenia in the southern region of the Peloponnesus had very good soil, and the central region of Thessaly encompassed a large plain surrounded by mountains, the plain of Larisa, which had such fertile soil that it was called the breadbasket of Greece. This agricultural environment imposed limits on productivity, which meant that population could outgrow its resources.

To adapt to the Mediterranean climate Greek peasants relied on winter wheat, planted in fall and harvested the following spring, as their staple crop, in a two-year crop-fallow cycle. They also grew barley, lentils, apples, pears, figs, pomegranates, and especially olives, which they learned to process at least by 1000 BCE. They also raised livestock, including cattle, sheep, goats, and poultry (including chickens which reached Greece from India probably about 1000 BCE). The Greeks did not make any great breakthroughs in farming technology: they used simple tools, mostly wooden, such as the ard, a simple type of plow that scratches the soil. They sowed grain by casting seed by hand, covering it with a hoe, and harvested with a metal sickle. They had wine presses and olive mills.

Farmers served as the basis of the Greek military and political systems. These farmers would fight wars between work seasons of sowing and harvesting to defend their lands or expand them on the borders, but would always end their wars in time to perform farm tasks. They served as "hoplites," armored soldiers who fought in rectangular phalanxes with spears.

The Greeks appear to have employed two types of agricultural systems. One, typified by Sparta, was servile, based on the forced labor or serfdom of a neighboring population, imposed by conquest and maintained by violence. The other system, exemplified by Athens, was based mostly on privately owned farms of various sizes. Such farmers did own slaves, but those slaves played a minor role in farm work and were not a separate social group upon whom all the farming obligations were imposed. Much more important was hired labor and a tendency for better-off farmers to form larger farms.

Sparta and the servile systems

The servile systems were apparently the typical pattern that most early Greek poleis or city-states employed. The early Greek societies of Mycenae and Minoan Crete relied significantly on serf and slave farmers. In all documented cases, however, all of these servile systems were at least partly reversed by natural disasters, rebellions, invasions, and apparently a nascent sense of human rights. During 1200–1000 BCE invading peoples of various origins, the Sea Peoples, devastated Greece. During the subsequent "Dark

Ages," from 1700 to 1000 BCE, Greek civilization declined into a period of subsistence production, and localism, but also transformed itself with the establishment of the poleis, self-governing city-states.

By the classical period, about 600–400 BCE, the polis of Sparta managed a servile system of farming more oppressive than other states in the region. The Spartans settled in the Peloponnesian peninsula in the tenth century BCE, and established an oligarchic state like other Greeks. Unlike them, however, the Spartans transformed their state into a military colony in which virtually the entire Spartan population trained or prepared for war. To support this system, and to insulate themselves from attack, the Spartans in the eighth and seventh centuries conquered and subjugated the peoples near them. These included the Lacedaemonians, who lived in the same valley as the Spartans, and the Messenians, who lived in a neighboring region that included the polis Messenia. By defeating them, Sparta gained 8,500 square kilometers of some of the best farmland in Greece.

The Spartans then turned these conquered peoples into "helots." This term is of uncertain origin, but the Greeks defined this group as "between free and slave." The helots were considered the property of the Spartans as a whole, and employed to farm the land of particular Spartan families. The helots could have families, possessions, and could maintain their own religion, but they had to work hard to feed and provide for themselves and the Spartans. They had to turn over half of their produce to the Spartans. The Spartans attempted to maintain their domination by intimidating the helots. The Spartan rulers declared a state of war with them every year and allowed, even encouraged, Spartans to attack helots with impunity, and sometimes kill them.

The Messenians did not accept this status willingly, and rebelled several times. In 464 BCE a devastating earthquake struck Sparta, destroyed most of the city and caused many deaths. This weakened the polis' fighting ability and provided the opportunity for helot communities to rebel. Sparta could not suppress this rebellion, and it ended only by a truce. Athens evacuated the helot survivors and settled them in exile communities far from Sparta. In 371–369 the polis of Thebes defeated Sparta and separated Messenia from Spartan territory. This became a new city-state, inhabited by the former helots and the descendants of the rebels of the 460s, who had maintained a memory of the rebellion and developed an ideology of freedom and equality. This ideology found classic expression in writings such as the "Messenian Oration" of the Sophist Alkidamas, which declared "God has set all men free; nature has made no man a slave."

The Spartans were not the only polis dependent on the forced labor of the neighboring population. Many Greek poleis relied on dependent laborers for their farm workers. Aristotle in his *Politics* even argued that in an ideal polis, serfs or slaves from other regions or not of Greek origin should do the farm work for the citizens.

Athens and Solon's reforms

During the seventh century BCE, Athens underwent a process of agricultural change that threatened to create a system similar to these servile poleis. In the Archaic period and at least up to the sixth century BCE, clans owned their lands collectively, and individual members could not sell their land or use it as collateral for loans. Farmers used their own persons and family as collateral. Such families would often end up as tenants of a wealthier farmer and have to turn over most of their produce to him. Such dependent families were called *hektemors*, a term which includes the concept of one-sixth, but it is not clear from the sources whether the hektemor paid the creditor one-sixth or kept one-sixth of the produce. If the hektemor reached the point that he could not pay the debt, he and his family by law would become slaves and the creditor could sell him and his family.

Environmental and demographic factors contributed to the small farmers' growing poverty and indebtedness. Athens occupied only 2,600 square kilometers, less than one-third the area of Sparta and with poorer quality land. Farmers in Athens early on cut down trees to clear farmland, which led to erosion and depletion of soils and declining crops. Athenians shifted from cattle raising to more extensive grain farming to produce more food for the large and growing population. Where the Homeric epics depict an abundance of cattle, by the classical period Greeks ate mostly grains and legumes, and raised mostly goats and poultry. Greek farmers generally produced little more than subsistence, and Athens especially was frequently short of food.

By 600 BCE Athens faced an economic and social crisis. Many Athenians had become hektemors, essentially debt peons to landlords and others, and many had been enslaved and even sold. The polis authorities or creditors indicated the status of the hektemors by stones, *horoi*, on the lands, apparently as an indication that these people's crops were already committed to the creditors and could not be sold.

To deal with this crisis, the Athenian elite selected one of their own, Solon, as *archon*, a leader with nearly dictatorial powers, in 594 BCE. Solon then introduced reforms that compromised between the interests of the poor – mostly hektemors and slaves – and the wealthy elite. Solon ordered the annulment of all debts and contracts indicated by the horoi stones and prohibited loans on the security of individuals and their families. He freed all those enslaved for debt and apparently brought back to Athens people who had been enslaved for debt and sold elsewhere. Athenians called this set of laws the *Seisachtheia*, the lifting of burdens. Solon also introduced policies to make the Athenian economy more commercial. He encouraged the export of olives and oil but prohibited all other agricultural exports, and he advised fathers to teach their sons non-agricultural skills and trades and invited foreigners to Athens to contribute skills to the economy.

These policies evoked considerable controversy in Athens. Many hekte-mors had hoped to obtain their lands back. Solon refused to introduce a land reform. Instead his policies forced poorer farmers to surrender their lands for debt and become tenant farmers or laborers, working on large landlords' lands or in Athens. Solon's reforms thus protected the poorest people from slavery, but also served the interests of those with property, and sup-ported manufacturing and export trade. This export trade enabled Athens to import grain to meet perhaps half of the polis' needs, to defeat the Persians (in alliance with Sparta), and to produce the cultural creations of the fifth-century classical era. The reforms also prevented the formation of an enslaved laboring group like the helots.

The Peloponnesian Wars of the late fifth and early fourth centuries BCE devastated Athens and brought important changes to farming. Many families lost their male workers, others came back less capable of work, and rich farmers and townspeople were able to acquire abandoned or indebted lands and worked them with tenants and slaves. This change affected mostly the regions near Athens and other poleis; in more remote areas small farm-ers still predominated. The pattern was established for the Hellenistic period.

During the fourth century BCE, Athens and other Greek poleis faced periodic food shortages, and their technology limited their ability to improve soils and yields. Few of these city-states could resort to colonization like Athens; most had to control imports and distribution. Athens, which was dependent on imports, appointed 35 grain wardens to oversee imports, prevent misappropriation of grain, and regulate the profits of traders, millers, and bakers to prevent speculation and keep prices low. Solon's law prohibit-ing grain exports remained in place and many other poleis duplicated it. The polis of Teos made it a crime punishable by death to interfere with grain imports or hoard grain.

The difference between the servile poleis like Sparta and more democratic and apparently humane ones like Athens clearly derived in part from decision by leaders and elites, and reflected pre-existing attitudes. They also derived from environmental circumstances. Sparta controlled a much larger area of land and more productive land than Athens. These lands' higher productivity meant that reliance on a dependent peasantry, such as helots, would still provide reliable food supplies even if the peasants were hostile and resistant. A modicum of coercion combined with the natural high yields of the land insured that these peasants would produce a reliable surplus.

In Athens, with small farms on poor land, production for subsistence became a tenuous and difficult struggle, and the society could not leave this matter to a recalcitrant servile peasantry. This uncertain livelihood in turn meant that farmers would have a direct interest in the polis' politics, since every decision could have a bearing on their interests and survival. Athens' shift to a more commercial economy and increasing reliance on trade, which began with Solon and intensified into the fourth century BCE, altered this pattern. Now Athens essentially gave up the struggle with the environment. The commercial elite grew in numbers and wealth, and ordinary farmers frequently became landless laborers, an economic stratification quite different from that of Sparta.

Rome and the first struggle for land reform

Rome began as an agrarian city-state, which the Romans called a republic, similar to Athens, with small-scale farmers who fought to defend and extend their lands. During its early history, 1800–1500 BCE, Roman villagers grew the Mediterranean agricultural complex of grains, olives, and grapes for wine, and raised cattle, sheep, goats, and pigs.

By the end of the early period, Roman society had become highly stratified. Debt played an important role in this stratification. Debts created long-term relations between people of different status groups, and became one of the main ways the wealthy elites extended social control over ordinary and poor people, almost all of whom were peasants. According to Roman laws as codified in the Twelve Tables, if a debtor did not or could not repay his debt on time, creditors could seize a debtor's property, sell the debtor into slavery, or impose debt-bondage, in Latin *nexum*, requiring the debtor to work for the creditor until the wages he earned paid off the debt.

The history of the Roman Republic, and especially its decline, is linked to agrarian history in several ways. From the sixth century BCE Rome had two main political classes whose status reflected in large part control over land. The patricians were the main landowners, the military officers, and exercised almost exclusive political authority. The plebeians initially included small farmers, and also tenants who worked the patricians' lands, served them as clients, and fought as their soldiers. Overlapping with these were six socio-economic classes, from the senatorial class, the wealthiest property holders, to the proletarii who owned no property.

During the fifth to fourth centuries BCE, in the "struggle of the orders," plebeians won concessions from the patricians that ultimately gave the plebeians power in Rome nearly equal to that of the patricians. The plebeians gained their own legislature, the Tribal Assembly, to balance the patricians' Senate, and the right to send elected tribunes to veto Senate legislation and propose legislation in the Tribal Assembly. The senatorial counterparts to the tribunes were consuls, who were the top military leaders of the Republic, but who did not have the right to intervene in the plebeian Tribal Assembly. By the second century BCE the distinction between plebeians and patricians had declined. Many plebeians had become wealthy and powerful, ranked as nobles, served as consuls and in other high posts, and could marry patricians.

Rome's military expansion also involved attacks on enemies' agriculture. This expansion had long-term effects on agriculture. From the fourth to the early second centuries BCE, Rome engaged in a series of defensive wars in which Rome conquered Italy and much of North Africa. The wars expanded Rome's territory greatly, leaving the state with vast areas of land. Roman armies often carried out mass enslavements of conquered populations to acquire their lands. The government distributed these lands to ex-soldiers or to the poor of the original Roman state. Romans employed many of the slaves to replace debt-bonded laborers, and in 310 BCE Rome abolished the practice of *nexum* or debt bondage.

The wars benefited recipients of land and brought wealth to Italy, but they strained the rural economy because the soldiers were away from home much longer than in the past, and sometimes did not return. Rome by the second century BCE had a population in the hundreds of thousands, many with money to buy marketed products. The big landowners, mostly patricians, capitalized on this market. Near the growing cities, these landowners acquired ever more land, often using subterfuges or debt to seize lands from soldiers' families. Now with much larger estates called *latifundia*, they employed slave labor to produce wine and olive oil for local markets. In more remote conquered regions, such as Sicily or North Africa, large estates employed slaves to grow grain for the cities.

These latifundia had not eliminated the peasantry, who still made up most of the empire's population. The latifundia were usually located near big cities, major trade routes, or ports, while in more remote regions small peasant farms still predominated. Also many latifundia did not operate as single large-scale farms. The term latifundium could refer to a group of several smallholdings owned by one owner, and often owners divided their estates into several smaller farms operated on a tenancy basis.

Slavery in Rome was not a uniform status: some slaves held responsible posts in managing farming estates or other enterprises and could earn their freedom and even end up owners of such enterprises. Some slaves worked in activities that did not impose great burdens, such as pastoralism. Sources from the republican period provide some of the earliest evidence of transhumance, or seasonal migration of shepherds with their animals from high-altitude summer pastures to low-altitude winter pastures. Some slaves also produced olives and grapes, which were again not the most strenuous jobs. In many of the newly acquired territories, such as Sicily, Spain, and former Carthaginian regions in North Africa, some owners employed slaves to perform difficult work growing grain and other crops and treated them extremely harshly. These practices led to rebellions by slaves, such as the Sicilian slave war of 136–132 BCE. Before the Roman legions crushed that rebellion, slaves controlled nearly half of Sicily.

The expansion of Rome had thus changed the country from a small republic of peasant-soldiers to a vast, complex, and socially polarized state that was rapidly depleting the old core agrarian group of small farmers. The small farmers' plight became the central issue for Roman leaders.

In the conquests Rome had confiscated large areas of land classified as "public lands" – *ager publicus* – which could be occupied freely. A law in the early second century BCE limited these occupations to 500 *iugera*, about 300 acres. Within a few decades of this law, however, many large landowners, senators, and other patricians, comprising fewer than 2,000 families, had violated this law and expanded their land holdings beyond those limits. They used debt, intimidation, and coercion to take lands from smaller landowners, plebeians who had become tenant farmers, or landless and fled to Rome or other towns to try to survive.

Both Rome and the countryside thus had many more poor people who posed a threat to social stability. Few poor men could be recruited for military service, and employment opportunities in construction or other projects declined by 150 BCE.

At the same time the countryside had many slaves farming on estates, with their potential for rebellion increasingly evident during the second century BCE. Some Romans blamed the expansion of slavery for depopulating the countryside as small peasants lost their land to illegal confiscations and could not find employment because large land holders relied on slaves. Slave-based estates produced olive oil and wine for Rome, thus shifting local land use from subsistence to market production. Contemporaries saw this situation as a threat to both Rome's subsistence and security. Rome had to rely on imported grain from slave estates in Sicily and North Africa, which left the city's subsistence vulnerable to slave revolts, while the apparent depopulation of rural areas reduced the pool of qualified men to serve in Rome's armies.

Some modern researchers have argued that rural areas were overpopulated. The wars stimulated a series of postwar "baby booms," which crowded Rome with more people than could be accommodated on the available lands. The illegal expansion of the big landowners exacerbated this problem. Rome had established colonies in conquered territories around the Mediterranean, but these colonies were not large enough to absorb the growing landless and potentially destabilizing groups.

Whether underpopulated or overpopulated, this circumstance was the context for the opening round in a conflict over land that plagued Roman society and politics for centuries. The fact that the Roman government had passed a law limiting land holdings already indicated concerns for this issue in the wake of the wars. During the early decades of the second century BCE Rome had distributed some one million iugera (approximately 600,000 acres) of land to 100,000 families, partly to soldiers and partly to colonies, but this began to exhaust the free lands available for distribution. By the 140s BCE one Roman consul, Laelius, proposed an agrarian reform law but was pressured by powerful interests to retract the proposal.

In the 130s and 120s BCE two brothers from a prestigious family of mixed plebeian and patrician origins, the Sempronii Gracchi, attempted to resolve this agrarian crisis through land reforms. In 133 BCE, Tiberius Gracchus, the older brother, was elected tribune after attacking patricians and the rich in Rome for taking advantage of the wars and government policies of distributing public lands to enlarge their private land holdings above legal limits. Tiberius proposed to resolve this issue with a law to enforce the 500 iugera limit, and distribute the confiscated lands in small units to landless farmers. He argued that this reform would provide an economic basis for recruiting more soldiers, and make Rome more reliant on small farmers and less on rebellious slave labor.

Tiberius introduced his law into the Tribal Assembly, because he knew that the patrician Senate would never approve it. The Assembly passed the land law after an intense political conflict, and set up a commission that included Tiberius to enforce it. To ensure enforcement, Tiberius announced a nearly unprecedented second run for tribune. Tiberius' opponents, including both senators and fellow tribunes, already aggravated by his agrarian reform law, now interpreted his actions as an attempt to seize greater power. Tiberius sought support from peasants and poor Romans, but a group of senators and their retainers attacked the crowds of Tiberius' supporters. In the mêlée that followed, hundreds of people were killed or trampled to death, including Tiberius.

Tiberius' law and his death divided Romans into supporters and opponents of land reform. A senate investigation of Tiberius' tribunate led to some punishments and executions of some of his opponents. The commission to enforce the agrarian law went to work in 132 BCE but by 129 BCE had redistributed all of the easily accessible lands and became bogged down in disputes and legal appeals.

In this context, in the 120s BCE Tiberius' younger brother Gaius emerged as new leader of the plebeians, based on a far-reaching series of reform proposals. He was elected tribune in 123 BCE and managed to serve two consecutive terms because of his great popularity. Gaius' agrarian law, as far as limited sources indicate, expanded the powers of the commissions set up by Tiberius; they could now redistribute public lands outside Italy including large allotments for new colonies. Gaius also introduced the first law in Roman history to distribute food to the poor in Rome itself at fixed prices every month, the *lex frumentaria*, after a slave rebellion and crop failures reduced grain supplies for Rome and raised prices. Gaius' law won popular support and somewhat weakened the hold of the rich over the poor. It also served as a tacit acknowledgement that land reform would be limited and that many poor in Rome would never get their land back. The law created a de facto state subsidy for large grain estates and grain traders who provided these supplies.

The Tribal Assembly passed Gaius' proposals, but again encountered opposition from other tribunes and especially from the senate. This developed within a few days into a small civil war in Rome. Gaius' forces were quickly overwhelmed, and he and 3,000 of his supporters were killed in the conflict or executed in the later "investigation." The senate reversed or undermined most of Gaius' laws, stopped the redistributions of public lands, and consolidated a system of private property.

Despite these failures, subsequent political leaders repeatedly confronted the issue of land reform. Tribunes in 100 BCE and 91 BCE again tried to introduce distributions of public land, and were again outmaneuvered and murdered. The senator and military leader Sulla took over Rome in 82 BCE, confiscated land in Italy, sometimes from his political opponents, and distributed it to 80,000 of his soldiers, crushing attempts to restore those lands to their original owners. In 62 BCE the senator Cataline ran for consul advocating debt cancellation and land redistribution. He lost the election, fled north of Rome, and assembled an army, but he and his followers died fighting senatorial forces.

Finally, during the crisis that would transform the Republic into an empire, Julius Caesar in his first act as consul in 59 BCE advanced a land reform proposal in the Senate. Many senators vehemently opposed his proposals, so he went to the Tribal Assembly, which expelled opponents and passed the law. Caesar then intimidated senators to swear to uphold the land reform law. He oversaw land distributions to veterans and the poor, less in Italy than in Spain, North Africa, and the eastern Mediterranean. Caesar also ordered the establishment of many new colonies.

A group of senators ultimately conspired to murder Caesar. In the civil war that followed the triumvirate of Marc Antony, Octavian, and Lepidas resorted to desperate measures of land redistribution to support and maintain the loyalty of their armies. They applied proscriptions to eliminate their opponents and take over their lands, and ultimately allotted to the armies 40 of the richest cities under Roman control for confiscation of land and property. This led to immense injustice and suffering. When Octavian defeated Marc Antony and took over Egypt for the Empire, he acquired great wealth that enabled him to discharge 140,000 troops and purchase land for them. For civilians, however, it appears that the land reform issue died.

Agriculture in the Roman Empire

Agriculture and rural society were central aspects of the transition from antiquity to medieval life in the Roman Empire and its successor political units. The agrarian history of the Roman Empire does not include any dramatic events like those involving the Gracchi at the end of the Republic. Instead during the Empire the number and importance of large farming estates gradually expanded, and the role of slaves in these estates declined in favor of a group whom Romans called *coloni*. Leaders beginning with the emperors Diocletian and Constantine introduced laws that imposed restrictions on increasing numbers of farmers, leading to the widespread serfdom of the early western Middle Ages.

No data exist on the numbers of large estates and small farmers, but it is clear that estates – latifundia – existed mainly in certain parts of Italy, North Africa, and Egypt. Estates employed both slaves and free workers, in the forms of both hired laborers and tenant farmers. Most estates apparently specialized in particular products. Some (especially in southern Italy) were essentially ranches raising livestock, others produced mainly vine and tree crops, for wine and olive oil, and yet others produced grain to supply Rome, Byzantium, and other large towns. Some of these estates employed hundreds of laborers of different statuses, and were quite sophisticated enterprises. Several Roman landlords even wrote books on how to manage these large estates. Others functioned as networks of smaller farms. Once the Roman emperors legalized Christianity and made it the official state religion in the fourth century, the Catholic Church acquired large land holdings, often worked by slaves.

These estates specialized in products in demand by urban markets or the government. The large grain estates were located in North Africa and Egypt, supplying Rome and Byzantium. Byzantium, like Rome a capital city, introduced grain rationing and distribution to the poor in the late Empire. The Roman government made monopolistic contracts with grain traders for years at a time to deliver grain to these towns.

Large estates had mixed economic effects. The Ptolemies, the Hellenistic rulers of the Middle East, developed Egypt, especially the Fayum region southeast of the Nile Delta, into a major producer of grain, wine, and other products for the imperial cities. When Rome conquered Ptolemaic Egypt, the country began to decline. The Romans maintained irrigation systems and food production, and trade revived. But the Romans imposed government monopolies on trade and shipped farm products, especially grain, to Rome as a tax without compensation. Roman authorities transferred many private estates in Egypt to government control.

By the second century Roman policies began to impoverish Egyptian townspeople and peasants. The land dispossessions culminated in the *boukoloi* (shepherds') revolt of CE 172, the first major Egyptian peasant rebellion against Rome since the conquest almost two centuries earlier. Many rebels were dispossessed peasants.

Efforts by later emperors to alleviate the situation had little effect. The grain tribute usually continued at a fixed level, though a few emperors reduced it when the Nile was low and the harvest small. By the third century Roman decrees described the country as infested with bands of dispossessed peasant men. Reports of abandoned villages increased into the fifth century, when a small number of great families and Church corporations brought large tracts of land and brought peasants living on them under their patronage. The Roman government acquiesced, and Egypt fragmented into local autocratic states that could not unify against the Arab invasions in the seventh century.

Slavery had peaked in the declining Roman Republic in the two centuries BCE during the Romans conquests. During the early Empire, Rome conquered few new regions, and the slave trade apparently declined. Yet Roman farming, despite the large estates, employed relatively few slaves. Roman agricultural writers held that slave labor best suited specialized crops, especially grape and olive production. Slaves often became specialist producers and could earn manumission for their work.

Most people in the Empire remained small-scale farmers. One emperor, Nerva in 96–98, redistributed land on a small scale. The available sources have little to say about these small farmers, but we know that many of them engaged in seasonal labor migration to find work to support themselves in the off season, much like peasants in modern developing countries. In the late Empire, surviving papyrus sources include more labor contracts between estates and laborers of various types than in all the previous centuries of Roman history combined. These contracts included sharecropping, direct tenancy for rent, and other arrangements. Some small producers raised livestock, especially sheep and goats, and during the first centuries BCE regularly drove the animals to lower-altitude pastures in winter and higher ones in summer. This pattern of transhumance spread all over the Mediterranean.

Increasingly during the Empire, sources refer to laborers on estates and other farmers as *coloni*, a term that in the early Empire meant renters of land on various types of leases. In some regions the status was inherited. A similar group, *inquilini*, could not rent land and could only be hired laborers. During the fourth and fifth centuries a series of laws changed the status of these groups toward one we would call serfdom.

These laws began with the objective of keeping people in their jobs and locations for taxation purposes and to produce necessary products. Starting with the emperors Diocletian and Constantine, in the fourth century Rome issued a series of laws requiring people to stay in their workplaces, and coloni to stay where they were registered for taxation. Subsequent laws required the return of coloni who "belonged to" a particular person but had been taken away by another, and the return of slaves, coloni, and their children who left an imperial estate. By the 390s laws declared coloni "slaves of the land," and denied them the right to sue landlords – except over rent. Later laws prohibited coloni from serving on juries, or in the civil service, the army, and holy orders. These laws finally assimilated slaves to coloni and prohibited their sale apart from lands. By 415 a law in Egypt required that peasants, not just coloni, who left their villages were to be punished and returned to their villages.

While ambiguities remain – some coloni owned slaves – these laws show that the Roman government considered it necessary to make sure that a large group of people remained in their villages, under the control of landlords both sacred and secular. Since most of the top officials in Rome were also major landlords, the legislators passed these laws in the interest of the landowning groups. We will see a similar pattern in the development of Russian serfdom several centuries later.

China

The agricultural history of China, like that of ancient Greece and Rome, began with small peasant farmers who lost their lands to wealthy landlords and became the impoverished basis of an expanding empire. This pattern had an even greater effect on Chinese history because of its much more volatile environmental context. Natural catastrophes, impoverishment of the masses of farmers, and abuses by landlords and officials provoked rebellions that twice overthrew governments during the Han dynasty.

Chinese agriculture developed in an environment fundamentally different from the Mediterranean. China is part of monsoon Asia: its rainfall usually occurs during summer to early fall when the ocean winds blow onto the land as a result of complex climate cycles connecting Asia and the eastern Pacific. During an El Niño event (a warming of the eastern Pacific) the monsoon rains can fall short or fail completely, causing drought and crop failures. A La Niña (cooling in the eastern Pacific) can cause a heavy and prolonged monsoon and flooding that sweeps away villages. Records over the 2,100-year history of Imperial China from 200 BCE to 1911 record some 1,800 famines caused by such disasters. Almost every year there was a flood, drought, infestation, or other disaster somewhere in the country. Some were so severe or widespread that they exceeded the relief capabilities of the government, and provoked rebellions when the government seemed especially incompetent.

Farming methods sometimes aggravated the environmental effects. From the earliest times, Chinese farmers cut or burned down forests to open land for farming. Deforestation always leads to erosion and topsoil loss, but in the first farmed region, northern China, it caused loess soils to be washed into the Yellow River. As the bed of the river rose, Chinese governments organized the people to build dikes that had the effect of raising the bed of the river above the ground level. Ultimately the river rose above the dikes. In CE 11 the Yellow River overflowed its banks and shifted course several hundred miles, causing immense destruction and loss of life.

Because of this dangerous environment, Chinese rulers attempted to alter the environment to protect against natural disasters and the resulting famines, and to increase farm production. In a famous example, the regional governor Li Ping built the Dujiangyan levee and irrigation system on the Min River in the central Chinese province of Sichuan to eliminate flooding around 250 BCE. The system took ten years to build and is still in use.

Chinese rulers have repeatedly described agriculture as the most important activity of the people and the most important concern of the government. Early Chinese writings reflect great fear of famine and of peasants fleeing farming to engage in "unproductive" activities like trade.

Farming developed in the context of China's basic two-part geography. In the first Chinese civilizations, in the north of the country, farmers grew millets, beans (including soy), barley, wheat, hemp, many vegetables, and raised the "six animals" – chickens, dogs, pigs, horses, oxen, and sheep. Only during the Han dynasties (CE 206–220) did significant numbers of peasants migrate to the warmer and more humid southern regions of the Yangtze River and begin growing rice. There they initially used a type of shifting or "slash and burn" cultivation in which they would burn the plants on a plot, seed it with rice, and then flood it to eliminate weeds, which the Chinese called "plowing with fire and hoeing (or weeding) with water." Each broad region had many subdivisions with different climates, soil types, access to water, and other characteristics.

Early Chinese agrarian structures

The earliest reliable sources on Chinese agrarian history, from the Chou (eleventh–third century BCE), indicate that in the period roughly from 1000 to 600 BCE many if not most Chinese peasants lived in a dependent relationship with local landlords who had a claim on a large share of what the peasants produced. One ancient Chinese source describes peasants essentially as serfs who worked under a landlord's agent, turned over their produce to the lord, and received rations from him.

Later Confucian writings described a pattern of peasant land use as the *tsing tien* or "well-field system." In this system fields were divided in a tic-tac-toe pattern with individual farmers cultivating the outside squares and the group collectively cultivating the central square to produce crops for the landlord. To the extent that this system existed (which is uncertain) it reflected landlord control, because these well-field farms were not held as private property.

These landlords in turn served higher-level regional rulers in a relationship similar to medieval European feudalism. The Chou dynasty declined in power in the eighth century BCE, and China divided into numerous small states that fought for dominance until the Qin defeated its competitors and established the Chinese empire. Starting in the sixth century BCE laws brought great changes. In 594 BCE a Chou successor state imposed the first land tax documented in Chinese history. These laws suggest that farmers had become sufficiently independent from local landlords or had enough income to pay taxes themselves, and were in the process of becoming an independent peasantry.

During these centuries of conflict, Chinese farmers introduced two innovations: iron tools and animal draft force. The new ox-drawn plows with iron shares enabled Chinese farmers to "break the plains" of the northern regions with their highly fertile loess soils. These and certain other agricultural techniques turned China into a region with large areas of land and few people. Chinese peasants became pioneers, reliant on nuclear families, ruled by their sovereigns through vassal lords.

By the fourth century BCE Chinese peasant farming based on the well-field system fell into decline, partly from soil exhaustion. Many peasants could no longer produce enough for their own needs or to pay taxes, and either fell under the control of large landlords or abandoned their lands. The Qin kingdom had substantial vacant land and tried to increase its wealth with a decree in 350 BCE that invited peasants to settle in the Qin kingdom, eliminated the well-field system, and made land into private property. The subsequent growth of highly developed farming and population enabled Qin to create the first Chinese empire in 221 BCE.

The Qin ruler, like his successors in later dynasties, tried to eliminate any competing authorities, such as the old local lords, who could interfere in the relationship between the rulers and their tax-paying, food-producing peasant subjects. Qin emissaries killed as many of the old nobles as they could find. But the Qin Emperor Shih Huang-ti imposed even more strenuous forced labor and taxation demands on the peasants to build irrigation systems and canals, which pushed peasants into a rebellion that overthrew the dynasty.

The Han dynasty and the failure of land reform

The overthrow of Qin and rise of the Han dynasty in 206 BCE caused significant disruption and loss of life. Early Han rulers were of peasant origin, understood that the security of the empire and the livelihood of the people depended on the peasants, and reduced government demands on peasants. By about 160 BCE, a significant famine occurred, with growing food shortages in many parts of the country, and declining reserves in government hands. A memorial prepared for the emperor emphasized that many small peasants, despite hard work, could not support their families in a normal year and had to borrow from moneylenders to pay taxes. In 155 the emperor reduced taxes to one-thirtieth of a farm's produce.

Rich officials and regional rulers, landlords, and merchants took advantage of peasant distress to take over their lands and employ them as tenants or even slaves. A long-lived emperor, Wu-ti (141–87 BCE), applied draconian measures to weaken these groups; he arrested regional leaders and confiscated their property, imposed high taxes on merchants as a pretext for taking their lands and freeing their slaves, and seized thousands of additional acres for later distribution.

After Wu-ti, however, landlords regained power over the villages. Later emperors worsened the situation by handing out land to their favorites. Most peasants lived in such poverty that in years of disasters they had to sell their possessions and even their children to make ends meet. In this period the first records appear of the "ever-normal granary" system (*cangping xang*), in which local officials would purchase grain from the population in years of large harvests, and release it onto the market in years of shortages, in order to drive market prices down. Still peasants' conditions worsened, and officials in CE 2 repeated earlier proposals to limit land holding and slave holding. Rich landlords and many officials opposed the plan, however, and it was never implemented.

In this context, a top official, Wang Mang, seized power in CE 7 and attempted to eliminate slave trading, nationalize the land, and set maximum land areas that members of different social groups could own. These edicts were part of a broader program of reforms, but were difficult to enforce or even monitor. They provoked opposition among landlords and confusion among all groups regarding land-holding limits.

Then in CE 11 a great catastrophe intervened; the Yellow River changed course, shifting its mouth from north of the Shandong peninsula to south of it, a distance of some 200 km. This catastrophe caused devastating flooding, cut off the Shandong peninsula from outside contacts, and overwhelmed government reserves. In Shandong groups of ruined and starving peasants formed armies that attacked government authorities in the province and, after the flood waters receded, outside it. They painted their foreheads red to distinguish themselves from their opponents, and for this reason earned the name "red eyebrows."

The change of the Yellow River's course caused all authorities to focus on this event. By CE 12 Wang Mang decided to rescind his agrarian and slave reform edicts as unenforceable. The rebels in Shandong defeated Wang Mang's forces and joined with others under a descendant of the former Han rulers. These armies defeated Wang Mang's forces in a series of battles during CE 23 and restored the Han dynasty the next year.

The leaders of later Han were beholden to the large landlords and their clans, who had financed their rise to power, and made no more plans for land reform. Critical writings of the CE first and second centuries complained that many people were moving away from farming into crafts and trade. This created a growing divide between the few rich who lived in luxury and increasing numbers of poor.

Gradual technological change came in agriculture as in other sectors. Evidence from tombs shows more iron plowshares and other tools, and suggests that the dominant farming method was a long plow pulled by two oxen and operated by one man. Several irrigation systems were also built in the later Han. Progress was not uniform, and many peasants in remote areas farmed with older equipment and techniques. Already in the last decades of the former Han, the newer farming equipment and irrigation installations were beyond the reach of poorer farmers who would fall into debt because they lacked access to these improvements. Wealthier and more powerful landlords would often acquire the land of such poor or indebted peasants through purchase, debt foreclosure, or intimidation. The poor farmers might become tenants but could also end up landless and displaced.

The Chinese government attempted to address these problems both out of a philosophical commitment to agriculture as the basis of society, and for economic and political reasons. As in the former Han, later Han rulers kept taxes low and tried to keep land registration accurate. Peasants and landowners in some cases rebelled against what they considered unfair assessments, and the government executed some officials who compiled false tax registers. Millions of peasants abandoned more densely settled and landlord-dominated northern regions, and moved to the frontier regions of the Yangtze valley and further south, sometimes under government resettlement plans.

The government also provided relief. Two dozen times in the later Han the government issued grants of grain to the elderly, widows and widowers, poor people, and victims of natural disasters. During the reign of Emperor Ho-ti (CE 88–106), when peasants in several parts of China and Vietnam faced drought, floods, locust infestation, and famines, the government remitted taxes, opened granaries, or issued money loans. China at this time was relatively stable and wealthy and the disasters were not too severe.

In the decades following Ho-ti's reign more peasants became impoverished, and the government could not command the resources necessary to alleviate these conditions. In 150 widespread locust infestations and flooding of the Yellow River induced hundreds of thousands of people to flee, and by 155 the state imposed requisitions on anyone who had grain to provide relief.

The central government and even regional officials steadily lost control over much of China, and local landlords exerted increasing control over local peasants. Meanwhile peasants, in desperation after disasters, formed secret societies based on kinship or on religious beliefs that promised a new world of peace and equality if they could overthrow the government and the wealthy landlords. Rebellions by several military leaders and peasant secret societies like the Yellow Turbans, combined with the ineptitude, weakness, and ignorance of the central authorities, helped to bring down this dynasty.

Conclusion

In the great ancient agrarian societies of Greece, Rome, and China, the rural majority had to contend with different versions of the dual subordination and different responses to it. In the Greek and Roman Mediterranean, great natural disasters were rare. The main problems that farmers often faced in this region were arid weather and saline soils, which they usually could manage with the methods they already knew. In China, farmers endured repeated catastrophes, frequently reaching a severity and scale never encountered in Europe, such as a major river changing course or multi-year droughts and floods. Successive Chinese governments established agencies to deal with emergencies and to carry out major long-term projects, employing tens of thousands of laborers in attempts to prevent the recurrence of such disasters. The success or failure of these measures was a barometer of the condition of the Chinese government.

While environmental factors, and government responses to them, differed between the two regions, farmers in both China and the West encountered similar versions of the rural subordination to powerful authorities outside their villages. In Athens and Rome farmers faced powerful landlords who could reduce them to slavery or throw them off the land. The results could include landless peasants crowding into the towns and slave rebellions, both of which threatened urban subsistence and security. While such rebellions could sometimes overthrow a servile system, it was more important that some government leaders recognized these problems and took measures to protect farmers from slavery or restore lands to them. The actions of Solon, the Gracchi, and others had limited effects at best, but they set a precedent of at least partly democratic political systems, which took into consideration the needs of poor and land-deprived farmers. The repeated efforts by Roman tribunes and emperors to introduce land reforms reflected a degree of "institutional memory" that kept the issue alive.

In China, the government did much less to mitigate the actions of land-lords against small farmers. Officials wrote reports to higher authorities, but policies depended on the attitudes of the emperors, shaped by court politics and personal characteristics much more than by the political demands of the population. Even when a Chinese leader did decide to introduce reforms, the power of local landlords and the wealthy often outweighed imperial direc-tives, as evidenced by the ineffectiveness of Wang Mang's attempted reforms. China's encounter with the dual subordination thus resembled Rome's, with the failure of attempted socio-economic reforms, but went beyond the West in the scale and frequency of the government's efforts to aid and protect farmers, and the towns as well, from serious natural disasters and famines. Yet in all of these regions, the claims of big landlords and other local authorities gradually overpowered and dominated farmers. The Roman Republic came much closer than any early Chinese government to implementing the land reforms that most of the farmers desired.

Further reading

Illuminating readings on Ancient Greek agriculture include Aristotle, *The Politics of Aristotle*, ed. and translated by Ernest Barker (Oxford: Clarendon Press, 1972); Signe Isager and Jens Eric Skydsgaard, *Ancient Greek Agriculture* (London: Routledge, 1992); Nino Luraghi and Susan Alcock, eds., *Helots and their Masters in Laconia and Messenia: Histories, Ideologies, Structures* (Washington, D.C.: Center for Hellenic Studies, 2003); Victor

Davis Hanson, *The Other Greeks* (Berkeley, CA: University of California Press, 1999).

Readings on agriculture and related issues in Rome include David Stockton, *The Gracchi* (Oxford: Clarendon Press, 1979); Nathan Rosenstein, *Rome at War: Farms, Families, and Death in the Middle Republic* (Chapel Hill: UNC Press, 2004); Jairus Banaji, *Agrarian Change in Late Antiquity* (New York: Oxford University Press 2001).

On Ancient China, Mabel Ping-Hua Lee, *The Economic History of China, with Special Reference to Agriculture* (New York: Columbia University Press, 1921), contains excerpts from Ancient Chinese writings. Good historical studies include Cho-Yun Hsu, *Han Agriculture* (Seattle: University of Washington Press, 1980); Mark Elvin, *The Pattern of the Chinese Past* (Stanford, CA: Stanford University Press, 1973); Francesca Bray, 'Agriculture', in Joseph Needham, ed., *Science and Civilization in China*, v. 6, pt. 2 (Cambridge: Cambridge University Press, 1984); also Bray's book *The Rice Economies* (Oxford: Blackwell, 1982).

Chapter 3

Agriculture in the post-classical period

The post-classical or medieval period stretches from 500 to 1450, almost a thousand years. The most important agrarian processes in this period, which this chapter will discuss, included:

- the prolonged decline of the Eastern Roman (Byzantine) Empire;
- the rise and decline of the Western European manorial system;
- the Muslim transfer of Asian crops to the Western European region;
- China's adoption of intensified farming to resist crop failures and famines.

The transfer of Asian crops introduces the first major global exchange of farm products, which had extremely important consequences. In Byzantium, Europe, and China, the dual subordination continued to shape agrarian life. In these regions, governments inherited from previous regimes the common problem of conflicted relations between small peasants and large landlords, which all of them attempted to resolve or control with limited success.

The environmental context: the medieval optimum

During the post-classical period, global climate underwent a gradual and intermittent pattern of warming from the fourth and fifth centuries that culminated in the medieval warm period or optimum. This warming peaked in three periods of 30–40 years during the eleventh to the thirteenth centuries, and was most evident in the northern hemisphere. This warming period almost eliminated the pack ice in the North Atlantic, which allowed the Norse in their small wooden boats to colonize Iceland, Greenland, and Vinland (North America). Greenland acquired that name because the warm climate reduced its ice cover enough to allow plants to grow on the coast.

The warming pattern affected agriculture. In Europe it made the weather more stable and regular, and lengthened growing seasons. Evidence of vineyards was found in southern England and at high elevations in central Europe, where viticulture would have been impossible in later centuries.

Disasters like droughts and heavy rains still occurred in this period, but less frequently and with less severity than later. In China, farmers grew citrus fruits and other warm-weather plants further north in the thirteenth century than in any other century. This medieval warming may have helped to support the Chinese agricultural transformation of the Sung period and its related population growth. Some evidence also indicates warmer weather in southern Africa, New Zealand, and North America, where archaeological evidence shows that native peoples in 1100–1200 were farming in regions that are now much too dry for crop production.

The West

Western developments split into two basic tracks during the fifth century. In Eastern Europe and the Mediterranean region, the Roman Empire survived as the Byzantine Empire and perpetuated Roman patterns and problems. In Western Europe, Germanic barbarians conquered Rome and began a process of transformation that led to the manorial system and serfdom.

Agriculture and the Byzantine empire

The eastern, Byzantine half of the Roman Empire survived the collapse of the western half in part because of its agricultural strength. Its farming regions, from Egypt to Syria, Anatolia, and Greece, produced grain, olive oil, livestock, and other produce. Its farmers were mostly peasant small-holders, although imperial, church, and private estates controlled perhaps close to half of the cropland. The senate of Constantinople consisted of 2,000 large landowners. These large farms produced in part for government contracts to provide grain subsidies for the poor in major cities in the eastern empire, continuing Gaius Gracchus' policy of 130 BCE.

The Roman Empire's succession wars during the third century significantly reduced the rural population. Peasants often surrendered their lands to landlords or fled to towns to escape taxation. Laws to protect smallholders had little effect. Efforts to revive the rural world had limited effects because of sixth- and seventh-century plagues that may have killed one-fourth of the population and disrupted farm production. Soon after these plagues subsided, Muslim Arab invaders took over the Middle East, Egypt, and the southern borders of Anatolia during the seventh and eighth centuries. Byzantium lost about two-thirds of its territory and population, the cities declined, farmers shifted to subsistence production, and the economy increasingly relied on barter.

The Byzantine emperor responded by dividing the empire into military districts called themes (*themata*), fortified with soldier-farmers whom the government settled relatively evenly over the territory, on lands taken from imperial and landlords' estates. Infantry soldiers received small plots, while cavalry received larger ones that employed tenants and hired workers. As a result of these and other reforms, the Empire recovered sufficiently to begin offensive wars against its former attackers; by the eleventh century the Byzantines made substantial territorial gains.

During this expansion, the Imperial authorities came into conflict with an emerging class of large-holding landlords on the Anatolian plateau. These estates' size and remoteness enabled them to resist Arab attacks, but also made it difficult for the government to tax and prevent them from appropriating small peasants' farms. Landlords took advantage of crises, such as famines caused by locusts and crop failures, in 927 and 963. Government relief efforts were not sufficient, and many farmers sold their farms to landlords, often military officers or government and Orthodox Church officials, and became renters of their former lands.

The government, fearing a decline in tax income that could weaken the army, issued a series of laws starting in 934 until the end of the century, requiring all lands obtained illegally or even legally from smallholders to be returned to them. One emperor even decreed that only the poor could buy land from the poor, and only the wealthy from the wealthy! Another in 996 prohibited government officials from acquiring land from smallholders, and ordered large landlords to pay the unpaid sum when smallholders defaulted on their taxes. Some evidence indicates that these laws were enforced: one of these laws even sparked a small rebellion.

From the eleventh century, military defeat, loss of territory, and the rising power of land owners and commercial elites ended enforcement of these land laws. Smallholders divided their lands among their children, and frequently had to surrender their plots to landlords and become tenants or laborers. By 1200 tenants significantly outnumbered independent smallholders, which weakened the Empire fiscally and militarily (since landlords could keep tenants out of military service). During the fourteenth and fifteenth centuries, civil wars and the Black Death in 1347–50 weakened the Empire, which lost more lands to Serbs and Turks. Landlords continued to acquire peasant lands until smallholders became rare. The Byzantine collapse in 1453 resulted from the Turks' military strength and from landlords' elimination of smallholders, which undermined the Empire's military and fiscal capabilities.

Medieval European agriculture

Medieval agriculture in Western Europe developed during the transition from the warm early medieval optimum to Little Ice Age. The period witnessed agricultural and economic changes including the formation of the manorial system, new farming technology, a shift from subsistence grain production to market specialization and from crops to livestock, and the emergence of Eastern Europe as a source of grain. The period saw the social and political transition from the early medieval invasions to the stability of the High Middle Ages, and the rise and decline of serfdom. These changes culminated in the dominance of a peasant agrarian system.

The early medieval period saw some technological improvements. In the sixth century and later, farmers developed the moldboard plow, which has a curved board behind the plowshare to turn over the soil to uproot and bury weeds. During the ninth century Europeans devised an improved horse collar (which Europe may have acquired indirectly from China) and horse shoes that allowed farmers to employ that animal instead of the slower and weaker ox. Europeans also gradually learned about crop rotations. At the earliest stage they inherited the old Mediterranean system of alternating crops and fallow, the two-field system. Some Europeans knew about or devised on their own the more productive three-field system, in which fields were rotated between fall and spring crops and fallow.

Introduction of these new technologies and methods took centuries, and medieval farmers for centuries knew little about fertilizers and crop rotations. Consequently the early medieval West had low food production. Good weather alternated with seasons of drought or cold and wet weather that destroyed crops. Plague and other diseases spread especially in the fifth to sixth centuries. Records show chronic crop failures and subsistence crises. Peasants surrendered their freedom for food. The Catholic Church tried to free such peasants, and political leaders tried to lower food prices. In 806, a year of scarcity, Charlemagne ordered his vassals to sell their surpluses at normal prices.

The early medieval economy became overwhelmingly rural. Cities declined in size and number, especially in northern Europe. Some regions had no real cities, just slightly larger settlements around nobles' castles. Elsewhere, as in Italy, towns survived and recovered from the ninth-century invasions, but even those towns were mostly rural in their economic focus. Among the main causes of this economic decline was the early medieval invasions, which disrupted European development for centuries.

In this context of invasions, natural disasters, epidemics, and famines, people sought security in remote settlements, a high degree of self-sufficiency, and protection provided by warriors. The manor or villa embodied all of these characteristics. The classic manorial system evolved in response to the conditions of northern Europe and England in the Carolingian period: mild, damp weather, heavy soils, dense forests, a localized economy with limited trade, much more exchange in kind than money, and local self-sufficiency. Medieval lords allotted manors to their cavalry soldiers on the basis of a contract called vassalage. Vassals agreed to provide military service in exchange for landed estates with peasant laborers to support their families while they prepared for and fought wars. Catholic Church officials and monasteries also held manors.

The manorial system was not universal in Europe: Italy retained the ancient latifundium into the twentieth century, the Muslim conquest of

Spain in 711 prevented its development beyond the northern Christian regions, and Eastern Europe developed it much later. Still, the manorial system in different variants dominated the rural economy in Western Europe, encompassing more people than any other system until its decline after 1350.

The manor ordinarily comprised a substantial house with dozens or hundreds of acres of fields legally attached to it. Part of these fields, called the *demesne*, the owner or landlord of the estate managed directly. The rest were held on several different terms of tenure by the local population. Manors were initially highly self-sufficient, producing not only food but also textiles, farm equipment, and other products. Landlords' dues often required peasants to make these items. In the early medieval period, manors were small in population and compact in area. A manor that expanded its cropland too far risked attacks from outside. In more secure periods, manorial peasants would undertake *assarts* or clearances by cutting down forests and reclaiming wetlands.

Peasant land allotments, most often called *manse*, usually had a few dozen acres. The concept emerged from the coloni of the Roman estate. In Italy the term coloni continued to be used well into the Middle Ages. A manse could be free or servile. Its status was created over decades according to a variety of circumstances. Peasants who accepted a manse on an estate took on obligations for providing the products and performing work associated with that manse.

The manse was not a homestead but rather a share in village lands. The functional unit of production was not the individual manse but the village as an agricultural complex. The villages were thus corporate and their residents were members of the village. Villages had established traditions and sometimes written bylaws for managing their affairs. Villages usually divided their lands into fields and the fields into strips. This practice reduced land disputes: everyone received portions of all types of field. It also served as a type of insurance: no family had all of its land in one field, and every family had plots in each type of field, so no one would have a total loss or exclusive benefit.

The peasants farmed the land according to a schedule agreed on by the village gathering of heads of households. In its simplest version, peasants grew winter crops on their strips in the winter field, spring crops in the spring field if they had introduced the three-field system, and left their strips fallow in the fallow field. They grazed animals on the fallow field and on the other fields after harvesting. Villages usually left some lands outside the regular rotations open for all, especially the poorest in the village, to use for a variety of purposes, including settlement, livestock grazing, and small-scale cultivation by landless villagers. In England these common lands became a crucial issue later on.

Many medieval villages in Europe periodically redistributed at least part of the lands among villagers to accommodate changes in family size, work capabilities, livestock holdings, and other considerations. By the late medieval and early modern periods in many villages land holdings became the fixed property or at least inherited holdings of a particular family, and this transition from collective to individual tenure was a crucial step toward agricultural modernization. The village as an institution and an intermediary between the peasants and outsiders lasted into the twentieth century.

The peasants were a complex group. Many were free smallholders or "customary tenants," often called "villeins." Villages were also divided by gender. Men, for example, usually did the large-scale farm work on the village fields with plows and horse teams, while women cultivated a household garden plot and handled all matters relating to clothing and small children. Some villages set aside land to be farmed for older widows; in others these women's fate was left to charity or the Church, although often such women could exchange services in which they were skilled, such as midwifery, for food.

Most peasants may have been "serfs," a difficult group to define. Some were freed slaves who retained certain obligations or free people who agreed to accept farming obligations in return for protection or other reasons, a process called commendation. Some people accepted serfdom to obtain land and equipment, which anticipated modern debt-peonage. Serfs were usually bound to the land or estate where they lived. They could not move to another location and were more or less completely subject to the will of the estate owner. A serf could be bought and sold with land or separately from it. The serf may not have been part of a larger village community, but he had home and family and was considered a human, unlike a slave.

The crucial serf obligation was cultivation of the lord's land or demesne. Lords usually farmed demesne "directly," which meant they supervised peasant work on the demesne, either themselves or through a bailiff or manager, often from among the peasants themselves. On Church and monastic estates, the owners would divide the demesne into territorial units called "granges," with groups of servile peasants assigned to produce crops on them, supplied from the institution's own reserves. Serfs were also ordinarily obliged to make certain payments to the lord, usually in kind from their own manse lands.

The obligations of serfdom usually formed over centuries through conflict and negotiation between peasants and lords. By the ninth century, much if not most of the Western European population was servile, ranging from 10 percent to 80 percent or more in different regions. In Europe's border regions, however, including Ireland, Scandinavia, and Eastern Europe, few if any peasants were serfs in the Middle Ages.

The high medieval period coincided with the peak of the medieval climate optimum, with warmer summers, milder winters, less precipitation, and drier weather than would prevail in the fourteenth century. The warmer climate and stable political conditions allowed the revival of trade and population growth. These developments in turn stimulated the main agricultural development of this period: the expansion of arable cultivation, both within Western Europe and on its borderlands.

Expansion took place in several ways. In established villages and manors, residents assimilated village wastes or other nearby uncultivated lands. Documents refer to numerous "assarts," waste and forest lands newly cultivated. In the Netherlands and along the French coast, people drained marshes and built seawalls, creating "polders," reclaimed farmlands, which had high fertility and productivity. In Eastern Europe, German crusaders claimed and settled lands in the Baltic regions, Poland, Belarus, and Western Russia, a process called the "Drang nach Osten," the push to the east. German, Polish, and Lithuanian nobles, bishops, and rulers recruited peasants, offering them freedom from serfdom and taxes for some years, and lower taxes afterwards, if they would take the risk of leaving their homes of long residence to start anew in an unfamiliar and wild place. Some new settlers would commend themselves to local authorities and end up with even heavier obligations. Catholic and Orthodox Church lords tried to settle Christians in the eastern territories, to farm and to proselytize.

This expansion continued until virtually all arable and even marginal lands had been cleared and brought under cultivation. This maximum was reached between 1250 and 1350 depending on the region. By 1300, and earlier in many places, villages became crowded, with multiple families often dividing a single manse. In both old lands and new eastern lands, this expansion led to deforestation. By the thirteenth century, population growth caused farmers to move into marginal lands that could not support long-term farming or produce yields adequate for subsistence. As more peasants moved to new lands in the east based on a promise of freedom, those in the central regions grew more intolerant of their servile status.

During this period, improved methods and farming techniques spread, including the three-field rotation, the plow with metal share, wheels, and mouldboard, and the use of horses with effective collars. Most manors built water-powered mills or windmills, which supported expanded grain production and freed peasants from the labor of manual milling and processing of fiber crops like flax.

By 1150 agrarian Europe had changed greatly from the time of Charlemagne: most of the land was settled, marshes were drained, forests were thinned, there were large vineyards, grain fields, increasing numbers of livestock, and substantial trade. A money economy had developed, networks of roads had been built, and towns had emerged at trade centers and road junctions. The beginning of regional specialization of farm production laid the basis for the diversification and specialization of the late Middle Ages. Peasants expanded cropland and pasture, which created core areas of livestock raising. They planted vineyards, flax, hemp, and other industrial crops.

This economic development led to significant social and political changes. Most important was the gradual dismantling of serfdom. By the twelfth century the status of serfs had improved. Lords increasingly shifted obligations from labor services to payments, making obligations of free and serf peasants more similar. Serfs now could sue in court, were included in local communities, and were increasingly recognized as people. The colonization of new land on terms of immunity from obligations and taxation attracted many peasants and persuaded lords to make similar concessions to peasants in old lands to keep them there. Peasants also began to purchase their freedom through the legal process of enfranchisement. Lords usually were agreeable to this because they could set or negotiate the price. While in some regions nobles practiced primogeniture, others divided their estates among their children, leaving their heirs poorer and weaker in relation to peasants. Many nobles controlled only a single village. Most lords in France had little to lose by commuting labor services to a payment, because only about one-tenth of their land was demesne, while peasants were farming the rest and paying dues on it anyway. The elimination of peasant servitude thus only represented a slight extension of tenancy. Peasants would often end up indebted to moneylenders instead of enserfed to a noble landlord.

Nobles also agreed to commute labor services to rents because their expensive lifestyles and activities, such as participation in the Crusades, had driven them into serious debt. Lords hired experts to manage their accounts, and began to dismantle their demesnes, dividing them and renting or selling the subdivisions. As a result villages were divided between multiple landlords. These nobles increasingly sought government offices financed by taxation, which depended on peasant participation in markets. The relatively self-sufficient manor was now an institution of the past. The grange system on Church estates went through a similar process under the pressure of market management.

England followed a different path. After the Norman Conquest, England came under strong central government authority. In the twelfth century, the English economy grew rapidly. Food production increased, as did the old sectors of wool and cloth. Land reclamation, drainage, and expansion of cultivation proceeded even faster in England than in France, and the English population more than tripled from 1066 to the Black Death in 1348. Yet the condition of most English peasants worsened. The Normans allowed their vassal lords considerable power over the peasants. During the eleventh and twelfth centuries the number of free tenants declined as lords imposed more demands. By the thirteenth century demesne occupied about one-third of the cultivated land on English estates, and many landlords reinforced serf obligations and required labor services from all peasants on their estates. Some English manors were entirely servile, with no freemen on their lands. Two abbeys, Ely and Ramsey, decommuted money payments back into labor services and increased them. Some landlords reduced burdens, but in general, in

England, labor services grew while they declined in most of continental Europe.

The Late Middle Ages in Western Europe began with the extreme cold and famine of 1315–22. Heavy rains began in May 1315 and continued through August all over northern Europe, and recurred through 1318 and in some places into 1320. Fields turned into ponds, and soldiers could not fight because the horses sank into the soggy fields. Crops were destroyed in vast areas; the 1316 European harvest was estimated at half of normal, and a "normal" harvest by the fourteenth century already was insufficient for the population. The result was described as "The Great Famine" and caused widespread deaths from starvation and disease. Even royal courts were short of food. The weather returned to normal only after an extremely cold winter in 1322. The crisis foreshadowed the Little Ice Age.

The first phase of the Little Ice Age began in the fourteenth century and lasted until a slight warming took place in the sixteenth century. The second phase returned with extreme cold in the seventeenth century followed by a gradual warming until the full-fledged warming phase began around 1850. The cold wet weather destroyed harvests and caused famines, which left people more vulnerable to the epidemics of the following centuries. Famines caused by cold wet weather preceded plague outbreaks in 1356, 1361, and 1374. These famines and plagues killed half to two-thirds of Europe's population during the fourteenth century.

The disasters of the fourteenth century surprisingly caused a long-term decline in the prices of grains, the main European food crops. In the famine years of 1315–18 prices rose up to ten times the normal level, but once Europe recovered grain prices fell and stayed low, mostly because of new sources of grain in Eastern Europe. Traders from Italy expanded their trade with Constantinople and the Black Sea, the connection that brought the Black Death to Europe, purchasing grain from Ukraine, Crimea, the Balkans, Crete, and Sicily for sale in Italy and France. Traders in the Hanseatic League, an association of trading states in the Baltic, purchased grain from large estates in Poland and Prussia to sell in Scandinavia, England, and the Netherlands. These shipments flooded Europe with grain and kept prices low.

Many European farmers understood the changes in the European economy and shifted to more profitable products, which created regional agricultural specializations that have survived to the present. Along the Mediterranean coast and the Rhine and Moselle rivers, for example, farmers increased wine production, while farmers near cities specialized in vegetables, fruit, and other high-value items. Other regions specialized in textile crops. Landlords and peasants responded to the vast areas of abandoned land and villages by shifting to livestock breeding. On the smallest scale, lords dug thousands of artificial fish ponds and raised stocked fish for Western European markets. Europeans especially favored sheep and raised tens of millions during the fourteenth and fifteenth centuries. Until about 1300 English wool was considered the highest quality, and the English supplied the textile producers of the Netherlands and Italy.

During the fourteenth century the English began keeping their wool for their own textile industry, and Italy and the Netherlands found a new source in Spain, where the Christian kingdoms had defeated the Muslim states. European demand stimulated the Spanish to turn their country into a giant pasture for merinos, a breed with high-quality wool. The sheep breeders had recently (in 1273) formed an association called the *Mesta*. To support the growing wool exports, the government extended privileges to the shepherds of the Mesta that restricted farmers' rights to interfere with the shepherds' routes of transhumance, or claim compensation from the Mesta for sheep-damaged farms. Spain became a grain importer like the rest of Europe. The Mesta, which lasted until 1836, held back Spain's economic development. Southern Italy also developed a sheep economy, under a similar association of sheep raisers, the *dogana*. Late medieval European agriculture thus shifted toward livestock, a pattern that distinguished farming in Europe and later America and Australia from most other agrarian systems.

The famines and plagues, the recovery of markets, and peasants' own efforts induced secular and ecclesiastical lords to concede peasants more rights and freedoms. This resulted in the decline and near-disappearance of the manorial system and serfdom. Since the thirteenth century, estates and rights over them had become highly fragmented. Running estates became costly, lords became indebted, and they increasingly surrendered management to peasant tenants. They imposed or enforced other obligations, including the "ban," to compensate. The ban required peasants on an estate to grind their grain in the lord's mill, bake their bread in his oven, and similar obligations, for set fees. Lords also imposed fees for life events, such as *heriot*, to allow a son to inherit from his father, or *merchet*, to allow a peasant's son to marry. These obligations, later called in French "*banalités*," were the last vestiges of serfdom abolished by the French Revolution.

Peasants who survived the Black Death used the scarcity of labor to demand better terms of employment and land tenure. Lords facing low prices for grain and high wage demands sometimes tried to reimpose servile obligations. The English parliament, mostly landlords, during the Black Death passed the Statute on Laborers, which required wages to be maintained at the same level as in 1346. Yet peasants were in a position to dictate their terms, and many lords reluctantly leased out demesne lands to them. Ultimately these concessions transferred management costs to the farmers and increased many lords' incomes; they also eliminated serfdom and manorialism in England.

In other cases, however, lords' attempts to restore servile obligations and government taxation demands provoked peasant rebellions, often involving considerable violence. In the Jacquerie of 1358 in northern France, peasants destroyed more than 150 noble castles and homes, and tortured and murdered hundreds of nobles and their families, until nobles and the royal armies defeated them and carried out brutal reprisals. In Catalonia, the last servile peasants, the *Remensas*, fought a civil war from 1462 to 1486, when King Ferdinand II of Aragon finally emancipated them. Ironically the same ruler who freed the Catalonian serfs authorized Columbus' journey to the New World and the establishment of even more oppressive systems there.

Islam: empire and agriculture

The Muslim empires began as a military–religious movement in the towns of southwest Arabia, the Hijaz, but contributed to the transfer of crops and livestock from Asia to Europe, one of the most important agricultural developments in world history.

Muhammad's successors in the seventh and eighth centuries brought under Muslim control or influence a vast region stretching from Spain and North Africa, across the Middle East to Central Asia and the Indus valley. Many of their policies had an agrarian component. Non-Muslim farmers had to pay the *jizya* tax or tribute that Muslims imposed in areas they conquered in order to retain their lands. During their invasions, Muhammad's successors tried to keep Arab soldiers and migrants separate from the conquered societies, partly to prevent the destruction of productive agricultural systems. In some cases, however, Arabs seized land if the owners refused to convert to Islam.

The two caliphates, the Umayyad, 660–750, and the Abbasid, 750–1258, retained and elaborated pre-existing systems of taxation and management of agriculture. The Umayyads overthrew Sassanid Persia but retained the Sassanid land tax and poll tax, and added additional taxes on the rural population, which sparked peasant rebellions against them. By the late seventh century, many Arabs had assimilated to the conquered regions, learned Persian, and became landlords or peasants. They were subordinated to local, sometimes Persian, officials, and subjected to the harsh taxation like the local population. By 735 these settler Arabs turned against the Umayyad caliphate and were the main supporters of the Abbasids who overthrew it.

The Abbasids relied on the previous tax system, but initially were much less rapacious. They managed a centralized bureaucratic system that operated through a *diwani* or finance minister, provincial governors, and local officials. The local authorities conducted surveys to determine the cultivated area and estimate production. Central authorities used these surveys to set tax quotas that local authorities collected. The farmers in the early phases of the caliphates were free private landholders.

This new empire supported movements of people, ideas, and goods, and a growing population, which expanded markets for agricultural products. Arab farmers met the increased demand with a wide array of crops, some new to the Mediterranean and others introduced recently: sugar cane, sorghum, hard wheat, Asian rice, sour oranges, lemons, bananas and plantains, coconut palm, eggplant, artichoke, spinach, watermelon, and many others for use as food, fiber, medicine, cosmetics, textiles, wood, and other purposes. These crops came from South and Southeast Asia and Africa. The Arabs were mostly intermediaries: they adopted the plants, learned to grow them, and helped distribute them through the region.

The introduction and spread of these crops brought important changes. All these crops required considerable water. The Muslim imperial lands were arid, and most did not have sufficient irrigation. Many farmers and officials from the eighth century began improving existing irrigation networks, building new ones, and introducing new methods, including waterwheels, the *shadouf* (a pail hung from a pole pivoting on a post), and the *qanat*, underground canals that moved groundwater while reducing evaporation.

These crops also changed land use. Traditionally in the Near East, Egypt, and the Mediterranean, farmers grew mainly winter-habit grains and legumes, planted in fall and harvested in spring, but very few spring crops. Yet Arab farming regions were nearer to the equator, and had more uniform temperature and weather conditions than Europe. As irrigation expanded, the new plants enabled farmers to grow crops all year round. Some, like spinach and eggplant, could produce four harvests a year; others that took longer could be alternated, such as rice, wheat, sorghum, and legumes. Arab farmers never used fallow but did employ a wide range of rotations that these short-growing seasons allowed. They also developed a much more sophisticated knowledge of soils than farmers had before, and were able to employ irrigation skillfully, enabling them to use almost any land for farming.

Arabs also held land as private property in this period. While they lived in villages, they did not have Europe's communal restrictions that required villagers to farm the same crops at the same time. The Arab farmers also worked in a highly developed market economy that used money rather than barter. Rich landowners and well-to-do peasants had capital to invest and lend, which facilitated long-term projects like waterworks and orchards. Arab rulers imposed taxes, but they were low and farmers could often evade them. At this phase Arab farming was less restricted, more adaptable, and open to markets than farming in early medieval Europe.

The Arab expansion depended on and contributed to significant population growth in the Muslim regions. This farming system supported several of the world's largest cities, including Baghdad, which may have been home to more than one million people. Rural areas also became increasingly densely populated, sometimes even decreasing the farmland, as along the Tigris River.

Arab crops and farming methods spread widely, as a result of the political unity that the Islamic caliphates provided in this period, and the Arab propensity for travel. The pull of demand also stimulated farmers to grow many of these new crops. As farmers produced more of these crops, demand spread down the social ladder, especially with cotton. Farmers and wealthy landowners also produced new crops in anticipation of a market, especially tree crops like oranges and lemons.

Ultimately Arab farming in the Mediterranean region declined. Partly this resulted from their intensive cultivation and heavy use of irrigation. Lands became increasingly saline and had to be abandoned. Farmers extended cultivation to marginal lands with thin and poor soils. Wars and invasion disrupted normal trade and monetary flows. The system also suffered from its very success. The farming population grew so much that farmers had to settle in locations unfavorable for trade and unprotected from invasion. By the tenth century, many settlements seem to have disappeared from the record.

External invasions also disrupted cultivation. In Spain and the Mediterranean, West European conquerors destroyed Muslim rule and drove out many Muslims, and with them much of the knowledge of how to grow many crops. Later rulers, for example, had to recruit foreigners to revive sugar cane production in Sicily.

Part of the decline also came from internal factors. As the Abbasids declined, regional authorities usurped power and intensified taxation. Driven into debt, increasing numbers of peasants commended themselves to local landowners, who assumed many characteristics of nobility, while peasants became increasingly servile. Various types of collective landholding emerged, such as the *waqf*, a land endowment for institutions, like schools or mosques. The produce of the land was to support the institution. New owners of waqfs lacked management skills but wanted to maintain their incomes. They hired managers who exploited the farming population on the waqf for their own benefit. These waqfs became increasingly widespread in Egypt and the Ottoman Empire, and stifled agricultural growth and innovation.

By the ninth century the Abbasid state declined significantly in power in part because of its policy of issuing tax-farms or *iqtas* to soldiers and officials. These military benefices or grants to military officers and other officials were accompanied by harsh taxation. These iqta holders took advantage of their position and maneuvered peasants into surrendering their lands to them. This procedure was called *taljia*, translated as commendation, or *himaya*, protection. The Muslim officials who accumulated such dependent peasants resisted and weakened Abbasid authority by depriving it of taxes. Privately held land, called *milk*, became ever scarcer.

Such conflicts seriously weakened the Middle Eastern economy. The Mesopotamian irrigation works deteriorated so much that the region became depopulated. Harsh taxation and manipulation by the iqtas and tax farmers weakened incentives for farmers to increase productivity. Iraq changed from one of the richest to one of the poorest regions in the Middle East until the twentieth century. While the Abbasids officially remained the rulers of the caliphate, the provinces came under rulers with varied approaches to farmers. Some perpetuated the exploitative iqta system, while others like the Seljuq Turks expanded irrigation and attempted to restore agriculture, until the Mongol invasions overthrew them in 1258.

The European Crusaders' conquest of Muslim lands also set back Muslim farming. Often the Muslim population was expelled from these regions or fled. Where they remained their land rights were curtailed. Former Muslim lands came under European methods of cultivation; this however caused less damage to the landscape and soils.

The discovery of the New World and Western imperial expansion in general reduced the importance of Arab agriculture. As Western European businesses produced the former Muslim crops in the New World and sold them at low prices in Europe and to Muslim countries, Muslim farmers could not compete. Production of these crops declined in the Muslim regions from the seventeenth century, as they became more dependent on imports from Europe. This pattern of domestic producers driven out of business by another country's foreign imports would recur in the nineteenth and twentieth centuries.

In the few cases in which Europeans conquered Arab regions, the Europeans replaced Arab farming with European systems. An important example was the Reconquista of Spain, an intermittent war of more than 200 years that ended with the European conquest of Granada in 1492. The new Spanish rulers, Ferdinand and Isabella, seeking to eliminate the Muslim and other foreign influences in their kingdom, expelled the Jews in 1492 and the Muslims in 1501. They also used a Catholic judicial agency and other "investigations" to find and expel the Moriscos, Muslims allegedly pretending to be Christian, in 1605. They thus drove from Spain most of the people who knew how to cultivate these Asian crops. When Europeans, a generation or two later, decided they wanted these crops, they had to re-import Arab farmers and farming methods that they had effaced earlier.

China: crises and innovations

Agriculture played a central role in Chinese history during the Middle Empire of the Sui, Tang, and Sung dynasties. Agrarian crises, rebellions, and recoveries shaped and sometimes determined the survival of empires. Natural disasters, crop failures, and subsistence crises tested the resources and resilience of Chinese leaders. In the Sung dynasty (960–1279) this led to the introduction of rapid-ripening rice varieties. Invasions and agrarian crises in the north led many peasants to migrate south of the Yangzi River for fertile land. By the Sung dynasty most of the Chinese population lived in the south.

After the Han dynasty, China disintegrated into separate states that attempted to solve the political and agrarian problems they inherited from the Han with little success. In one of these states, Western Wei, the ruler rebuilt his army by recruiting soldier farmers who would support themselves with their families' labor. This system became the "divisional militia" that Chinese governments employed intermittently into the eighteenth century. It provided a military force of 200,000 men. The Sui dynasty (581–618) began with efforts by Chinese emperors to weaken big landlords with the extension of divisional militias and land redistribution to peasants.

The Sui dynasty was aggressive and militaristic, exploiting millions of peasants to build the Grand Canal and restore the Great Wall. Chronic agrarian and subsistence problems persisted, and the first Sui emperor restored the ever-normal granary system. In this system, the government bought surpluses from peasants when harvests were abundant and prices low, and then released grain during shortages to drive prices down and supply the hungry. Yet the dynasty was overthrown, in part because the emperor pursued a luxurious lifestyle while many peasants starved during a famine.

The Tang dynasty (618–907) began with recovery from the disasters of the Sui dynasty. The new Tang emperor asserted government control over land use, prohibited the sale of land, and tried to introduce an equalizing land distribution policy based on the old equal-field system. By the reign of the second emperor, however, the government began receiving official reports that the rich were "eating up" the lands of the poor despite the prohibition on sales. Successive emperors repeatedly ordered all lands illegally purchased from poor peasants to be returned to them, and even allocated funds to local officials to buy these lands back from the big landowners. The repeated promulgation of these laws, however, indicated that the problem continued.

The equal-field system failed because it was difficult to implement and could not be used for rice cultivation in the Yangtze River valley. Rice cultivation required long-term investment in land, but the equal-field system depended on redistribution of lands. The Tang dynasty had chronic crop failures from droughts, floods, and infestations that caused serious famines. Like the Sui dynasty, the Tang government relied on the ever-normal granary system and relied on it for famine relief.

Military developments also had an effect on Tang agriculture. The divisional militia was unpopular, and many Chinese evaded recruitment or fled, so the government ended it in 749. This abolition eliminated one of the last obstacles to the expansion of holdings by large landlords. It also obliged the Chinese government to rely for its border defense on local armies. One of the leaders of a local army, An Lushan, took advantage of a series of natural disasters and famines in the early 750s to initiate a rebellion. This eight-year rebellion (756–63), and the famines the government could not eliminate because of the rebellion, were estimated to have killed more than 30 million people, more than half of the population. After defeating the rebels, the government undertook to revive agriculture. The regime settled most soldiers on farmland, prohibited the rich and influential farmers from enlarging their estates or controlling water supplies, and distributed seed and food to small farmers.

The agrarian economy recovered, but the problems of the wealthy appropriating the poor peasants' land reappeared. The government introduced a tax reform, but this did not solve the problem. The wealthy continued to appropriate lands legally and illegally while the poor increasingly abandoned their farms. In the late ninth century, the emperors' powers declined as provincial authorities fought rebel groups formed by desperate peasants. The Tang dynasty collapsed in the early tenth century, succeeded by another sequence of small short-lived states for which little evidence survives.

The Sung dynasty (960–1279) that reunified China has an extremely important place in agrarian history as the first example of a government-supported "Green Revolution." The first Sung emperors faced a China with its agriculture in decline and disarray, after decades of environmental crises and military conflict since the late Tang dynasty. Population and productivity had both fallen, and the countryside had many deserted farms since so many peasants had fled taxation and war. The new government began with the usual array of policies to help farming recover. It settled soldiers on farms, distributed food relief and seed, published farming guidebooks, and attempted a series of administrative and land reforms with tax exemptions to encourage production. By the time of the third and fourth Sung emperors, conditions had improved, but inequities appeared: large landlords evaded taxation, lived luxurious lives, while poor peasants paid more than their share. Peasants faced declining yields from soil exhaustion, and large land areas in many provinces remained uncultivated.

In 1011 a drought destroyed rice harvests in parts of the lower Yangtze and Huai River valleys. The Emperor Zhenzong (997–1022) in 1012 transferred seed to the drought regions, a type of relief applied by previous governments. This time, however, he sent seed from Fukien province (on the southeast coast of China) that derived from a rice variety from Champa, now Vietnam. This variety ripened in 100 days instead of the usual 150 days required for most other rice varieties in use at the time. Champa rice also could withstand drought conditions better. Its rapid ripening and ability to grow both in wet-rice paddy fields and as a dry-land crop, like wheat, allowed farmers to produce two crops on the same fields in one year. The introduction of Champa rice encouraged Chinese farmers and officials to seek out more early-ripening varieties in subsequent years. These varieties had somewhat lower yields than the full-term varieties, but the opportunity they provided for double cropping substantially increased total farm production possibilities.

While these new varieties promised great improvement in food production, their use spread only gradually. The government encouraged their use by distributing guidebooks to farmers. Farmers used the new varieties widely only in four central rice-growing provinces around the lower Yangtze River before the Mongol conquest in the thirteenth century. Their main expansion apparently took place in the Ming and Qing dynasties.

Chronic problems of poverty persisted and held back farm production. The introduction of the new varieties did not bring about an immediate transformation. Serious crop failures and famines continued to occur. A famine during the reign of the Emperor Renzong (1022–63) exceeded the government's capacity to provide relief because of military supply needs. Officials estimated that more than half of the famine victims died. Farmers' poverty hindered the spread and effectiveness of new varieties. Often farmers lacked the resources to fertilize and weed their fields adequately. Emperor Renzong attempted to alleviate these conditions by eliminating taxes on farmers who settled on unused land, limiting land holdings, and introducing the "square-field system," essentially a type of tax reassessment. It proved impossible, however, to cut back large land holdings, the square-field system proved unworkable, and poor farmers needed more aid than the government could provide.

During the eleventh century, the varied environmental and economic conditions in different provinces gave rise in some cases to servile agrarian relations. Sung dynasty laws prohibited landlords from tying peasants to land, and thus enserfing them, but many landlords ignored these laws. While China in the Sung dynasty was not a "manorial" economy, landlords in certain provinces had large holdings. Some of these were consolidated estates like those of medieval Europe, which could be managed from a central point. Others consisted of many small dispersed holdings which a landlord could not reasonably expect to manage and from which he could only receive rents. The tenants had varying and uncertain degrees of subordination. Tenant-guests were the highest status group, with legal rights to resist landlords. Land-guests were more like servants, had fewer rights, and were more often subject to subservient relations. Field servants could be hired laborers but were more often bondservants, who had surrendered their status as free men (liang-min) for a period ranging from a single day to several years, to pay off a debt or earn money or food by working as indentured laborers. A limited number of slaves worked mostly in non-Han Chinese populations in inland China.

These different servile groups probably never reached half of the total population, but in some central provinces they were much more numerous than in the more commercially developed provinces in the east. In regions where servile relations prevailed, land-guests and sometimes even tenant-guests often worked under conditions that resembled serfdom. They could not leave the lands where they worked, and if the landlord sold that land they would be sold with it. These tenants had to pay rents, work as forced laborers in certain tasks for the landlord, and had to pay fees, for example to permit a child to marry. Such bondage may have been the dominant practice in Hunan and Hubei, in southern inland China, and it was also found in many parts of Fukien province. Chinese law also made land-guests and field workers, and sometimes tenant-guests, legally unequal, penalizing them more harshly than free people and especially landlords.

Other areas had few or no servile groups. In the highly commercialized areas around the Yangtze Delta, there were few large land holdings, and farm land was a less attractive investment than urban land. These regions had more small private land holders producing for the large markets of the towns. Landlords with large holdings were absentee owners who allowed their tenants to run their farms. In these areas land prices changed frequently and it was in landlords' interest not to bind tenant-guests to the land. These areas had very few land-guests but many tenant-guests, who worked much more autonomously than tenant-guests in Hunan. They had unpaid obligations and were still in a highly subordinate legal status.

This was the social context for the chronic Sung dynasty problems of vacant lands and extreme inequalities of wealth between landlords and masses of poor peasants. Peasants exhausted their lands desperately producing crops to meet their tax, rent, and food needs, while landlords' lands often produced larger harvests because they were not so intensively cropped. Large landowners used their local power to evade taxation, while poor peasants paid what they owed and more. This situation in turn reduced the government's revenues and strained its supplies.

To address these problems, in the 1070s, a top minister, Wang An-shih, instituted a wide range of reforms: including a system of loans to peasants to protect them from rapacious moneylenders, and policies to fix commodity prices. This program did not work out as well as hoped. Both officials extending the loans and many of the farmers receiving them did not fully understand the consequences of the system. Officials pushed loans on farmers even though any interest payments for them were difficult to pay. When poor peasants could not repay, the government required their richer neighbors to cover the repayment, which often required those neighbors to sell their main assets.

In the midst of this reform, another famine in 1074 drove peasants to flee their lands to escape worsening debt and find food. Wang's enemies at court replaced him with an old official who abolished the loan system. As famine deaths continued, this official decided that no existing policy could solve the peasant–landlord conflict, and adopted a policy of "watchful waiting" for a better idea.

Over the next decades and into the Southern Sung dynasty, Chinese leaders tried every traditional policy to increase farm production: improving irrigation, reorganizing fields, reviving and abolishing Wang's loan system, reclaiming land, and settling soldiers on open lands. Crop failures and famines recurred, but the needs for relief came to exceed the granary system's capacities. In the last century of the dynasty, emperors resorted to more extreme expedients to restore agricultural production. Emperor Xiaozong in the late twelfth century dismissed officials of provinces that had bad harvests, and applied measures such as seed loans, irrigation construction, and tax cuts. Peasants continued to abandon lands, however, and tax revenue fell. Emperor

Lizong (1223–64) ordered the outright abolition of large land holdings through government purchases, which also failed because officials often offered below-market prices in depreciated paper currency, and bankrupted many formerly successful landlords. By 1280, Sung China had an empty treasury, rebellions, brigandage, and no defense against the Mongol invasions.

Servility, freedom, and agricultural transformation in the post-classical period

During the thousand years after the fall of Rome and the Han dynasty, the dual subordination of farmers underwent a complex transformation. This period witnessed chronic struggles between peasant producers and large landowners over autonomy and subsistence. Large landowners tried to retain and expand their land holdings and power at the peasants' expense, but met resistance from peasants and certain governments. In Byzantium and China, emperors or lower officials tried to restrain the growth of large land holdings and even to restore appropriated lands back to smallholders. These governments also attempted to supplant landlords with militarized peasants, as in the Chinese divisional militia and the Byzantine Theme system of farmer soldiers, with limited success. In all of these cases, governments and peasants attempted to resist the trend of socio-economic subordination of farmers.

Europe in this period endured economic decline, political fragmentation, and invasions. Many farmers sought security at the price of subordination in serfdom. After the invasions ended, the agrarian economy expanded to its geographical limits, with a large population farming marginal lands, but also with a money economy and cities with growing and diversifying demand. The cumbersome and inflexible manorial system became a costly obstacle to the necessary agricultural changes. The crises of the fourteenth century provided peasants with the opportunity to force landlords and governments to accommodate at least part of their interests.

European governments in this period, however, undertook few if any steps to defend the peasants at the expense of the landlords, like the Byzantine and Chinese governments did. For the most part aristocratic governments viewed the peasants as a potential problem and threat. Peasants won partial autonomy and in a few cases emancipation only through hard economic negotiations, political struggles, and sometimes rebellion. Ultimately only the Enlightenment, the great shift in European intellectual life in the eighteenth century, would motivate European governments to emancipate most of the peasants.

Environmental factors played important and sometimes decisive roles in agriculture and the lives of farmers in this post-classical era. China and Byzantium had chronic disasters that destroyed harvests and caused famines. European conditions were more favorable initially, but ended the period with the Little Ice Age, a vast agricultural and demographic crisis that would linger for centuries.

Partly in response to these environmental hazards, the post-classical millennium saw slow but progressive agricultural changes. The Muslim Arabs who created empires from Spain to India also helped spread a diverse array of Asian and African crops throughout that region. Europeans' taste for several of them later led to the formation of the plantation complex, a crucial development in world history, in the following centuries. China's Sung dynasty leaders initiated a long process of agricultural intensification by introducing Vietnamese rapid-ripening rice. The rice varieties that derived from that beginning would make possible the massive expansion of the Chinese population, economy, and empire. The Sung dynasty's efforts to improve rice seeds, sometimes described as a "Green Revolution," appear to have been the first effort in history to use a technological "fix" to help farmers resist their subordination to environmental disaster.

The territorial expansion and trade of the Muslim empires increased agricultural connections between East and West. Still, European and Asian agriculture continued to diverge: China and most of Asia emphasized intensification and crop production, while Europe increasingly emphasized extensive farming and livestock. Europe's focus intensified the region's dependence on trade for food supplies. Even within large states, regional specialization and trade shaped farming, as in the Byzantine Empire, with its regular import of Egyptian grain, and China, which relied on the Yangtze valley farmers for rice to feed the north via long-distance shipments on the Grand Canal. The European pattern of regional specialization and reliance on grain imports from the East would lead to the much larger globalization of food production in the modern period.

Further reading

On Medieval Europe, good readings include Renée Doehaerd, *The Early Middle Ages in the West* (Amsterdam: North Holland Publishing Company, 1978); Georges Duby, *Rural Economy and Country Life in the Medieval West* (Chapel Hill, NC: University of North Carolina Press, 1968); Warren Treadgold, *A History of the Byzantine State and Society* (Stanford, CA: Stanford University Press, 1997). The classic study of the Arab agricultural contribution is Andrew M. Watson, *Agricultural Innovation in the Early Islamic World: The Diffusion of Crops and Farming Techniques, 700–1100* (Cambridge: Cambridge University Press, 1983).

On China, see the sources listed for the previous chapter, and also Joseph McDermott, "Charting Blank Spaces and Dispute Regions: The Problem of Sung Land Tenure," *Journal of Asian Studies* 44(1) (1984), pp. 13–41.

Chapter 4

Early modern agriculture and European agricultural dominance
1500–1800

During the fifteenth to the eighteenth centuries farmers in most of the world lived under worse environmental conditions than in previous centuries. The Little Ice Age brought extreme cold weather with breaks of warmer periods. Environmental factors created recurrent crises, especially in the northern hemisphere: cold summers, freezing winters, serious crop failures, and famines.

Farmers also lived under several different types of servile systems. Some of these systems formed through small-scale actions that almost imperceptibly transformed free farmers into dependants. In the Muslim empires of South Asia, the Ottomans and the Mughals, initially free peasants came under the growing power of local landlords. In East Asia, government actions and market forces combined to reduce the numbers of servile farmers significantly. In China and Japan, small-scale peasant farmers, smallholders, and tenants prospered in the growing economies of the region, but suffered greatly from political conflict and natural disasters.

In contrast to Asia, Europe consciously maintained or created highly servile systems. In Eastern Europe, peasants came under a new and intrusive domination often called the "second serfdom." In Western Europe serfdom declined to a few isolated locations, but most peasants remained subordinated by a variety of traditional practices, reassertions of noble authority, and the growing power of governments. Western European explorers, traders, and imperialist politicians created a "plantation complex" that harnessed the conquered American territories and enslaved Africans and Indians in a mass-production system of luxury commodities.

The Little Ice Age

The long-term cooling pattern of the Little Ice Age ran from the fourteenth century well into the nineteenth century. The pattern was not uniform but cycled between warmer and cooler periods. During the cooler times, such as 1680–1730, glaciers expanded into lower altitudes all over the world, and extreme weather caused many problems. During the fifteenth century, falling temperatures eliminated grape growing and wine production in England.

During the 1590s, cold weather brought crop failures, high prices, food shortages, and food riots in England and the continent. In 1709 the extremely cold winter caused ice floes to block rivers and obstruct the French government's efforts to transport grain to relieve famine in several provinces. Similar crises recurred repeatedly in these centuries. Extreme cold in seventeenth-century China destroyed the last orange groves in Jiang-Xi province.

Causes of the Little Ice Age included increased sunspots, a decline in the flow of the Gulf Stream, and more frequent large-scale volcanic eruptions. In 1600 the Huaynaputina volcano in southern Peru erupted in a gigantic explosion on the scale of the Krakatau volcano of 1883. Ash from Huaynaputina, detected in ice cores from Greenland to the South Pole from 1600 and afterwards, made the summers of 1601 and the following years the coldest in centuries, or even millennia, all over the northern hemisphere. This weather caused crop failures and famines, such as the great famine of 1601–4 in Russia. Scientific studies indicate that while the Little Ice Age affected the northern hemisphere more than the southern, its effects were global.

The Little Ice Age created an environmental context that made subsistence uncertain. Crop failures and famines in Europe led to food riots and popular rebellions against taxation and local or central government authorities. China, Japan, and other East Asian countries endured some of the worst droughts in their history in the seventeenth century, which contributed to rebellions and other political crises. Extreme and variable weather and the resultant crop failures affected governments by decreasing taxation, hindering supply of armies, and supporting the resistance of regional rulers. Among the objectives of government agrarian policies were measures to reduce the threat of agrarian protest and avert or prevent food crises.

Agrarian Asia: rising and declining servile systems

Asian agrarian societies during the fifteenth to eighteenth centuries came under two main cultural-economic spheres of influence: the Muslim empires of South and Central Asia, and the Chinese sphere of East Asia. Both spheres included peasants and landlords in different ways. The Muslim sphere began this period with its inheritance of diverse food crops and primarily small-scale private farmers. In the Chinese sphere, governments supported peasant farmers as the economic basis of the nation, but landlords had a strong tendency to force peasants into a state of dependency when the government weakened. This period brings the reversal of both patterns.

Farming in Muslim empires: The Ottoman agrarian system

The Ottoman Empire that formed in Anatolia in the thirteenth to fifteenth centuries relied on cavalry forces or *sipahis*, and a "new army" infantry or *janissaries*, recruited from the conquered peoples. The Ottomans granted the sipahis landed estates, *timars*, in Anatolia, but tried to reduce potential military threats from them by keeping them occupied in military campaigns and by rotating the timars among recipients.

In all of their conquered areas, the Ottomans attempted to weaken landlords and support peasant farmers. They invaded the Balkans, for example, in the early fifteenth century during a conflict between Serbian nobles and their serfs. The Ottomans took over the estates, eliminated the nobles or incorporated them into the Ottoman elite, and abolished the peasants' serfdom, requiring them to pay only a relatively light "plow tax."

The Ottomans declared that all the lands belonged to the Sultan or were transferred by him to the government. Ottoman laws specified that as long as peasants cultivated their lands regularly, they could not be dispossessed and could pass them on to their children. The Empire also tolerated varied peasant farming systems. In Egypt peasants lived in corporate villages, were taxed as a village rather than individually, and in the south even repartitioned their land every year to equalize distribution. They observed these practices until a new Egyptian government privatized the villages in the nineteenth century.

The Ottoman Empire reached its peak in the sixteenth century and then began a slow decline. In agrarian life this intermittent decline involved processes of increasing taxation and growing power of local elites. During the sixteenth to eighteenth centuries the Empire nearly doubled in population, while the area under crops grew only 20 percent. This in turn created overcrowded villages, unemployment in towns, and food shortages. The government increased taxes to cover its frequent wars and growing court expenditures. The taxation and rural overpopulation forced peasants to resort to local moneylenders, or to flee the villages for the towns.

The fiscal burdens also fell on local land holders, the timar-holding sipahis, as well as tax farmers and other officials whom the government sent to the provinces to collect taxes. These officials often extorted illegal taxes and forced labor obligations from peasants. In some cases peasants sued the officials in the Ottoman court system, but many simply fled. If a timar holder or another landlord could find the peasants who fled, they could use the courts to force the peasants to return to their timar lands.

In the seventeenth century, the Ottoman leadership tried to make the Empire self-sufficient and prohibited exports, but traders smuggled goods out relatively easily. This clandestine trade raised land prices, and many janissaries, corrupt officials, and timar holders acquired large land holdings to profit from this development. These new landlords, called *ayans*, often formed their estates on land abandoned by peasants who had fled to towns. Many ayans recruited fleeing peasants as laborers on these estates, or purchased slaves in the slave markets of the Middle East. The ayans increasingly evaded state control and formed their own small armies of janissaries. Many peasants ended up subjected to the kinds of servile obligations from which the Ottoman conquest had freed them, including forced labor and requisitions of crops, livestock, and money.

Some peasants resisted this subordination and formed bands with former soldiers. The Ottoman leaders tried to alleviate the situation with reduced taxes, but sharply raised taxes whenever they fought a war. This again led to peasant flight to towns, crowding, food riots, and rebel bands. Conflicts over land, peasants' rights, and agrarian taxation would be important factors in Ottoman decline after the sixteenth century.

South Asia and agriculture under the Mughals

Before the Mughal Empire, South Asia had only two brief periods of unification: the Maurya Empire (322–185 BCE) and the Gupta Empire (CE 320–550). South Asia in other periods fragmented into numerous smaller and shorter-lived dynasties. The few sources that have survived from these eras indicate that early rural South Asia had peasants and landlords, but their identities and relationships found expression through the South Asian caste system, in which every individual was born into a particular social and kinship group that determined his or her role and status in society. In some cases the lowest caste groups, *sudras* or outcaste "untouchables," worked as laborers for high-caste Brahmins. Hindu temples, like European monasteries, sometimes held substantial estates. Farmers had to pay a range of taxes.

The Mughal Empire as a stable state really begins with the reign of Akbar (ruled 1555–1605), the first Indian state from which substantial sources have survived. Based on the plans of his main economic advisor Todor Mal, Akbar introduced a tax system based on ten-year averages of production for the main regions of India down to the local level. Preparing these estimates was a major accomplishment for India at that time. The system exacted one-third of grain production and a larger share of other crops, but initially peasants produced enough to leave them with more than subsistence food supplies in most years.

In Mughal India, as in the Ottoman Empire, the Mughal sultan was the official owner of the land, but peasants could buy, sell, and inherit land, and could not be removed from their lands under ordinary circumstances. An extensive survey of land-holding patterns in the nineteenth century showed that almost nowhere did peasants or other cultivators hold lands in common or collective tenure. In the Mughal period and before, virtually all land holding was private and individual, but under the Mughals the peasants could not leave their lands. Laws and repeated decrees required peasants who left their lands to return or to be returned to their home territories. Since India in this period had considerable open land and relatively few peasants to farm it, the government enforced these laws to retain peasants on estates to pay taxes and support the Mughal elites. Peasants had security of tenure but lived in a status of "semi-serfdom."

Peasants lived in villages under the authority of a village council or *panchayat* and a headman or *muqaddam*, but the most important authority for peasants was the landlord or *zamindar*. The zamindars (the term derives from the Persian word for landlord) comprised three groups: the former local rulers or rajas whom the Mughals conquered or co-opted into their government, local or regional tax officials who held their own land, and most often, small-scale local landlords. Under Mughal law, a zamindar was not the final owner of the land, but held rights to produce and payments from cultivators, and could sell and buy land. Mughal officials often viewed zamindars as tax gatherers and lumped them together with local tax officials, but they treated the zamindar's land holding, or *zamindari*, as his private property. If he failed to pay taxes or rebelled, the rulers allotted the zamindari to someone else. Zamindars often had armed retainers and exercised despotic power in their districts, but usually did not have the military capacity or unity to threaten Mughal authority. A few former rajas and especially powerful zamindars became a real threat to Mughal authority.

Agriculture under the Mughals had high but variable productivity. Less than half of the present crop land was under cultivation, for a population of approximately 140 million. Indian peasants used advanced techniques including seed drills (which enable farmers to control the spacing and depth of planting) and transplanting of rice. Most noteworthy, the subcontinent's seasons were defined not by temperature but by the monsoons, the heavy rains that fell most summers. Skillful use of irrigation and crop selection allowed some farmers to produce two to three crops per year. Generally farmers grew wheat and millet in the west and northwest, and rice in the east and south. They also grew many other crops for consumption and sale, including cotton, hemp, jute, indigo, opium, fruits and vegetables, and increasingly New World crops including chilis, maize, and tobacco. Because much land remained uncultivated, farmers also raised livestock for draft forces and food. Villages processed sugar and textiles as well.

Foreigners' impressions of India contrasted the country's apparent wealth of produce with the poverty of its peasants. India exported large amounts of valuable farm products such as spices, sugar products, and silk and cotton cloth. Many regions of India developed specializations in particular products. Yet India chronically endured terrible famines, usually after monsoon failures. The worst such crisis occurred in 1630–32, under Shah Jahan, whose wife Mumtaz Mahal died in childbirth in 1631. Shah Jahan, apparently more moved by his wife's death than by the starvation and deaths of millions of Indians, began building the Taj Mahal to commemorate her in the midst of the famine. He devoted to that purpose millions of rupees that could have saved lives.

The suffering and loss of life that famines caused under the Mughals suggests that India's apparent wealth concealed a generally low level of farm production and subsistence. These famines reflected the frequency and severity of natural disasters as well as Mughal land and tax policies. The Mughals used conditional grants of estates to military servitors to reward and retain supporters. They tried to prevent these estates, or *jagirs*, from becoming the basis for opposition by rotating them among their recipients, or *jagirdars*, every few years. This pattern encouraged jagirdars to extract from estate peasants not only the taxes due to the Mughal government but as much as they could for themselves. Government reports from Akbar through Aurangzeb reported that jagirs and other officials oppressed peasants, who would flee, leaving land uncultivated. François Bernier, a French physician who served Aurangzeb, reported that much land was left uncultivated because peasants had fled or died from officials' abuse. Yet the Mughals often left zamindars with nothing themselves after imposing especially high taxes to finance wars and construction.

In response to these abuses, both peasants and zamindars rebelled, in some cases jointly. In 1661 the Mughals conquered the western district of Kooch Behar and imposed much harsher taxes than the previous raja (local ruler). Peasants rose up and expelled the Mughals from the region. Caste identity and the new Sikh religion unified many peasant rebellions. Zamindars often resisted paying taxes and resorted to rebellions, which encouraged them to moderate their treatment of their peasants in order to rely on their support against the Mughals.

Mughal rulers could not easily solve the causes of rebellions. In the earlier decades of their rule, they could punish oppressive jagirdars or move them to another estate to protect the peasants from their depredations. By the late seventeenth century, however, Aurangzeb was caught between chronic rebellions of the Marathas (a large Hindu ethnic group from Western India) and other groups against Mughal authority and taxation, and his need to retain supporters by granting jagirs to military officers and defeated opponents. In this context the condition of the peasants became a low priority. Yet the Marathas and other rebels, while relying on peasants for troops, could be just as oppressive as the Mughals and jagirdars they replaced. The Maratha leader Shivaji demanded revenues from his territories double those the Mughals had exacted. Peasant rebels often ended up exploiting their fellow peasants. These rural conflicts along with the political conflicts of the late seventeenth and eighteenth centuries created the circumstances that allowed the British to establish imperial control in South Asia.

In these Muslim empires, Ottoman and Mughal authorities fought about the division of groups of villages among themselves and exploited the rural areas for products, labor, and soldiers. Very rarely did they view the rural sector as deserving any contributions from them for support or improvement. Even famine relief appears to have been weak at best. From the peasants' standpoint, these regimes combined frequent environmental crises with ill-regulated plunder.

China: the Ming–Qing transition and the end of Chinese serfdom

China's pattern of political change was closely connected to peasants and agriculture. Dynasties often began in the wake of chaos and loss of life from wars and economic crises, with abandoned lands and insecure subsistence. New dynasties would make concessions to peasants to encourage them to farm more land. The new Ming dynasty, for example, in 1372 allowed peasants to claim as much land as they could cultivate in the areas devastated by the succession wars. Such dynasties also restored the relief granary system to deal with famines.

As a dynasty matured, however, sooner or later local officials and landlords took advantage of waning central power to subordinate peasants to servile status. In the Ming dynasty they made peasants into bondservants. Generally landlords living on their lands had field workers who were bondsmen, while absentee landlords relied on free tenant farmers to cultivate their lands, supervised by bondservant-managers. The Ming dynasty tried to stop this pattern with a law in 1397 that prohibited commoners from having servile laborers. Commoners then had to adopt the bondservants. Ming and Qing documents show that many rural people were bondservants and many were free peasants. There is not sufficient information to determine relative numbers.

In the course of the Ming dynasty, the status of bondservants declined. They were classed in Ming law as "base people," below commoners, punished more harshly for violations of laws and denied access to government posts and education. Bondservant managers at least had the opportunity to make money, even though they resented their low status. Bondservant field workers, even though they were often adopted by their masters' families, endured harsh treatment. Masters often made them work with too little rest and food in bad weather, abused their wives and daughters, and confiscated their property and sold off their family members after the bondsman's death.

As the dynasty declined in the late sixteenth and early seventeenth centuries, natural disasters caused famines. "Poor households" and "hungry people" plundered granaries and sometimes the houses of wealthy families. The Ming authorities responded with tax relief, and some gentry landlords organized collective relief. These efforts were insufficient, and in 1630 a famine in the central province of Shaanxi led peasants to support the peasant rebel leader Li Zicheng. During the 14 years of Li Zicheng's rebellion, his forces equalized land between rich and poor in the provinces they controlled, killed many rich landlords, and plundered and destroyed many estates. His rebellion overthrew the Ming dynasty in 1644, but then lost power to the Manchu invasion a few years later.

The Manchu conquest and the associated interruption of government activity during repeated famine crises caused massive loss of life. China's population had grown approximately from 80 million in the fourteenth century to 150 million by the early seventeenth century. By the late seventeenth century when the Manchus had defeated the last resistance to their authority, the population had declined to an estimated 90 million.

Soon after coming to power, the Manchu leaders began to reward their relatives, followers, and military officers, called bannermen, with estates, usually about 50 hectares, supplied with ten bondservants under a headman. Peasant bondservants had begun rebellions against landlords in the last years of the Manchus, and after the Manchu conquest they rebelled against their new Manchu-imposed masters. These rebellions ranged from group demands to have the bond of servitude annulled, to violent attacks on gentry families and their estates. Population growth contributed to this unrest: the estates that the Qing allotted within a few decades could no longer support their growing servile populations.

By the early eighteenth century the Manchus began to dismantle the servile system to reduce peasant discontent. In laws issued in 1727, 1728, and 1744 the government raised the status of bondservants from "base people" to commoners. By the 1750s bondservants played an insignificant role in the Chinese economy. In association with this reform and with the expansion of the Chinese economy, Chinese farmers in the early Qing increasingly produced for growing urban markets, based on an intensified employment of family labor.

With the decline of Chinese serfdom, by the late eighteenth century most farm units in China were peasant family farms, either smallholders or tenants. The landlords included the previous rural gentry and scholar officials and also successful traders who saw farms as a source of cotton and cloth for finishing in town enterprises. In this period the peasants differentiated regionally and economically. In remote inland areas they focused more on food production, but in urbanizing areas like the Yangzi delta, they increasingly shifted to commercial crops for the growing market, above all cotton. Few if any peasants in the Yangzi delta grew cotton in the fourteenth century, but by the nineteenth century virtually every peasant farm grew it, supporting a boom in textile production and exports of tens of millions of bolts of cotton fabric every year.

Yet this commercialization was based on peasant family farms that could rarely escape a basic subsistence level of existence. The fast-ripening rice varieties of the Sung and Ming dynasties reached a limit of productivity by the seventeenth century that Chinese agriculture could not surpass until the Green Revolution of the 1970s. As their population increased from the eighteenth century onward, Chinese peasant households saw their land allotments shrink in each successive generation. They had to employ as many family members as possible, even in jobs that earned very low wages, in order to bring in more income. This pattern of "self-exploitation" is still prevalent among many low-income groups worldwide, especially peasants.

The high productivity of Chinese agriculture and textile production was thus based on desperate efforts by poor Chinese peasants to survive.

Still, during the first century of Manchu rule Chinese peasants survived fairly well. China recovered the population lost in the Ming–Qing transition and reached a population estimated at 300 million by the end of the eighteenth century, or double the peak level of the Ming dynasty. One factor in this growth was the improved famine-relief system under the Manchus. During most of the eighteenth century the granary system functioned effectively, allowing the government to alleviate the famines of the late seventeenth and eighteenth centuries.

Japanese farmers: from hereditary servants to market individualism

Agriculture in Japan can be dated back to 1000 BCE with rice cultivation modeled on Korean and Chinese practices. Initially Japanese farmers used shifting cultivation, but as the population grew and governments established control, land became scarcer and a valuable commodity; peasants acquired tax, labor, and military obligations.

In the seventh-century Taika reforms, Japanese rulers attempted to abolish private property in land and impose a system of state land ownership borrowed from China. This reform conflicted with traditions of private land holding, and Japanese farmers evaded it so much that the ruler abandoned it. Instead, private landlords and Buddhist monasteries acquired so much land that by the twelfth century private landlords or *shoen* controlled half of Japanese lands.

The shoen were masters of a *sho*, the Japanese counterpart to the western medieval manor, but shoen did not have a demesne (as discussed earlier, the portion of a European estate farmed directly by the landlord). In practice peasants living on the sho disposed of the lands as though they owned them, except that they paid dues in kind to the shoen. The consolidation of this system from the twelfth century coincided with intensification of farm production in Japan, including double cropping of rice and other crops and the expansion of irrigation systems. Still, Japanese farming remained highly vulnerable to weather conditions that could destroy crops and cause famines.

Over the following centuries the shoen landlords came into conflict with the emerging provincial rulers or *daimyo*, and during the late fifteenth and sixteenth centuries, the *sengoku* or warring states period, most of the shoen were brought under the control of daimyo. During the late sixteenth and early seventeenth centuries a series of leading daimyo defeated all the others, culminating in Tokugawa Ieyasu's establishment of the Tokugawa shogunate. The new rulers of Japan conducted comprehensive cadastral surveys that confirmed private peasant land holding as the basis of the Japanese agrarian system. The Tokugawa brought peace, stability, and economic growth to Japan, and also an agrarian transformation.

The Japanese agrarian system by the sixteenth century was based on peasant family networks and private land holding. While some families acquired more land, others had more children than their land could support. To save their families from destitution, and to provide opportunities for their children, these poorer families would sell or give these children as *fudai* or hereditary servants to families who held more land. During serious famines poor families would sell thousands of members, including adults, as fudai. The shogunate repeatedly prohibited such sales, but in crises grudgingly allowed them. The fudai contributed labor to their new families and benefited from the opportunities that the family could provide, including education and inheritance. Perhaps ten percent of Japanese villagers in the seventeenth century were fudai.

Villages also had landless people who became *nago*, a much larger class of farmers who were dependent on the larger peasant land owners, or *oyakata*. Like European serfs, nagos and their families received small allotments of poor quality land, and the minimal means necessary to cultivate it, including livestock, tools, fertilizer, seed, and water, from the landlord. In return they had to work the landlord's lands and perform other tasks for him. In the seventeenth century land owners had no restrictions on employment of nago labor, but had to provide often considerable support to maintain the nago especially in time of crop failure and famine. Nago may have comprised half of Japan's rural population.

Japanese farming in the early Tokugawa shogunate was based on these large family and servile groups. Families would designate one son as the head of the family and allot to his family a disproportionate share of the land and assets. The other sons and kin would receive less. In farm work, however, all of the related families and servants worked together, flooding, planting, and cultivating each paddy or field in succession because water supply and weather conditions required that all jobs be completed as rapidly as possible. This farming system of family collectives increased both productivity and population. From 1500 to 1700 Japanese population and cropland tripled.

Urbanization and economic development stimulated agricultural growth. Japan's urban population grew even faster than the general population. Edo (later Tokyo) grew from a village in 1590 to half a million people by 1730, possibly the largest city in the world. Many other towns grew substantially in this period. Such large cities required vast supplies and relied on big markets for food and textiles. Villages responded by producing more food for town markets, growing cotton or mulberry trees for silkworms on part of their lands, and employing family members to work with silkworms or weaving cotton fabric. All of these processes involved market-based exchanges: purchases of seed, fertilizer, spinning and weaving equipment, and sale of products at different stages of production to other families, middlemen, or townspeople directly.

The publication in 1697 of a large guidebook for farmers, *Nogyo zensho*, by Miyazaki Antei, reflected farmers' efforts to increase production. Antei, an experienced farmer, spent years studying different methods and learning from farmers all over Japan. His book became a classic unsurpassed for centuries, and inspired several imitations during the Tokugawa period. Many farmers read it and applied its ideas. The technological improvements introduced by farmers included greater use of fertilizers, which became expensive and often in short supply, extension of irrigation, regional specialization in particular crops, improved crop rotations, and improved varieties of the main crops, which would have dramatic consequences in the twentieth century.

These methods had an important unforeseen effect. They made farming in Japan much more complex and intricate, requiring more careful work. As a result, once a farm exceeded a certain small size, it became difficult for a single owner to manage, and diseconomies of scale set in. As noted, Japanese farmers routinely divided their farms among their family heirs, and as the population grew this pattern continued. Many larger farms remained, but by the eighteenth century they often could not make ends meet. This pattern undermined the older tradition of large kin-based holdings, servile nago labor, and collective work.

During the eighteenth and nineteenth centuries, the large-holding peasants increasingly divided their holdings into tenant farms, and made their nago dependants into independent tenants paying rents. Apparently no law abolished the nago status, and some people were still nago in the twentieth century. Still, from the eighteenth century onward, nago disappear from the cadastre surveys, replaced in the lists by tenant farmers.

Servile Europe

In Asia during the fourteenth to the eighteenth centuries, free peasants in West and South Asia fell under increasing dependence, and servile peasants in China and Japan were emancipated or at least improved in status as a result of new laws and market forces. During the same period, the agrarian systems of Europe followed similarly divergent patterns of subordination. In western continental Europe the market-oriented changes that undermined serfdom in the medieval period reached a limit and left an underproductive, hierarchical system oriented mainly toward the incomes of the lords and the state. In most of Eastern Europe peasants fell under a new type of subjection similar to the former western serfdom but enforced and regulated by central governments. Finally, farmers in the Netherlands and England (and a few other areas) developed an agrarian system oriented toward market sales more than or even rather than subsistence, and that increased productivity and enhanced resources. This chapter examines the first two systems as examples of Early Modern servile systems; the next chapter examines the third category as the "agricultural revolution."

Western Europe: the Ancien Re'gime

The late medieval peasant rebellions and conflicts over land, status, and wages freed most Western European peasants from servile status, although more than a million peasants remained serfs in isolated districts. Even free peasants still owed a wide range of old customary obligations to noble landlords and the government. Western European agrarian society remained hierarchical and grew more so in the eighteenth century. A small noble elite dominated land and wealth, while most nobles were poor and differed little from peasants. Similarly a small group of elite peasants dominated the villages (against considerable resentment), which included larger numbers of smallholders, and even more poor and landless peasants. More egalitarian groups, such as the peasants of the Moselle River valley who held their lands in common and repartitioned them periodically, as in the Russian village commune, were highly unusual.

In principle and in law, governments, nobles, and churches owned almost all European lands. As in the Middle Ages, such ownership often overlapped and fragmented individual villages. Still, this ownership carried with it rights to traditional dues, which ranged from including rental payments like the *cens*, labor obligations, fines for inheritance, tithes to the church, to the *taille* tax in kind and labor duties for road construction to the state. Nobles had reciprocal obligations to peasants, such as relief in times of famine, but a serious famine could overwhelm their ability to provide relief.

Peasants' dues in money and kind usually totaled half of their income and often more. These high payments left peasants with much less than they produced, and weakened most peasants' capacity and incentives to work efficiently and productively, or to make efforts to improve their lands or equipment. This significantly contributed to the low productivity of European farming in this period.

Europeans raised more grain than any crop, and rye and oats more than wheat because they withstood weather and soil conditions much better in this generally cold period. Even then, no crop could survive in the bad years such as 1709, 1740, and 1772. Some noble landlords and even governments tried to introduce new crops but peasants often resisted, most notably in the case of American potatoes in the eighteenth century.

Peasant farming methods in continental Europe rarely advanced beyond medieval practices until the nineteenth century. The medieval three-field system remained the dominant cropping pattern throughout continental Europe, with the crucial exception of the Netherlands. This system left a substantial part of the fields available for livestock but empty of crops, even clover or grasses. The system also retained the medieval pattern of peasants holding many small plots scattered over the village lands.

The open fields and scattered plots had agricultural and economic advantages and drawbacks. Growing crops in multiple fields provided some security in bad weather because certain fields might be more affected than others, and distribution of different types of land among villagers helped to eliminate resentments. Multiple fields required peasants to spend time and energy moving from field to field and to follow the village crop rotation on those fields. The main drawback of the three-field system was its use of fallow to "rest" the land between grain crops. In France as late as 1789 one-third to two-fifths of the arable was fallow every year. The key innovation in the Netherlands and England was to use this land without depleting it, thereby eliminating the three-field system.

Farming methods were also old fashioned: peasants sowed by hand, used old wooden plows, and harvested with sickles or scythes that could cause grain to shatter onto the fields. Women and children had to glean – manually gather the shattered grains – after the harvests. Peasants had access to very little fertilizer, mainly obtained by allowing livestock to graze on the harvested fields and fallow land. Their crops had low yields, often only three to five times the seed, which meant that most of what they produced went for subsistence and in-kind taxation, and left little reserve for profitable sale or improvement. Consequently peasants were poor.

Peasants' diets consisted mostly of grain, and much less of other foods. They often ran out of food in late spring and ate surrogates or starved until the harvest. They lived in primitive housing, often with their domestic animals, and wore homespun clothing. Despite the general pattern of poverty, peasants' conditions varied by economic or social status. Small numbers of prosperous peasants lived in sturdy houses and owned more clothing and better food. A much larger group of poor peasants, sometimes one-third of the population, abandoned villages and became beggars, vagabonds, and criminals. Many poor lived in the villages as landless laborers. Some 50,000 of 122,000 adult male peasants in Bavaria were in this landless group, according to a survey in 1796. Peasants' conditions worsened during the eighteenth century in part because their population grew while the land areas available to them increased much less or not at all, despite large potentially usable lands held by nobles.

Landlords in Western Europe generally had little or no demesne, and let out all or most of it to peasant tenants. Most nobles had little interest in improving production on their estates. They were more concerned with maintaining their status of superiority to the peasants, whom many lords considered backward and stupid, almost sub-human. In Eastern Europe this sometimes reflected a nationalist bigotry, as when Polish nobles ruled Ukrainian serfs. Some nobles and other elites did recognize that peasants appeared this way in part because they were victims of an oppressive system.

During the eighteenth century a conflict over peasants and agriculture, often termed the "noble reaction," developed between nobles and monarchs in Western Europe. Nobles attempted to collect dues more strictly and completely, revive older obligations that had fallen into disuse, seize peasant lands, and ignore laws restraining them. Peasants often resisted these demands. In most countries even enserfed peasants had self-governing institutions and often some representation in government. In the Swiss cantons, parts of Germany, and France, peasants were represented in the estates (when they met), and peasants in most areas had long-established and often electoral institutions of self-government.

The complex of medieval farming practices, the dominance of the noble landlords, and the pejorative attitudes of the elites toward the peasants all combined to create a backward, exploitative rural society that was slow to change and develop. There were some progressive farmers who employed different rotations and other innovations. Most farms, however, were suspicious of new ideas and practices.

Russia: the second serfdom

The agrarian systems of Eastern Europe, including the eastern German states, the Baltic states, Austria, Hungary, the Balkans, and Russia, were sparsely settled in the medieval period. Nobles and governments in those regions offered favorable terms to peasants who would settle there to farm and raise families. Events in the late medieval period gave rise to a new type of servile system.

The crucial event was the Mongol conquest of Russia in 1237–40. This conquest established the Golden Horde, the northwestern part of the Mongol Empire, for more than a century, after which the Russians freed themselves from Mongol rule in decades of battles and other conflicts. The Mongols forced the Russian city-states to exploit their populations to pay tribute, and to compete with each other to become the Mongols' vicar in Russia. Moscow won this competition and took over the other city-states, supplanting the Mongols as the rulers of a unified Russian state, Muscovy.

The Muscovite ruler, from the fifteenth century called *tsar*, Russian for Caesar, at first relied on an army of nobles, allotting lands with peasant villages to them in order to keep their loyalty and support their families. To maintain this system and also retain a taxpaying population, the tsar had to insure that the peasants on these estates would not flee. During the serious economic and military crisis in the late sixteenth to early seventeenth centuries, part of which was the interregnum period called the "Time of Troubles," the tsars passed laws temporarily prohibiting peasants from leaving their lands. By 1649 the nobles managed to pressure the tsar to issue a law code that allowed nobles to reclaim fugitive peasants with no time limitations. This completed the establishment of serfdom in Russia. The government also applied a similar type of domination to peasants outside nobles' estates.

West of Russia, Eastern and Central European nobles rejected peasant demands for freedom, and instead imposed stricter demands. From 1487 to

1645, governments in Denmark, Bohemia, Poland, Hungary, Prussia, Austria, and other East European states passed laws that made peasants serfs, denied them civil and political rights, and tied them to the land or the serf owners.

These countries imposed this new serfdom for economic, political, and military reasons. The Baltic region had large estates producing grain for growing Western European markets. Poland was dominated by nobles who sought to consolidate their rural power and status. In Russia the nobles were weak but the government used serfdom for military recruitment and imposition of labor dues to build urban fortifications, so in this case serfdom met national security as well as subsistence goals. In all cases, enserfment made the nobles in effect the lowest rung of government authority, responsible for tax collection and implementation of government policies.

Eastern European serfdom often imposed much greater demands than the milder servile status of Western European peasants. In Denmark, nobles required serfs to work 200 days on the estate, with their own horses. In many places serfs had to work several days every week, and more during the harvest. Usually Eastern European serfs also had to pay dues in kind or money, which required them to turn over to the lord part of the products they produced on their own small farms in their limited time off from labor on the demesnes.

In Russia peasants' dues depended on the region of the country. In the southern regions of the Volga and Ukraine, it was possible to produce a profitable grain surplus, and serfs' main obligations there were labor services on nobles' lands, called *barshchina*. In northern regions such harvests were rare, and nobles mainly required money dues, called *obrok*. Nobles permitted peasants to move to towns to sell estate products, and a few of them became wealthy enough to purchase their own freedom.

Most Russian peasants, however, declined in status in the eighteenth century. Rulers from Peter the Great (1694–1725) to Catherine the Great (1761–96), while supporting westernization for the nobles, eliminated the peasants' basic rights, including the right to petition state authorities about nobles' abuses, allowing nobles to punish them brutally and exile them to Siberia. Russian nobles sold serfs just as American planters sold slaves. The government made peasants living outside noble estates into state peasants, a less oppressive type of serfdom. The Russian government also subjected serfs to military recruitment, requiring every 20 families to surrender one young man to the government every few years for long military service. The village would "celebrate" the youth's departure for military service with a funeral. Other Eastern European regimes similarly deprived peasants of basic human freedoms.

Yet the Russian peasants had an institution that protected them by intervening between peasants and outside authorities: the corporate village commune, called *mir* or *obshchina*. The terms are revealing: mir means "world" and "peace," reflecting its role in settling village disputes, while obshchina means "the common affairs of all the peasants," referring to peasants' management of village lands. Nobles and the government imposed dues, labor, and taxes on the commune, which periodically repartitioned and redistributed land plots among village families to share the burden of these obligations more equally. Most other villages in Eastern Europe had similar corporate institutions.

Servile peasants and European life

The underproductive and servile farming systems of early modern Europe contributed to recurrent famines and rebellions. Despite rumors in eighteenth-century France of "famine plots," in fact famines resulted from natural disasters, usually the Little Ice Age pattern of cold and wet weather, and insufficient reserves. Governments provided relief, but in bad years their reserves were not enough. The famines of 1601–4 in Europe and Russia after the Huaynaputina volcanic eruption were extreme cases. According to one writer, the famine of 1739–40 killed more people in France than all the wars of Louis XIV.

Rebellions were less frequent than crop failures but could acquire massive proportions. Russia had four major rebellions in the seventeenth and eighteenth centuries, from an unusual source. Many peasants fled serfdom in central Russia to the south and became Cossacks, military groups who lived along major rivers. The Russian rebellions all began as Cossack rebellions against the growing demands of the Russian state, and acquired substantial peasant followings. The largest was led by Emelian Pugachev in 1774–76, whose armies approached Moscow before Catherine the Great suppressed them. Russian leaders feared a new Pugachev revolt for decades afterwards.

European agriculture provided relatively unstable subsistence. The semi-servile peasantry in Western Europe did not regularly produce enough for themselves, let alone for many of the larger towns. These countries often had to import food produced by Eastern European serfs. The cultural flowering of the Renaissance, the Reformation and the wars of religion, the scientific revolution and the Enlightenment, all were fed in large part by these subordinated farmers. By the late eighteenth century increasing numbers of educated Europeans, east and west, began to consider this system to be unjust.

The Atlantic plantation system

If we view Eurasia as a whole, servile agrarian systems declined in some regions and expanded in others, with the most oppressive system forming in Russia. These systems produced the basic, staple food supplies consumed in these countries, and to a limited degree exported these goods to nearby countries or beyond. None of these systems, however, approached the violence and exploitation of the New World plantations, or the globalization of their inputs and exports. Consumers from England to China obtained luxury foods from the servile plantation system in the Americas. This "Atlantic system" or "plantation complex" combined agrarian characteristics of the pre-Columbian Americas and Europe.

Pre-Columbian American agriculture

The two major American societies contemporary with Early Modern Europe, the Aztecs or Mexica, and the Inkas, relied on unique American food complexes of maize (corn), beans, potatoes and other tubers, capsicum peppers, and certain animals. Both imposed types of servility on the farmers.

The Mexica migrated from upper Mexico to what is now Mexico City around 1280, and in return for military services, received from the local Tepanec people some islands in the large Lake Texcoco in the valley. The Mexica farmed in part using *chinampas*, floating gardens fertilized with dredgings from the lake and animal and plant waste. Chinampas produced quite high yields of maize, beans, and other crops, and then gradually settled into the lake. In the fourteenth century Mexica society expanded sufficiently for them to build a capital city, Tenochtitlan, with large temples to their deities, including Huitzilopochtli, for whom they practiced human sacrifice.

Mexica society consisted of territorial clans called *calpulli* that collectively paid tribute and taxes, owned lands or *milpa*, and redistributed them periodically. In 1370 a council of calpulli leaders appealed to a prestigious neighboring Toltec city-state to send them a leader, who became the first Mexica king, or *tlatoani*. Soon these kings and their family members became an elite caste who acquired tribute, including land with peasants settled as serfs. Successful warriors, merchants collecting state tribute, and high religious officials could also acquire estates.

By the 1420s, the Mexica conquered their neighbors and founded a regional empire. They established the worship of their sun god Huitzilopochtli as the state religion. According to this belief system, the sun god fought the forces of darkness every day, and constantly needed human blood from human sacrifices to survive until the next day. The Mexica leaders took on the duties of war, conquest, and sacrifices to support Huitzilopochtli in warding off darkness and the end of the world. This ideology brought a sharp increase in human sacrifices, a ritual practice in earlier societies in the region. The Mexica apparently ate body parts of the sacrificial victims as ritual cannibalism. They also fought almost continuous wars to obtain prisoners for sacrificial rites. In the process the calpulli sector declined; the newly conquered lands became serf estates and the dominant economic sector for production and tribute.

The empire soon reached its subsistence limits. The chinampa system could not keep up with the urban population growth that followed imperial expansion, and periodic droughts worsened shortages. The state began a large program of land reclamation and built raised farm plots, which still could not prevent chronic food shortages and famine. The Mexica took more and more people from the conquered provinces to sacrifice to the sun god, undermining their productive capacity and provoking resistance and rebellions. The Mexica would usually defeat these rebellions, massacre part of the subject population, and impose even higher tribute than before, in goods, food, and people for sacrifices. This process thus undermined food production and extended hunger into the conquered territories as well as the Aztec cities. The Mexica nobility, meanwhile, expanded and accumulated more servants and retainers, overburdening the state and the economy.

In an attempt to overcome the capital's food shortages, the next-to-last Aztec emperor Ahuitzotl, in the late fifteenth century, built a large aqueduct to channel water to Tenochtitlan to support the chinampas. The project caused a flood that devastated the capital. Ahuitzotl died in 1503 and his successor Motecuzoma II fought futile and costly wars against rebellious subjects and neighboring peoples, in the midst of food shortages, until the arrival of the Spanish conquistador Hernán Cortés.

The Mexica developed an environmentally sustainable agricultural system, but then conquered an empire that outgrew their food production capacity and provoked rebellion because of their violent religion. The Inka constructed a similarly oversized empire, based on a different food system, which collapsed from internal contradictions.

The Andean region where the Inkas built their empire, stretching from present-day Ecuador to northern Chile, has three geographical regions. The arid coastal plain has oases formed by rivers. The *altiplano*, the plain of the Andes Mountains, extends from present-day southern Peru to northern Chile and western Bolivia. The inland plain consists mostly of rainforest drained by the Amazon. The peoples here adapted to the different regions with a wide variety of crops. The early peoples raised corn, beans, fodder crops for llamas and vicuñas, the main native animals, and cotton in the coastal oases. By 1000 they had long irrigation canals and terraces in the altiplano. They also domesticated many varieties of potatoes, which became one of the most important crops in the world, as well as other types of tubers. They used the cold, dry mountain air to freeze-dry potatoes into *chuno* which could last for years.

The Inkas began as one of several peoples living near Lake Titicaca in the highlands of Peru. From the thirteenth century, they formed local kinship-community groups called *ayllu*. The ayllu allowed members to cultivate as much land as they needed for themselves, but required members to produce crops for dependants, such as elderly people, widows, and orphans, and also for religious rites. This principle of mutual obligation laid the basis for the labor taxation that later supported the Inka state.

The Inkas believed in a sun god, Inti, worship of whom required them to worship their own ancestors, a practice they carried to an extreme. In their early history the Inkas defined a main leader as "the Inka." In 1438 the son of the ruling Inka defeated an invasion and took over the government as the Inka Pachakuti. Under Pachakuti the Inkas established a system of "split inheritance." The Inkas divided their lands between state lands and the lands of the Inka ruler, which supported him and his *panaqa*, a group consisting of his other sons and relatives, and his dependants and former officials and their families. Each Inka, in other words, headed his own ayllu, which functioned like those of the peasants. When the Inka died, one of his sons became his political successor and inherited his political power, but not his land and property. Those lands and assets remained the property of the dead Inka and his panaqa, which could have a thousand members, each of whom held lands with peasant villages, servants, and a luxurious lifestyle.

This system of split inheritance and maintenance of the dead Inkas' panaqas imposed significant economic demands on the Inka Empire and motivated its expansion. In order to acquire land for himself and his panaqa, each new Inka had to conquer new territories. The periodic wars and conquests imposed heavy demands on the state and the population to serve as soldiers, farmers, and other jobs. Each succession of a new Inka withdrew more territory from the economy. Finally, when the last full-fledged Inka died, his legitimate heir, Huascar, decided to eliminate ancestor worship. His half-brother Atauhualpa, supported by panaqas and other Inkas who observed ancestor worship, fought a seven-year war for the succession and won, causing great destruction and loss of life, only to encounter the Spanish invasion led by Francisco Pizarro.

This unusual history of the Inka polity took place on the basis of an economic system almost as remarkable. The Inkas discovered the fertilizing effect of guano, formed from seabird droppings that accumulated for millennia on the coast, and used it widely. Their terraces, canals, and reservoirs demonstrated high-level water management. Yet their technological level barely surpassed the late Neolithic period. They did not have the wheel, iron, or the harness. Their main agricultural implements were the *taclla*, a small digging tool of stone or bronze, a wooden mallet to break clods, a small hoe, and a knife for harvesting. Yet this farming system supported the largest empire in the Americas before Columbus. The empire relied on a system of taxation in labor. This labor service was called *mita*, and included farming on state and panaqa lands, military service, transport, guarding warehouses and postal relay stations, construction and repair of irrigation canals, terraces, wells, roads, and other activities. The Spanish conquerors retained mita in name and in principle.

The food systems of the Americas seemed extraordinarily rich and productive to the Europeans who came in the sixteenth century. The diversity of crops shows that these peoples maintained highly innovative and creative agrarian societies. The dispersal of these crops, during the Columbian exchange of the sixteenth to eighteenth centuries, sharply increased food production in many countries. Yet these systems supported these pre-Columbian American empires poorly, with low productivity, and episodic or chronic food shortages. This low productivity resulted from soil exhaustion and from the exploitative, servile character of these governments' relations to peasants. The Aztec and Inka systems stretched the limits both of the environment's agricultural capacity and of the peasants' capacity to produce for their own needs, as well as fulfill the exorbitant and often violent demands that these governments imposed. The civil wars that Cortés and Pizarro encountered suggest that neither of these empires would have survived long even if the Spanish conquistadors had not shown up.

The native empires did not realize the potential of American crops or of the farmers who produced them, mainly because of their religious and political ideologies. The Spanish, Portuguese, and other European explorers and entrepreneurs who came to the Americas in the sixteenth to seventeenth centuries rapidly grasped the agricultural potential of the region and its crops, and by spreading production of these crops to other continents they substantially altered world agriculture. The Europeans' exploitation of Central and South American farming, however, almost equaled the violence of the Native American systems, albeit with much greater food productivity.

Europe, the Americas, and the formation of the plantation complex

Spain and Portugal based their plantation complex in Central and South America in the sixteenth to seventeenth centuries mainly on medieval Iberian farming systems and Arabic crops. This medieval farming system derived from the last vestiges of serfdom in Spain. During the twelfth to fifteenth centuries, the Christian Spanish fought a prolonged series of wars and crusade against the Muslim states in the south, called the Reconquest (*Reconquista*). As the Reconquista added new regions to Christian Spain, Spanish rulers transferred numerous large estates that the Muslims had preserved from the early medieval period to Spanish lords who employed slaves and *solariegos* or serfs. Because of the peninsula's mostly arid climate, Spanish rulers decided to emphasize pastoral production under the management of the Mesta. They freed the slaves and the Remensas of Catalonia, and granted the solariegos more personal rights and reduced obligations to their lords. Ironically, on the eve of the imperial expansion that would create the largest slavery-based agrarian system in history, the Spanish had freed their own slaves, emancipated their serfs, and subordinated crop production to pastoralism in the country's economy.

The key Arabic crops that the plantation system produced were sugar, initially the most important, and coffee. Sugar cane originated in South Asia and reached the Mediterranean during the Roman period. Under the

Muslim caliphates, sugar production spread and expanded into both Muslim and European markets. European Crusaders encountered large sugar farms in Palestine and Syria. Spanish and Portuguese businessmen established sugar plantations in Cyprus in the late Middle Ages, employing European serfs, slaves purchased in the Mediterranean slave trade, and hired labor.

In 1543 the Ottoman Turks' conquest of the Byzantine Empire forced the Portuguese and Spanish to move sugar production west. The Portuguese set up plantations in Algarve in southern Portugal, and then from 1450 on the Atlantic islands of Madeira, Cape Verde, and São Tomé. Portuguese agents on these islands, and Spanish agents on the Canary Islands, built sugar plantations and brought slaves from Africa and the local populations to work them. International competition began for the European market as successive colonies and later independent states tried to outproduce and undercut each other in production of sugar, coffee, and other luxury crops. By 1490 Madeira was the top sugar producer for Europe, by 1530 the Canary Islands topped Madeira, and by 1550 São Tomé topped the Canaries. The Americas dwarfed these islands and drove them from the market as major producers.

In this context of the formation of competitive markets in Europe for exotic foods, Columbus' discovery of the western hemisphere for Europe in 1492, followed by the conquests of the Aztec and Inka empires by Cortés and Pizarro in the early sixteenth century, and the Portuguese discovery of Brazil in the same period, soon dramatically altered world agriculture. The Americas provided the Spanish and the Portuguese with vast territories well suited for farm production and large subject populations. Because the Iberians came first and in the sixteenth century, the colonial exploitation of these regions derived from Spain's and Portugal's medieval farming systems, which had only recently and incompletely ended serfdom, and contemporary plantations in the Mediterranean and the Atlantic islands, which relied on slave labor.

Columbus and his successors repeatedly tried to establish slave-run sugar plantations on Santo Domingo island, with little success. After the conquests of the Aztecs and Inkas, the Spanish initially assigned the native population to Spanish agents or nobles on the basis of a system of *encomienda* or entrustment. These agents often treated the native people as expendable slaves in farm work. This abuse combined with diseases from the Europeans caused massive mortality. Complaints to the Spanish rulers by humanitarian churchmen like Bartolomé de las Casas brought the abolition of encomienda, but native people continued to die in large numbers from disease and impoverishment. Spanish and creole (American born but of European ancestry) farmers and others who needed laborers found indentured labor from Spain to be too expensive, and appealed to the Spanish rulers to import enslaved Africans.

In response to these demands for labor, and indirectly in response to the growing demand for sugar in Europe and the new colonies, trading companies, initially Portuguese but later Dutch, British, and others, established trading bases at several points on the West African coast and eventually on the East African coast. Slave trading was an ancient business in Africa, and Spanish and Portuguese traders had participated in this trade from the fifteenth century. In the sixteenth and seventeenth centuries Europeans took over the westbound slave trade and expanded it significantly. The Europeans obtained slaves mostly in exchange for textiles, especially cotton cloth from India and China. They also bought slaves with gold and silver mined in the Americas, or other products, like rum, produced from American sugar, so the trade was circular and self-supporting.

The slave traders purchased slaves over several months from ports all along the African coast. The traders crammed the slaves by the hundreds into cramped boats and often chained them to the under-decks. They fed them local foods, or the slaves would all have died of scurvy before crossing the Atlantic. When the boat could hold no more slaves because they were jammed under the decks and piled on top of each other with practically no room to move or even breathe easily, the traders embarked on the three-month voyage across the Atlantic. During the trip many slaves died of disease, while others sometimes rebelled and were shot by the crew, many of whom also died on the voyage. Some tried to escape through suicide by jumping off the boat. Nonetheless, and quite remarkably, ordinarily between 80 and 90 percent of the captives survived to reach the Americas to be sold to work in the plantations or other jobs.

This economy of sugar, coffee, tobacco, and other luxury crops, unnecessary for subsistence and in most cases harmful to consumers, relied on a vast global network of exchanges of goods and people. Traders made enormous profits: slave ship captains had incomes of hundreds of thousands of dollars in modern terms. The unpaid labor of slaves and the underpaid labor of free workers who produced these luxury crops provided the basis for this wealth.

The history of the American slave-agrarian system involved three continents: the Americas, Africa, and Europe; at least five major European participants: Spain, Portugal, England, France, and the Netherlands; and several different crops: sugar, coffee, cotton, and cacao. The history developed through three overlapping periods. The first period comprises the creation of the system, from 1550 to 1700. In the second period the system peaked, at different dates depending on the region and the crop, but generally in the eighteenth to early nineteenth centuries. The emancipation of slaves defined the third period, which began in the late eighteenth century and lasted into the 1880s, overlapping with the system's peak.

The Spanish colonies in Mexico and Peru, and the Portuguese colony of Brazil, were the first regions to receive African slaves, in the mid-sixteenth century. In Mexico and Peru, after the encomienda debacle, the Spanish landlords adapted the European estate to America with a type of combined ranch and farm called *hacienda*. The imported slaves were employed on such farms and throughout the economy. Mexico and Peru, however, received few slaves and their production was small scale and limited to local markets.

The first large-scale export-oriented plantation system began in Brazil in the 1550s. Portuguese entrepreneurs, seeking locations to grow sugar for European markets, found suitable conditions in the northeastern regions of Pernambuco and Bahia, and by 1580 had established more than 100 *engenhos*, or sugar plantations, in the region. The plantations comprised a group of fields surrounding a central processing plant that included a mill, usually water powered, to crush the cane, and boilers and other equipment to refine and package the sugar and other products. The fields grew not only sugar but also the subsistence crops, mainly corn, necessary to sustain the slaves. As Brazil's economy developed, other farms and even regions would specialize in subsistence production, allowing the plantations to focus on sugar. Into the 1570s these Brazilian engenhos employed mostly enslaved local Indian labor. Smallpox killed so many natives that by the 1580s the planters shifted to African slaves. By 1620 the plantations relied almost exclusively on the labor of Africans or their American descendants.

Portuguese-Brazilian sugar production depended for marketing on Dutch shipping through a charter mercantile company, the Dutch West Indies Company. During 1580–1640 Portugal came under Spanish control, and Brazil then became a target for the Dutch as part of their resistance to the Spanish Habsburgs. The Dutch controlled the sugar regions in northeastern Brazil from 1624 until the planters rebelled in 1645. In order to compete with Spain, the Dutch transferred mill technologies, credit, and slaves to the Caribbean islands under British and French control.

The British and French seized several Caribbean islands from Spain during the mid-seventeenth century. The islands provided excellent agricultural conditions for sugar plantations worked by slaves. By 1670, the first major British sugar island, Barbados, produced most of the sugar sold on British markets. It soon consisted mostly of large plantations and had a majority population of African descent. British and French traders also extended sugar cultivation to Jamaica, Hispaniola, and other islands. The British and French eliminated Dutch competition in the carrying trade through naval wars in 1652–70 and tariffs. By the 1680s the British and the French dominated production, shipping, and marketing of Caribbean sugar.

The peak of the Atlantic agrarian system began with the Treaty of Utrecht that ended the War of the Spanish Succession in 1714. By this Great Britain obtained from Spain the *asiento*, the authorization to trade in slaves. In 1789 Spain extended this right to every country. Because of these changes and the growing demand for sugar, more slaves were brought to the Americas in the eighteenth century than in all other periods of the Atlantic slave trade combined, between six and seven million. The slave trade declined only in the early nineteenth century when Britain outlawed it and deployed its navy in the Atlantic to apprehend illegal traders. Despite this the slave trade continued into the 1870s, and three million more slaves reached the Americas between 1800 and 1880.

The peak of slave-based sugar production involved a succession of centers. The first great producer was the French colony of Saint Domingue (now Haiti, the eastern half of the island of Hispaniola). This colony was the largest, most productive, and most efficient producer of sugar in the world, based on the harsh labor of 450,000 slaves by 1780. The British colony on the neighboring island of Jamaica attempted to compete but never came close. The Haitian revolution of 1791–1804 eliminated this country from the sugar market. Cuba became the new powerhouse. This island came briefly under British control at the end of the Seven Years' War in 1763. The British began a plantation system for sugar and other crops that the Spanish continued when they regained control of Cuba after the war.

Despite the dramatic and profitable export trade, in all of these colonies much of the farm labor force, free and slave, produced food crops and other products for domestic needs. The Brazilian city of São Paolo, for example, was surrounded by slave plantations that produced corn, livestock, and other foods for the city and the other plantations. Corn was the staple crop of the slave trade: it was the main ration on the slave ships, and it became the staple of many African states, and of the populations in most of the slave colonies.

The majority of the slaves taken from Africa to America went to Brazil or the Caribbean. During at least the first century of the plantation complex, slaves lived and worked in extremely difficult conditions. Cutting and carrying cane was exhausting work. Plantation managers punished resistance ruthlessly, often by public flogging to intimidate others. In this period planters usually found it cheaper to buy new slaves than to care for the ones they had or to make it possible for slaves to raise children. This failure helps account for the volume of the slave trade. Yet many slaves escaped, many were freed, and many had families and children, contributing to rapid population growth from the eighteenth century. At the peak of what was at root a slave system in the nineteenth century, most plantation workers were non-slaves, partly because Spanish and Portuguese authorities early on granted slaves *coartacion*, or the legal right to buy their own freedom. The British and French granted slaves the right to buy their freedom in the early nineteenth century.

A crucial consequence of the establishment of the Atlantic agrarian system was the Columbian exchange: the transfer and production of crops and livestock between the Americas and the rest of the world. This exchange resembled the medieval Arab agricultural exchange, but had much larger and more serious consequences.

Europeans brought to the Americas not only sugar, but also European crops like wheat and oats, and also weeds, as well as livestock including cattle, horses, and pigs. European crops often grew poorly in the Central and South American tropics, but farm animals thrived. The initial European attempt to settle future Argentina in the early sixteenth century failed, but the small number of horses and cattle left there multiplied to millions when Europeans returned several decades later.

In the reverse direction, the Europeans brought several important crops from the Americas to Africa, China, and South Asia. Corn and tobacco spread most rapidly; potatoes and tomatoes spread more slowly but soon became important crops in Europe, Africa, and Asia. Capsicum peppers became extremely popular in Africa and Asia, where local farmers developed new varieties. Peanuts, called groundnuts in Europe because they ripen underground, became an extremely important food and oil crop, especially in the colonies that European imperialists established in Africa in the nineteenth century. American crops may have been the main agricultural factor behind the demographic transition, the world population expansion that began in the eighteenth century.

The plantation complex played an ambivalent role in early modern world history. It successfully employed a relatively small number of people to produce and process an enormous amount of crops and other goods for large numbers of consumers in Europe, the Americas, and elsewhere. Later European imperialists emulated elements of this system in Asia and Africa in the nineteenth and twentieth centuries. Yet it contradicted Europe's humanitarian ideals, from Christianity to the eighteenth-century Enlightenment, even more than Eastern European serfdom. Its main redeeming feature, for most of the period only in the Spanish and Portuguese colonies, was the law of coartacion that allowed slaves to buy their freedom, which hundreds of thousands of them did from the eighteenth century onward.

Conclusion: the peak of servile agriculture

Farmers experienced the dual subordination in its most extreme form in the early modern period. The Little Ice Age made farming riskier than before or since, especially in the northern hemisphere. Servile farmers probably comprised a larger share of all farmers, and produced a larger share of the world's agricultural goods, than at any other period in history. Yet this period also saw significant emancipations in Asia.

In Russia, the Muslim Empires, and the Americas, rulers and landlords attempted to extend their power and control by maintaining or imposing servile agrarian sectors to provide a secure tax and subsistence base. In China, Japan, and eventually in Western Europe, governments perceived the value of allowing peasants to live under a less restrictive system that enabled them to respond to the market and increase their production and sales. The combination of laws and market forces that freed Chinese bonded laborers and changed the Japanese nago into tenants resembled the European pattern in the Middle Ages, but the process in East Asia apparently proceeded more peacefully and more rapidly.

Most of these regions also had chronic food crises, crop failures, and famines, caused by the Little Ice Age as well as by specific natural disasters. Some leaders, such as the Russian tsars, considered constraints upon peasant mobility necessary to ensure that peasants would continue to produce in order to accumulate reserves and overcome subsistence crises. In contrast, the expansion of markets and the diversification and intensification of farm production persuaded Chinese political leaders and Japanese landlords that freeing peasants from servile status would stimulate production.

The incorporation of the Americas into world agriculture involved paradoxical results. On the one hand, slave plantations produced vast quantities of many crops, especially luxury ones for export, at great human cost in the slave trade and in harsh plantation labor conditions. No other society in this period created a system as violent and exploitative. Russian serf owners in the vast majority of cases did not approach the cruelty of the American plantation system in their treatment of serfs. The system also exploited its consumers by selling them products that many people at the time recognized as harmful and addictive. This pattern of exploiting cheap labor and public taste to make a profit for a few governments, entrepreneurs, and shareholders anticipated the twentieth- and early-twenty-first-century agribusiness food system. On the other hand, the exchange of European and American crops and livestock have provided essential subsistence for billions of people and have enriched human experience in mostly positive ways. These crops and livestock will be central in dealing with world population growth.

Peasants, serfs, and slaves frequently resisted this expanding domination. Their reactions ranged from outright rebellion and flight to modest efforts to use customary and traditional practices to mitigate or undermine exploitation. Exploited farm workers' attempts to defend themselves, and efforts by urban educated elites to defend them, both discussed in the next chapter, facilitated the great emancipations of the nineteenth century and the agricultural developments that followed.

Further reading

Two key studies of South Asian farming are David Ludden, *An Agrarian History of South Asia* (Cambridge: Cambridge University Press, 1999) and Irfan Habib, *The Agrarian System of Mughal India* (New Delhi: Oxford University Press, 2001). Stanford Shaw, *A History of the Ottoman Empire and Modern Turkey* (Cambridge: Cambridge University Press, 1977), contains considerable information on rural life. Jerome Blum has published two major studies on European and Russian serfdom: *Lord and Peasant in Russia* (New York: Atheneum, 1969) and *The End of the Old Order in Rural Europe* (Princeton, NJ: Princeton University Press, 1998) is a classic. G. W. Conrad and A. A. Demarest, *Religion and Empire* (Cambridge: Cambridge University Press, 1984), provides a uniquely detailed insight into Inka and

Aztec agrarian history. Two excellent studies of Atlantic slavery are Philip Curtain, *The Rise and Fall of the Plantation Complex* (Cambridge: Cambridge University Press, 1998) and Herbert Klein and Ben Vinson III, *African Slavery in Latin America and the Caribbean* (Oxford: Oxford University Press, 2007). Useful studies on East Asia include Philip Huang, *The Peasant Economy and Social Change in North China* (Stanford, CA: Stanford University Press, 1988), also his *The Peasant Family and Rural Development in Yangzi Delta* (Stanford, CA: Stanford University Press, 1990); and Thomas Smith, *The Agrarian Origins of Modern Japan* (Stanford, CA: Stanford University Press, 1959).

Chapter 5

Agriculture in the nineteenth century

Emancipation, modernization, and colonialism

This chapter surveys the first part of the vast modern transformations of agriculture in the nineteenth and twentieth centuries. These transformations were part of the broader processes of the formation of European capitalist economies and the rise of European and then American economic and political dominance. In the nineteenth century these changes included the emancipation of the great majority of servile farmers and laborers in the Americas and Europe. They also included the development of agricultural systems oriented toward market production. This development, often called the "agriculture revolution," involved less a revolution than a different path taken by those involved in the farming systems of the Netherlands and England. Such systems found their ultimate expression in the agriculture of the United States and Argentina.

The chapter then examines the agricultural systems of Africa, Asia, and Latin America as they came under increasing European domination or colonial control. That control involved European attempts to adapt traditional farming to European methods and to involve these regions in the emerging Europe-centered world economy. One of the main results of this process was ironic: the same civilization that abolished slavery and serfdom created conditions that drove vast numbers of farmers into debts that oppressed and limited them almost as much as the old servile systems.

The environmental context

The nineteenth century saw the transition from the Little Ice Age to the beginning of global warming. Illustrations from the Alps from the seventeenth to the nineteenth centuries show glaciers retreating, a process that could have happened only with substantial warming. Russia had twice as many warm days in the second half of the nineteenth century as in the first half, and rivers in Russia and the Arctic Sea to the north had much less ice by the late nineteenth century than previously. The last major crop failures from cold and wet weather occurred in 1816–17 and in 1845–48.

One example of the interaction of environment and agrarian society was the great Irish potato famine of 1845–48, which also affected much of northwest Europe. Ireland by the early nineteenth century had a large population, eight million by 1845, most of whom were small-scale tenant subsistence farmers who survived by growing a small plot of potatoes. Their diet of five to ten pounds of potatoes a day with some milk was relatively nutritious, and better than that of most urban workers in Britain. The Irish farmers, however, had little or no reserves beyond each year's crop. Ireland as a whole had limited supplies – its main export to England was cattle. In 1845, a mysterious blight ruined about half of the potato crop. In 1846 it recurred and destroyed virtually the entire crop, and it recurred in 1848 with less intensity. This blight was found later to be a particularly virulent strain of the fungus *phytopthoria infestans* brought accidentally from the United States. The cool, damp weather conditions and wind spread this disease to Scotland, England, the Netherlands, and other regions in northern Europe. Those weather conditions also reduced grain harvests widely in Europe, contributing to the discontent and anxiety that triggered the revolutions of 1848. Irish and British authorities expanded relief efforts from late 1845 to 1847. By that time Ireland had become a massive net importer of food. Nonetheless more than one million Irish died, and perhaps two million emigrated under desperate conditions to the United States and Canada.

As the climate warmed, European observers noted another pattern, now called the El Niño Southern Oscillation or ENSO. This vast global teleconnection, or climate pattern connecting two remote processes, tied the increasing frequency of monsoon failures in South and East Asia with the concurrent warming of the eastern Pacific Ocean off the coast of Peru. British meteorologists first noticed this climate teleconnection, which has subsequently been extensively documented.

After the European cold weather crises of the early nineteenth century, the main and more dramatic environmental crises in agrarian history were the monsoon failures and subsequent famines of the late 1870s and 1900s. These intense droughts devastated large regions in India and China, parts of eastern Africa, and the Sertão of northeast Brazil. These monsoon failures caused widespread famines in India and China, with millions of deaths. Serious environmental crises, such as droughts and other extreme weather conditions, also affected other countries such as Russia and the United States. These disasters disrupted the extensive global commodity trading system that had developed by the mid-nineteenth century.

These disasters fortunately also stimulated research and technical efforts to alleviate and prevent these crises. Governments and scientists developed a much better understanding of these events and a greater commitment to help the victims and improve production with irrigation systems, drought-resistant crops, and improved transport. These measures were the origins of the large agricultural development programs of the twentieth century.

The great emancipations

The emancipations of West European peasants, East European serfs, and American plantation slaves during the late eighteenth and nineteenth centuries comprised the largest, most prolonged, and most effective liberation process in human history up to that time. Governments implemented these reforms with the support of progressive-minded people, usually middle class, and peasants or slaves, and against the opposition and resistance of landlords and serf- and slave-owners.

Emancipation in Europe

By the late eighteenth century, the modernizing agriculture of the Low Countries and England, with their improved crop rotations and higher yields, showed that farming in most of Europe was backward and inefficient. The British farm journalist Robert Young criticized the prevailing open-field system for weakening incentives for higher productivity. Yet only Denmark carried out land consolidation and enclosure in the eighteenth century.

Educated Europeans and writers from the French philosophes to Russian radicals described the peasants' poverty, filthy and deprived living conditions and chronic starvation during the "hungry season" before the harvest, and their tax and service obligations. Many peasants ended up as vagabonds, while noble privilege or state laws denied them large areas of farmland. Isolated attempts by Enlightened Absolutist monarchs and nobles to introduce reforms failed against the resistance and poverty of most peasants and nobles. Many nobles tried to reinforce existing demands on peasants and revive old ones. This "seigniorial reaction" only increased peasants' discontent. By the late eighteenth century the rural world threatened to explode, with large rebellions in Russia and defiance and resistance against servile obligations in Europe.

European governments finally emancipated their peasants during 1771–1884, against weak noble resistance and often in the context of peasant rebellions. Often large political crises forced governments to emancipate peasants in the service of broader goals. The "abolition of feudalism" during the French Revolution in 1789 was an influential example. The calling of the Estates General in 1789 led many peasants, already worried because of crop failures the previous year, to attack noble estates and destroy records to weaken seigniorial (noble) domination. The Constituent Assembly of nobles, churchmen, and commoners sought peasant support against royal authority. On 4 August 1789, noble delegates renounced their privileges and voted to "abolish feudalism." The radical Convention on 17 July 1792 abolished all seigniorial rights without compensation.

The Revolutions of 1848 in Central Europe supported peasants' demands for emancipations. In Austria and Hungary, newly elected legislatures, which included peasants, emancipated servile peasants. The Austrian Reichstag freed the serfs after peasants stopped paying dues and fulfilling service obligations. The Hungarian Diet freed them after a rumor that 40,000 armed peasants were coming to attack the delegates, a rumor later shown to be false!

The largest emancipation, of the Russian serfs and state peasants in 1861–66, had been long anticipated, or dreaded, by different groups in Russia. Tsars Alexander I (ruled 1801–25) and Nicholas I (ruled 1825–55) saw serfdom as an evil and prepared reforms, but held back from implementing them out of fear of rebellion. Russia's defeat in the Crimean War (1853–56) persuaded even conservative nobles and the new tsar, Alexander II, to agree with the vast majority of educated Russians that freeing the serfs was necessary to overcome Russia's backwardness.

Most of the emancipations allocated peasants some land but treated it as noble property for which nobles had to be paid back. Russian peasants paid redemption payments for decades until the 1905 revolution. The Austrian government, pressured by peasant deputies in the Reichstag, paid the indemnity to the nobles. The emancipations also initially restricted peasant mobility, out of fears that peasants could leave and deprive local landlords of labor, or could become a dangerous rural proletariat. Some peasants protested, disappointed with the reforms, but most focused on taking advantage of their new rights and lands. Some nobles adapted to capitalist farming, but many others lost their estates, which ended up rented or sold to enterprising peasants or townspeople.

Emancipation in the Americas

Slave emancipation in the Americas derived in part from the paradox between the inhumane character of slavery and the legal right of slaves to self-purchase. During the eighteenth century the Iberian colonies freed so many slaves that by 1800 in most colonies freedmen (and women) outnumbered the slaves. Fewer slaves gained freedom this way in the British and French colonies until the nineteenth century. Many slaves fled their plantations for free slave colonies, called *quilombos*. Brazil, with the largest slave population and the largest territory, had the most quilombos. Some quilombos fought government attacks, but others produced and even traded crops with the cities.

Spanish and Portuguese colonies thus had an outlet for discontent that French and British colonies lacked. The slaves in the French colony of Haiti, the top sugar producer in the world by 1780 and one of the most exploitative slave systems, began the era of emancipation with a dramatic and violent rebellion in 1791–1803. The French Revolution of 1789 gave civil rights to free blacks and mulattos (people of mixed African–white ancestry). Subsequent conflicts among Haitian whites, free blacks, and mulattos distracted the planters from the slaves.

A Jamaican slave named Boukman, a religious leader who knew about events in France, met with slaves in the main sugar-producing region, and organized a surprise rebellion. In August 1791, the slaves rebelled all over the north, and destroyed most of the plantations in the region. Boukman died in the rebellion, but his successor, the educated freed slave Toussaint L'Ouverture, led rebel Haitian slaves to defeat British, Spanish, and French armies. By 1803 the slaves liberated Haiti and proceeded to destroy the sugar plantations.

The Haitian revolt led colonial governments to reinforce control over slaves, but Enlightenment writers had been attacking slavery and demanding emancipation for decades. From the 1770s, European countries and the northern United States began to abolish slavery. The Haitian crisis stimulated the British abolitionist movement, which managed in 1807 to persuade Parliament to declare the slave trade illegal and deploy British ships to enforce this ban for the next 50 years. Strikes and rebellions by slaves in Jamaica in 1831–32 helped persuade Parliament to pass the Slavery Abolition Act of 1833 that freed slaves throughout the British Empire. The French abolished slavery in their remaining colonies only in the 1848 revolution.

Conflicts between planters who sought to maintain slavery and abolitionist townspeople and free people of color who supported emancipation prolonged slavery in Latin America. Cuba and Brazil held out the longest. Cuba continued to import slaves until 1864, despite British efforts to stop the slave trade. Cuban sugar producers benefited from the Haitian revolution and increased output steadily. In 1870 Cuban cane workers, including African slaves, indentured Asians, and free workers, using the latest steam-powered mill technology, produced 700,000 tons of sugar, more than 40 percent of world production. The slave colonies competed in other crops as well. Cuban and Brazilian planters competed in producing coffee, Brazilian and U.S. planters in cotton.

During a Cuban rebellion against Spain in 1868–78, Spain passed the Moret Law that freed slaves. Spanish forces enforced this while suppressing the rebellion. In Brazil in the 1870s a widespread popular movement created free cities and provinces, and managed an "underground railroad" to transport slaves to free regions. These movements, coupled with the unwillingness of the police and army to capture and return fugitive slaves, persuaded the government to free the slaves in 1888. This law finally ended slavery in the Americas.

The emancipations of slaves in the Americas and serfs in Europe both took decades and were achieved against often significant opposition. In Cuba, Brazil, and other countries, rebellions by former slaves persuaded governments to free the remaining slaves without conditions. The massive simultaneous emancipations in Europe and the colonies initially disrupted agricultural production, but farm output recovered rapidly and increased in most regions. These former servile regions shifted their approach to farming to combine free labor, private land holding, and market-oriented production in emulation of Europe and the United States, considered the most successful agrarian systems.

The entrepreneurial path

The "Agricultural Revolution" in Britain, similar to the earlier market transformation of farming in the Netherlands, was gradual, episodic, local, and cumulative, and much less rapid than the term "revolution" implies. In contrast to servile systems on the continent, farmers in these countries worked under few restrictions from the village or landlord. This path led farmers to focus on production for markets.

The breakthrough to capitalist farming came first in the Netherlands. From the fourteenth century, this country had a large and highly urbanized population whose wealth and market demand could support diverse farm production. The key innovation that made intensive production for this market possible was the elimination of fallow, the only means that most medieval farmers knew to restore a field's productivity. From the 1320s Dutch farmers began to replace fallows with lentils, clover, turnips, and other crops to feed animals and improve the soil. They alternated food crops with grass or clover (convertible husbandry), grew crops in rows to make weeding easier, and applied several types of fertilizers. These methods required more work and more inputs, and farmers had to charge higher prices to cover their costs. The sixteenth-century "price revolutions" raised most prices, however, and the generally higher incomes of Dutch consumers enabled farmers to earn a profit despite their higher costs. The one exception to this pattern was grain crops, prices for which declined from the mid-fourteenth century. The Netherlands supported intensive livestock farming by importing grain from the Baltic. Servile labor in Eastern Europe thus made possible the market-oriented intensive production of free Dutch farmers.

As their farming became increasingly oriented toward sale off the farm, Dutch farmers bought inputs and even much of the food they themselves consumed from sources outside their farms. This farming by the early modern period had more in common with later factory-based industry than with contemporary subsistence farming in neighboring France and Germany. Entrepreneurial Dutch farming resembled that of entrepreneurial Chinese peasants in the early Qing dynasty, except that the Dutch farmers focused much more on livestock.

The English "agricultural revolution" took place gradually and unevenly over several centuries. English farming, like the earlier changes in the Netherlands, shifted from subsistence to market production and an industrial-style farming system. The English transformation derived from unique circumstances. European demand for British wool grew in the medieval and early modern periods. Increasing numbers of English landlords sought to emulate the high productivity in Dutch farming. A large domestic market emerged in London and other towns in the sixteenth and seventeenth centuries.

English landlords and farmers responded to the demand for wool with enclosure, which meant evicting peasants from the common lands of a village and constructing a fence or hedge around that land. The manor lord thereby removed this land from the village rotation and used it for other purposes, such as raising sheep. Some landless peasants denied access to the former common lands ended up as beggars and vagrants. Many of the evicted peasants worked as laborers on the enclosed lands.

Regional differences also supported the English agricultural changes. In the central regions, English villages followed traditional open-field farming practices with village control over farm work. In the eastern and southwestern regions, however, villages had more privately-held land and enclosures, and farmers there were more independent in their farming and responsive to market trends. These regions had a market in land, partible inheritance, and many smallholding peasants who had to work for the few large-holders. Landlords and farmers in these more market-oriented eastern and southwestern regions led the transformation of English farming.

The English adopted the Dutch practices, replacing fallow with forage crops and alternation of crops and grasslands, and used their own innovations such as "water meadows," in which a meadow would be surrounded by raised earthen ridges to prevent water runoff, and submerged under several inches of water the whole winter. This flooding improved yields in ways similar to East Asian wet-rice cultivation. The farmers used their increased forage to breed much larger animals with meat that was "marbled" with fat, which people preferred.

These and other improvements in English farming relied on enclosure, which expanded to 70 percent of English farmland by 1700. While humanitarians and politicians condemned enclosure, and peasants resisted it fiercely, landlords continued to enclose in response to growing markets and environmental crises. In the late eighteenth and early nineteenth centuries, especially during Britain's wars with Napoleon, cold spells from the fading Little Ice Age caused crop failures and famines. Parliamentary surveys disclosed an overall shortage of food in 1800, and rioters in towns demanded lower food prices. Parliament responded with more than 4,000 enclosure acts that enclosed 6.8 million acres. Many landlords used enclosures to produce food crops, particularly during the wars. In Scotland, the Highland Clearances, "lairds" (landlords) drove the "crofters," the small tenants, off the land to raise sheep to profit from high wool prices.

Improved farming methods and enclosures raised productivity and drove prices down. Landowners in parliament passed import tariffs on grain, called Corn Laws, to protect British producers. They became a major political issue between towns and countryside until their abolition in 1846, because they kept food prices and wages high in the towns. While some small farmers survived catering to the large urban demand, most British farms were much larger than those of continental Europe. They were owned by landlords and run by tenants (the original "farmers"), who hired laborers to perform most jobs. Despite the high crop yields, laborers tended to be poor, malnourished, and had lower intelligence and more physical deformities than the general population. Yet mid-nineteenth-century English farming was the most advanced in Europe, the agricultural counterpart to England's status as the leading industrial and colonial power.

Agriculture in the United States of America

The entrepreneurial path of the Dutch and British farmers reached a peak in U.S. farming. The future United States, with its long growing season, reliable precipitation, and good soils, had greater potential for farm production than perhaps any other country in the world. It also began its modern agrarian history with a commercial orientation. English colonists began selling tobacco to England and the Caribbean colonies soon after settling along the eastern seaboard, and expanded to rice, sugar, and livestock.

The new United States had distinct agrarian regions. During the nineteenth century, farmers in the north spread through the "old west" of Ohio, Indiana, Illinois, and Missouri and reached the Great Plains. This region became a "feedlot empire" where farms raised corn and livestock for urban markets. The South developed an extremely productive cotton plantation system. Southern farmers had relied on African slaves since the seventeenth century. They bought few slaves but provided sufficient food and housing for them so that by the nineteenth century the U.S. had more slaves than any other country in the Americas, almost all of them in the South. Slave labor and the cotton gin, which separated the cotton from its seeds, made possible the explosion of U.S. cotton output from 100,000 bales in 1801 to 5.4 million bales by 1859. This supplied the textile mills of the Industrial Revolution in Britain and elsewhere.

The American South's plantation agriculture was oppressive and many slaves resisted the planters' domination. Nonetheless its enormous production resulted from disciplined and productive work by slaves, achieved through both coercion and incentives such as food and status. The main food source for this system was corn, which covered more cropland than cotton. Corn was a domestic cash crop, grown by small family farmers who rarely had slaves. Since corn was deficient in B vitamins and protein, Southerners subsisting on corn risked pellagra, a deficiency disease that can cause neurological decline, and death. Despite the South's great farm productivity, Northern firms managed most of the trade and processing of Southern cotton. The South functioned like an internal colony that enabled Northern businessmen to accumulate the assets necessary for the massive industrialization of the United States after the Civil War.

The Civil War, in great part an agrarian conflict between the North and South over slavery, eliminated Southern opposition and allowed the establishment of the United States Department of Agriculture (USDA), land grant universities to advance agricultural knowledge, and an agricultural extension service to improve farming methods. The South eventually recovered from the war and the region became a major cotton exporter again. The former slaves ended up working on the old plantations as sharecroppers, in reality debt peons, forced to work at extremely low wages to retain their plots.

After the Civil War, the U.S. became the dominant agricultural power in the world, mainly through assimilation of the West. The Mexican–American War of 1844–46 opened the region to U.S. settlement. The Civil War began a boom in the region as American and British businessmen set out to raise cattle for the army, and after the war for growing U.S. cities. Soldiers and cattle raisers slaughtered millions of buffalo, and drove the Plains Indians into reservations. Cattle barons shipped European breeds to the plains and hired cowboys – poor southern men, black and white, and displaced Mexican ranchers – to graze the cattle and drive them to the train heads. The cattle were routed through the new Chicago stockyards and other meat-processing centers. Cattle production operated on a boom and bust cycle, because of glutted markets and disastrous weather. The worst case was the great freeze of 1886–87, when four months of temperatures 40 below zero froze millions of European cattle on the plains. The sector recovered and reached a peak of production in 1900.

Simultaneously, homesteaders had already begun moving into the plains after the Civil War, supported by Homestead Acts, construction of railroads, and improved equipment like the steel plow developed by John Deere. His plow was the first that could cut the dense roots of prairie grass. The homesteaders, poor farmers or townspeople or European emigrants, endured arid and unpredictable plains weather and the great farm depression of the 1870s–1890s. Despite many failures, they made the U.S. the top wheat-producing country in the world.

In another important region, California, which became a state in 1850, farming evolved from large "bonanza" grain farms using the latest technologies – and that went bust in the 1880s – to more valuable fruit and vegetable crops and livestock. By 1900 California showed immense agricultural potential that relied on emigrant Asian and Mexican labor.

U.S. industrial development and the national market created by the railroads made farmers into specialist producers and dependent on outside businesses and agencies for inputs and marketing. These agencies included the USDA, factories producing tools and equipment, railroads to ship their products, and traders to purchase and process their products. The most important trader was the firm of Cargill, which by 1900 dominated Midwestern grain purchases. During the late-nineteenth-century agricultural depression, when farm shipping costs stayed high while produce prices fell, farmers organized political movements, such as the People's Party, to cut shipping costs and raise tariffs. The U.S. government opposed intervention in the economy and businesses like Cargill opposed import tariffs, for fear of retaliation from countries that imported U.S. produce, so the government provided little if any protection for farmers in this period.

The farmers of Argentina were important competitors with U.S. farmers. Argentina's main farming region was the *Pampas*, similar to the U.S. prairies. Like that region Argentina began as a livestock empire managed by the Argentine cowboys or *gauchos*, supported by brutal military action against Indians in 1879. Like the American Great Plains Argentina also endured a major livestock disaster, hoof and mouth disease in 1900. After this Argentina expanded grain farming, but unlike the U.S., Argentina had large landlords and did not encourage homesteading. Improved international transport enabled Argentina to sell in Europe at low prices, and to recruit poor peasants from Italy and Spain to migrate to Argentina to work as tenant farmers. They endured deprivations and frequent bad weather, but expanded the wheat area to 15 million acres by 1910. One emigrant, Giuseppe Guazzone, acquired land and became the single largest wheat producer in the world.

Nineteenth-century Europe

By the mid-nineteenth century, European farmers had generally high product prices and low wages for farm laborers, because industrial development in the continent was not advanced enough to compete with farms for labor. This stability and profitability supported the European emancipations.

Developments in science and business in this period modernized and commercialized agriculture with enormous repercussions. German soil scientists such as Justus von Liebig (1803–73) found that plants needed specific chemicals. Their research led to a vast fertilizer industry. Specialized companies, such as Leopold Dreyfus in Switzerland and Bunge in the Netherlands, dominated European markets, as Cargill did in the U.S., expanding from grain into new sectors. Farmers increasingly had to sell their products to these firms in order to market them. European and U.S. industry introduced advanced industrial technologies, which increased industrial demand for agricultural products. These advances produced large steam-powered ships and refrigeration which allowed transport of much larger amounts of commodities much more rapidly than before. The United States, Argentina, Australia, and India all could now compete on international markets at low prices.

This combination of factors created the late-nineteenth-century "great depression" in agriculture. Competition drove down farm prices, farmers' profits fell, and debts rose. U.S. and European farmers resorted to political action. While the U.S. and most European countries were democratic, their developed and diverse economies and politics forced the agricultural interests to accommodate other groups' demands in diverse ways.

The British commitment to free trade left tenant farmers little alternative but to demand that landlords reduce rents. Farmers used rent strikes and boycotts, and fought landlords' attempts to evict them, so fiercely in Ireland that it was called the Irish Land War. These protests finally induced Parliament to legislate reforms, such as tenant rights, which required landlords to reimburse tenants for farm improvements they made. Still, farmers could not overcome the resistance of industrialists and workers to any increase in food prices. Increased British reliance on food imports, with trade routes protected by the British Navy, led many farmers either to abandon farming or specialize in dairy products and vegetables. British farming and agronomic education fell behind.

In Germany the farm sector was much larger and more important politically. German politicians worried about dependence on imported food. Large landlords and small peasants both supported protective tariffs. Chancellor Otto von Bismarck favored tariffs to keep small farmers from being driven by the market into the cities as potentially rebellious workers. Germany consequently imposed tariffs on most food imports, and supported agricultural education and research, modeled in part on the U.S. Other European countries, such as Italy and France, similarly resorted to import tariffs, expanded agricultural education, and developed extension systems modeled on the U.S. The reforms supported increases in production of grain and other crops.

This agricultural depression also had an unanticipated effect: it drove many big landlords out of business or forced them to lease their lands to tenants, while small farmers and peasants managed to survive. In Russia, for example, the serf emancipation left nobles with more and better land than the peasants. Despite several crop failures and famines, by the 1890s Russian grain exports competed with U.S. exports. Yet this increased production was accomplished mostly by peasant farmers, who owned or rented nearly 90 percent of cropland by 1910. This led to theoretical and political disputes over the superiority and viability of small farms versus large farms. The most extreme defenders of the peasants were the Russian Populists, a small group of radical students who felt guilty that their privileged lives depended on exploited peasant labor. Yet the Populists saw the peasants as the hope for Russia's future, because they considered the peasants' traditional practice of land repartition to be primitive socialism. These attitudes led them to try to incite the peasants to revolution, first by going directly to villages. When that failed, the Populists unleashed a campaign of terror that culminated in the assassination of Alexander II, despite the fact that he had freed the serfs. No rebellion took place, but Populists and some socialists continued to believe that the Russian village commune could enable Russia to bypass capitalism and move directly to socialism.

These views were an extreme version of agrarianism, a broad pattern of thought in Europe and the U.S. that idealized the peasant or farmer as the true and fundamental representative of the nation. Adherents of this view considered peasants and farmers better than urban people because they worked on the land, producing the crops and livestock that satisfied civilization's basic needs, uncorrupted by towns, capitalism, and foreigners. These attitudes found expression in art, such as the work of the French painter Millet, and music, in composers' use of peasant folksongs. These attitudes, so different from the earlier derogatory views of servile peasants, idealized the primitive peasantry as it disappeared under the influence of modernization. The agrarian image of peasants viewed them as self-sufficient when industrialization had eliminated the market for peasants' cottage production of textiles and other goods. Urban industrialization had deindustrialized European villages and it would do the same in India and other colonies.

Colonialism, the new colonialism, and agriculture

The world beyond Europe and the U.S. came under varying degrees of European domination and incorporation into the developing world markets by the late nineteenth century. Yet these regions retained a significant degree of autonomy in the agricultural sectors.

In Africa, Britain substantially reduced the transatlantic slave trade by the mid-nineteenth century. Yet slavery survived, as exemplified in the nineteenth-century Sokoto caliphate of the Sahel region, the largest state in Africa before colonialism. Slaves comprised at least half of the Sokoto caliphate's population and were employed widely, mostly in farming. The caliphate had large plantations owned by landlords or officials with hundreds or even thousands of slaves. Plantation slaves had a status similar to European serfs: they had their own lands on the plantation, received housing and other supplies from the owner. They supported themselves, but also had to work regularly on the landlord's land. The owner–slave relationship was less adversarial and exploitative than in the American plantations, but owners still required substantial labor and many slaves fled, worked badly, or stole crops from the owner's land. Some African states resembled Sokoto, but others, such as the Gold Coast (now Ghana), relied on a free small-scale peasantry.

European powers invaded and conquered large regions of Africa in the late nineteenth century. Finance ministries resisted funding development, so colonies needed to find commodities for Africans to produce to pay for the colony. The powers resorted to mining and agriculture, specifically cash crops for export. While Africans had produced crops for local sale and export long before colonialism, the Europeans' demands for cash crops posed problems of time, labor, and subsistence, especially in savannah regions that had to devote much more time to growing their traditional subsistence crops. Often women farmed while men had other jobs, or else farm labor involved everyone in intensive seasonal work. Cash crops strained labor and threatened subsistence.

In some regions Africans responded to markets actively and successfully, specializing in particular crops that suited environmental conditions. The Gold Coast, through the initiative of an African grower, developed an export cacao industry that grew from £27,000 in 1900 to £8.2 million in 1925, and became the top cacao exporter in the world. Africans produced large amounts of several other crops, especially oils, and colonial production of all commodities for Europe sharply increased before the First World War. In general the British policy of indirect rule did not initially alter existing economic patterns.

On the other hand, some colonizers did attempt to "remake" forcibly the African economies and cultures. In Tanganyika (now Tanzania) in Southeast Africa, the German East Africa Company employed indirect rule but imposed heavy taxes and forced villagers to grow cotton for export, which threatened traditional practices and subsistence. This provoked a series of rebellions by Africans, which culminated in the Maji-Maji Rebellion in 1905 in the Kilwa district in southeast Tanganyika against cotton cultivation, inspired by a belief that water, in Kiswahili *maji*, would make them impervious to bullets. The Germans suppressed the rebellion by destroying Africans' crops, creating a man-made famine that lasted two years. Afterwards the German administration was more tolerant but the rebellion set an extremely tragic precedent for colonial agriculture.

In the African colonies, a few European firms came to dominate the cash crop export trade. Some ran their own enterprises in the colonies, such as the large British soap company Lever Brothers, which had palm oil plantations in the Congo and the Solomon Islands. These enterprises were colonial counterparts to the large grain trading firms in Europe and the U.S.

Southeast Asia came under extensive European colonial domination during the nineteenth century, under methods similar to colonialism elsewhere. Dutch imperialism in Indonesia provides an example of a colonial system that moderated its exploitation in response to changing circumstances. The Netherlands' government took control from the Dutch East India Company (VOC) as the company declined economically and militarily in the seventeenth to nineteenth centuries. To cover costs, in 1830 the government introduced a policy of forced cultivation called the Cultivation System. This required peasants to plant 20 percent of their land with a cash crop, usually sugar, indigo, and coffee, and to work two months for the government to cultivate these crops.

By the 1840s farmers produced so many cash crops that "Java" became a common word for coffee, and Indonesia competed with Cuba in sugar. Dutch government income from the Netherlands reached one-third of the

Dutch budget. The effects on the peasants were mixed and unclear. In 1844–48, however, monsoon failures destroyed crops, and Dutch authorities reduced their cultivation demands and provided famine relief. Widespread criticism of the Cultivation System for oppressing the peasants and closing Indonesia to private investment during the 1850s induced the government to dismantle the system. The regime eliminated obligatory cultivation and opened Indonesia to private entrepreneurs. The government abolished compulsory sugar cultivation in 1870 and closed the last government coffee plantation in 1915.

South Asia

The British conquest of India in the eighteenth and nineteenth centuries brought under England's control numerous different rural societies, which many Westerners viewed as primitive and backward. Some colonial personnel, however, recognized the skills of earlier governments and Indian farmers in solving difficult environmental and economic problems, such as irrigation.

The British government and colonial authorities faced demands from home industry for raw materials and food supplies at low prices. Parliament was reluctant to spend much on this new colony, preferring that it be self-supporting. Increasingly India became a source of revenue from taxation, cheap raw materials, and sales of British goods. Indian agriculture and farmers were the main group who had to fulfill London's economic objectives, because they comprised the vast majority of the population, and because the British did not want Indian craftsmen to compete with British products.

Initially the British colonial authorities, in the form of the British East India Company (EIC) until 1858, imposed heavy taxes and other payments that reached the limits of the population's paying capacity. In 1769–70 Bengal, the EIC's headquarters, endured a severe drought that destroyed crops. Since many peasants had little or no reserves, the result was one of the worst famines in Indian history. Mortality may have reached one-third of Bengal's population of 30 million. After several abortive attempts to reform the agrarian tax system, Lord Cornwallis, the EIC's new governor general in 1786–93, decided that India needed security of property and stability of taxation to increase its farm production. To this end, he issued the Permanent Settlement of Bengal in 1793. This law defined the zamindars in Bengal as landlords who owned their landholding or zamindaris, and fixed their tax obligations in perpetuity. Cornwallis and his supporters believed that fixed taxes would motivate zamindars to invest in their lands and increase production.

The reform had mixed results. In line with the Permanent Settlement, the government auctioned the lands of zamindars who failed to pay their taxes, which created a land market. Indian officials and wealthy townspeople bought land and became absentee landlords who pressured peasant tenants to raise cash crops. Later British conquerors and officials, aware of many problems in the Permanent Settlement, imposed in newly conquered areas the *ryotwari* system in which the government taxed each peasant farmer. This system also had difficulties because of the small British staff and the corruption of local Indian officials.

In both systems, the EIC imposed high money taxes which forced peasants to devote part of their limited lands to growing cash crops. Some sectors of Indian agriculture adapted to this cash crop system profitably. A small privileged group of farmers in Bengal grew poppies, grown ever since Alexander the Great brought them to India, to produce opium, used as a medicine and a recreational drug. The British EIC began to export or smuggle opium to China, Southeast Asia, and Britain itself in the seventeenth century. These exports grew from over 100 metric tons in 1767 to 2,000 metric tons by 1837.

For producers of other crops, British rule involved heavy taxation of both peasant cultivators and landlords. Resentment of British taxation and other policies exploded in the 1857 rebellions and the Indigo or Blue Mutiny. The 1857 rebels included local landlords, such as the *talukdars* in the central Ganges region of Oudh, whom the British deprived of their lands in 1856. Peasants sometimes had higher tax obligations to the British than they had to their former landlords. They often had to borrow from oppressive *mahajans*, or moneylenders, who sometimes ended up taking possession of peasant lands. Consequently, in 1857 peasants often rebelled against the British under the leadership of resentful landlords. In other regions, such as Bengal and Punjab, peasants and landlords benefited from British policies, and sided with the British against rebels who sought to restore abusive old systems.

After the suppression of the 1857 revolts, in Bengal a long-brewing conflict exploded over indigo, an ancient Indian crop (the name derives from "India") that became the main source of blue dye for Britain by 1800. By the 1850s planters and processing factories controlled large land areas rented or purchased from zamindars, and employed *lathiyals* or guards armed with *lathis*, long sticks with metal tips, to beat or intimidate peasants into growing indigo. Bengali lawyers and zamindars could not stop these abuses. In 1859 peasants began attacking planters' factories and taking the planters to court. By 1861 they managed to destroy indigo planting in Bengal. Indigo production continued in other provinces but planters learned from this "blue mutiny" to avoid these practices.

After these rebellions, the extensive penetration of railroads incorporated the Indian economy into the growing world economy. The British tried to increase cotton and wheat production in India to compensate for uncertain production and prices elsewhere. Britain in the early nineteenth century obtained most of its raw cotton from the American South. The U.S. Civil

War and Northern blockade of the South reduced supplies so much that British cotton mills laid off masses of workers who ended up starving. Desperate industrialists worked with British colonial authorities to find regions in India suitable for cotton. One was the south-central province of Berar, where taxes and merchant-moneylenders induced peasants to grow cotton, but British purchase prices were so low that cotton farmers wore rags.

In the Narmada River valley in central India, the extension of the railroad made possible large exports of wheat. Local merchant-moneylenders again pressured peasants to accept advances for wheat production, and appropriated the lands of peasants who defaulted on these loans. Wheat production boomed in the 1880s, peasants expanded cultivation, so Britain in 1887 decided that land values had increased and raised land taxes in the region. In 1891 grain from Argentina and Punjab came on the market, Narmada exports collapsed, and peasants fell into debt to moneylenders and the government. By 1905 Narmada depended on imported food.

Despite such crises, on average during the nineteenth century Indian farm production slowly increased. Yet frequent droughts – perhaps a result of developing global warming – as well as floods, locust infestations, and other environmental disasters destroyed harvests and often caused massive famines and vast mortality in different regions of the country. Major famines took place in 1837, 1876–78, and 1899–1901, while others only slightly less severe occurred in many other years. British tax policies often weakened the resistance of poor peasants and laborers to such disasters. Many British officials also accepted the views of classical political economy that government aid during a famine could make it worse and undermine peasants' self-reliance. Consequently their main relief programs were public works, in which recipients had to work a full day in order to receive rations. Such programs often reached only a minority of famine victims. In some cases the British refused to import food, but allowed food exports from famine regions.

Yet British authorities undertook major programs to alleviate and prevent famines. From the 1820s, the British began restoring old and building new irrigation systems, explicitly with the goal of mitigating droughts and famines and improving farm production. These programs grew rapidly after 1857, supported partly by peasants' taxes and famine victims' labor in public works. By the early twentieth century one-sixth of Indian farmland received irrigation from these projects. In the wake of the great 1876–78 famine, Viceroy Robert Bulwer-Lytton established a famine commission in 1879, the first such agency in Indian history, which drew up the first of several famine codes to guide government policies in such crises. Lytton's public works projects during the famine built dams that enlarged India's irrigation system, which he saw as necessary to help India produce a surplus that would prevent famine.

The government also undertook to improve Indian agriculture with provincial agricultural departments from the 1880s, which developed new crop varieties and improved equipment, and with an Imperial Council for Agriculture Research in 1905 to guide research. These measures would have significant consequences in the twentieth century.

After famines, or even under less drastic circumstances, peasants also frequently had to rely on local moneylenders to pay taxes and obtain food or other needs, and often lost lands to them when crop failures or low income prevented them from paying back their debts. Many peasants ended up as bonded laborers, a widespread status by 1800. Later British efforts to stop this practice had only limited success because the bondage relationship was often concealed.

China

China was an agricultural paradox. It was the largest agrarian society in the world, with private land holding and markets, and extremely productive in good years. Yet it was extremely vulnerable to frequent natural disasters, especially droughts from monsoon failures and floods from the silt-carrying Yellow River. At such times the population desperately needed effective government intervention, and government failure or abuse could lead to major rebellion.

During the eighteenth century the Qing dynasty had sufficient organization and legitimacy to cope with the numerous disasters and crop failures, relying on the granary system to aid peasants. By the end of the century, however, the Qing encountered the recurrent Chinese pattern of corrupt officials, increasing taxation, and declining reserves. In 1796 a secret society, the White Lotus, rebelled in northwest China against taxation, with massive peasant support. The government took eight years and tactics such as blockading villages to suppress the rebellion. The White Lotus set the pattern of growing religious-utopian peasant movements challenging a weakening government.

China by 1800 had two main agrarian regions: the north with more subsistence farming and private land holdings, and the south with more cash-crop production and much more tenancy. In both regions peasants faced frequent economic downturns and often had to resort to money-lenders. Chinese peasants also faced growing environmental problems. Political stability and economic growth in the early Qing supported popula-tion growth that drove peasants into previously uncultivated regions of the north and west. By 1820 most of the forests in these regions were gone. This significantly increased erosion and runoff, and the government had not renovated river-control systems for two centuries. In the late 1830s, floods began and intensified until in 1855 the Yellow River overflowed and shifted its course hundreds of miles from south of the Shandong Peninsula to north of it, destroying thousands of villages and killing hundreds of thousands of peasants.

Peasants' increasing numbers had also forced them to divide their lands into smaller holdings. Many shifted to cash crops such as cotton or mulberries (for silkworms). While their small plots would not produce sufficient rice for subsistence, with cash crops they made enough money to support themselves. This imposed more demands on the government granary system during crop failures, while the Qing administration declined in competence and grew in corruption. Investigations repeatedly found low or empty granaries despite state orders to refill them. In 1848–49 during a famine in south China, officials held back granary reserves to speculate, and the government had to suppress the subsequent peasant rebellion with military force.

These circumstances served as background for the vast Taiping rebellion in southern China (1850–64). This rebellion began when a peasant family's son, Hong Xiuquan, failed the examination for entrance into government service. Under the influence of western missionaries, Hong formed a Christian-Chinese secret society that acquired millions of followers based on its egalitarian ideals and emotional appeal. Its followers included peasants fleeing the Yellow River's course change, famine victims whom the government could not aid, poor peasants and laborers who could not survive in the competitive market situation of the period, women from poor peasant families, and many others suffering from Qing decline.

The Taipings were at root a peasant movement and their ideology espoused equality, in particular promising the expropriation of landlords and equalizing land distribution. Yet their military control over much of southern China relied on components of the Qing system. When landlords had been removed, the Taiping officials would grant the peasants rights to the land. Where the landlords remained, Taiping officials demanded that peasants continue to pay rent. The Taipings imposed high taxes and other obligations, like the Qing. All of these compromises ultimately undermined their peasant support. Simultaneously another peasant rebel group, the Nien, formed in central China, fought the Qing for more than a decade before they were defeated.

Both of these movements involved vast numbers of peasants, but neither alleviated peasants' conditions. Instead they weakened the already declining government and its institutions, such as granaries. Military defeats by Western and Japanese imperialists further weakened the Qing regime and brought large areas of China under foreign domination similar to imperialism. Consequently when China endured the two severe El Niño-caused famines in 1876–78 and 1899–1901, the government was too corrupt and too weak to cope with it as it had a century earlier. China entered the twentieth century much weaker and much further behind the West than it had ever been.

The Middle East

The Middle East resembled China in being a region dominated by a declining empire, with a predominantly peasant economy, and threatened by

European imperial expansion. The most important agricultural country in the region was Egypt. In the seventeenth and eighteenth centuries Egypt was a province of the Ottoman Empire ruled by a Viceroy and dominated by Mamluk landlords who harshly exploited the peasants, driving many to flee their lands. Yet Egypt was an important producer of food for the Ottoman Empire. During the French Revolution Egypt exported wheat when it had good harvests.

In 1811 a new Ottoman Viceroy, Muhammad Ali, ruthlessly massacred the Mamluks and began a program of westernizing Egypt. To pay for imports from Europe he introduced a system of forced labor to induce the farmers to grow long-staple cotton for export. Muhammad Ali's successors continued these practices. Cotton production grew massively, but the peasants endured the El Niño-caused failure of the Nile floods and subsequent famine of 1876–78 with little government aid. Peasants earned too little to pay the high taxes the government imposed, and most ended up working on the landlords' cotton estates to pay their debts to moneylenders. Peasants' discontent with the moneylenders was one of the main factors in the Urabi rebellion in the late 1870s that overthrew the Egyptian rulers and led the British to establish a protectorate over Egypt.

Under the British protectorate, the cotton plantations operated, as they had for decades, on the 'exbah system, in which peasants would accept a small farm in exchange for raising cotton on the plantation. Sometimes the landlord or *pasha* would advance the peasant money to move onto the estate. The peasant would end up too poor to pay off the debt, and his work on the cotton farm would be credited to the debt so he would not earn anything. The circumstances of these Egyptian peasants resembled those of black sharecroppers in the U.S. South after the Civil War. Yet despite this, Egyptian cotton exports increased rapidly and competed well with U.S. cotton. Egyptian peasants also grew sugarcane and other crops.

Latin America in the late nineteenth century: neocolonialism, banana republics, poverty

Latin American economies after independence and the emancipations remained agrarian and dominated by plantations or large landowners, although many smallholders survived. Benefiting from Latin America's natural agricultural productivity to produce both traditional products – sugar in Cuba, coffee in Brazil – and new ones, these landlords were the main income earners and export producers; they dominated the region politically. Mining and manufacturing industries developed but remained less important politically until the Great Depression forced these countries to diversify their economies.

Mexico's farm system resembled that of most Latin American countries. After Mexico won its independence in 1821, Mexican leaders began efforts to restructure the country's economy based on nineteenth-century liberal ideology that favored private property and civil rights. These reforms included laws to privatize the lands of the Catholic Church and of the peasant villages, but government weakness and resistance by Church authorities, peasants, and conservative interests prevented their enforcement. Then in 1856–59, a new liberal government led by Benito Juarez, who was of peasant origin, introduced strengthened versions of these laws in a period called La Reforma. This included the Ley Lerdo of 1856, which required the Church to sell most of its lands and villages to privatize or sell theirs. This law infuriated conservatives, and provoked the brief War of the Reform (1858–60), which led the government to nationalize and sell Church lands.

The law also applied to traditional peasant village lands, which the peasants called *ejidos*. Legislators extended the Lay Lerdo to established private property in Mexico, but because peasants often had no legal documentation of land ownership, landlords and speculators used this law to deprive many peasants of their lands. In areas with less attractive lands, some villages managed to evade these laws, but in more attractive areas most peasants were expelled from their lands by wealthy Mexican and foreign, especially U.S., businessmen. This process intensified under the dictatorial presidency of General Porfirio Díaz (1876–1911). Peasants at first used legal means to resist expropriation, but the bias and corruption of the legal system led many to resort to rebellions that landlords and the government suppressed with military force.

Most peasants ended up as *peons*, bound by debt to work on haciendas, which survived from the colonial period. Haciendas combined subsistence farming and market production for the Mexican domestic market, limiting exports as well. Haciendas recruited labor by offering peasants a land plot for subsistence and a cash advance, which tied the peons to the hacienda until they could pay them off. In northern and central Mexico peons sometimes manipulated the haciendas, which needed them as workers, by asking for increased debt-advances in exchange for labor. Landlords often complained that the peons demanded debt-advances that they never intended to pay off. Debt bondage eventually disappeared from northern Mexico by the late nineteenth century.

In southern Mexico many haciendas exploited peons, and provoked chronic rebellions. In the Yucatán, planters raised henequen, a type of agave plant with thick leaves containing long fibers, called sisal, used to make twine heavily in demand by U.S. cattle ranchers and industry. Under Díaz, production grew from 40,000 to 600,000 350-pound bales for export. The millionaire planters used the Ley Lerdo to make Yucatán's Mayan peasants into landless and indebted laborers, working in debilitating conditions for long hours, often in chains and shackles. Subsistence crop production fell in the region, requiring planters to import food. These abuses provoked 50 years of Caste Wars of these Mayans against planters and people of

European origin. Similar conditions prevailed in the sugar plantations of Morelos. Despite laws against slavery, southern Mexico may have had 750,000 slaves working on these plantations. Other large estates in southern Mexico, such as coffee plantations in Chiapas, recruited migrant workers from Indian tribes of the nearby Sierra mountains with very little coercion.

Similarly impoverished and landless peasants worked on landlords' estates to produce export crops in many other Latin American countries. Estate owners often included investors from the United States and Europe. The landlords used their political power to orient these countries toward export production, in the process making the countries dependent on foreign markets, a relationship often described as "neocolonialism." In all cases the wealth of these estate owners depended on poorly paid and often coerced or servile peasant labor, even if their production processes were modern.

Science and the commercialization of agriculture

While agrarian systems during the nineteenth century gradually and ambivalently ended their reliance on servile labor, agricultural scientists achieved the first systematic understanding of the chemical and biological processes of farm production. The innovators in agricultural sciences included researchers and breeders. The soil scientist Carl Sprengel in 1828 showed that plants need specific chemicals, and that insufficiency of any of these would prevent the plant from growing normally. Justus von Liebig called this idea (without crediting Sprengel) the "law of the minimum." Liebig also wrote the first substantial analysis of agricultural chemistry, his classic textbook, *Organic Chemistry in its Application to Agriculture and Physiology* (1840), which went through many editions. Another crucial figure overlooked in his time was the nineteenth-century Austrian monk Gregor Mendel, whose studies of the inheritance patterns of pea plants led to modern genetics.

An early example of the commercial application of scientific research to agriculture involved nitrogen fertilizer. By the 1820s European farmers saw their crop yields declining from soil exhaustion and sought fertilizers to increase yields. Von Liebig wrote his book on agricultural chemistry on commission from the British Society for the Advancement of Science, in order to find a chemical explanation and solution for declining soil fertility. The German naturalist Alexander von Humboldt found in 1800–04 that Peruvian farmers used dried bird droppings, which they called guano, from the coastal Chincha Islands to increase harvests. Samples of this powder tested in Europe proved that it was an effective fertilizer. The British government soon claimed the islands, and British businessmen recruited desperate Chinese men as ostensibly free laborers, to work in virtual slavery on the islands mining guano. The exposure to this substance caused every conceivable kind of respiratory, gastro-intestinal, eye, and skin illness.

Many committed suicide or took opium. Their foremen used whips to induce them to work. Ultimately these methods produced some 13 million tons of guano from the islands before the deposits were exhausted in the 1870s.

The U.S. Congress passed the Guano Islands Act in 1856, and by 1900 American businessmen had claimed 91 islands around the world for guano. They seized one from Haiti in the 1880s and put laborers to work there in near-slavery conditions. After a few years the workers rebelled, killed a foreman, and were found guilty of murder in Maryland in 1887. Newspaper descriptions of their working conditions led an appeals court to overturn their sentences. In the end, this guano had been leached of nitrogen compounds by exposure, so all the workers' efforts and suffering were in vain.

The soil depletion–fertilizer issue remained significant. Henry Carey, an early American social scientist, argued that the long-distance trade between rural areas and towns worsened soil depletion, and von Liebig agreed. These ideas influenced many others, including the revolutionaries Karl Marx and Vladimir Lenin. Both criticized "capitalist" agriculture for separating town and village and exhausting the soils by neglecting fertilizer sources from towns. They apparently were unaware that Chinese reliance on such fertilizers, including human waste or "night soil," caused widespread parasite infections that held back all aspects of the Chinese rural economy.

Breeders employed careful observation and increasingly scientific research to develop new agricultural varieties. Robert Bakewell, an eighteenth-century British livestock farmer, bred large sheep and cattle whose meat tasted better than previous varieties, and Luther Burbank, a late-nineteenth-century American botanist, developed more than 800 new plant varieties. An extremely important version of breeding in the late nineteenth century involved a new version of the international transfer of varieties. In the Columbian exchange of the sixteenth century, plants and animals from remote locations became staples in regions where they had never grown before, such as cattle in South America and potatoes in Ireland. In the late nineteenth century, breeders employed different varieties of the same plant from remote areas to solve serious production problems found in the old varieties.

In one case, French vineyards began to have low harvests, and research found the cause to be a tiny aphid-like insect called phylloxera, inadvertently transported to France from the United States. By 1880 it had devastated vineyards in France, Spain, Italy, and Algeria. Research found that certain California grapevines were resistant to it. European growers had to import California vines and graft their local varieties onto them to obtain a plant with at least some of the European plants' character and the California vines' resistance to phylloxera. Since then vine growers all over the world have constantly struggled against phylloxera, using California vines as their first defense.

In another case, farms in the Great Plains frequently endured extreme cold, drought, or blights that destroyed their crops and drove farmers out of business. The main blight was black stem rust, a fungus spread by wind that could reduce harvests to a fraction of normal, as in 1877 in Kansas. The solutions came from Mennonite farmers, who emigrated from Russia to the U.S. in the 1880s with Turkey Red wheat, and the research of a USDA agronomist, Mark Alfred Carleton, who brought Kubanka wheat from the Central Asian steppe. Both varieties proved much more resistant to cold, drought, and rust than any U.S. variety, but they were durum or "hard" wheats, impossible for existing U.S. mills to grind, and best used for pasta. Most U.S. wheat was soft spring wheat grown for bread-making. Carleton began a one-man campaign to persuade millers to develop steel roller mills, European pasta producers to purchase U.S. durum wheat, and U.S. consumers to try pasta. After successful harvests of Kubanka in 1904 despite a black rust infestation that ruined other varieties, Russian durum wheats became basic to U.S. farming.

Trade in farm produce also underwent a significant transformation as part of the nineteenth-century expansion of global trade and mass markets. For most of history farmers sold their own crops, or relied on small-scale middlemen. Middlemen faced hostility from peasants for offering low prices for their products and from townspeople for high market prices. Governments regulated and sometimes arrested middlemen for charging high prices that could potentially cause food riots. In the late eighteenth century political economists, such as Adam Smith in *The Wealth of Nations*, argued that grain traders' high prices served to ration food during a dearth and attracted other traders whose competition would lower prices. On this basis British officials during the famine years of 1794–95 and 1799–1801 told poor people protesting high prices in the towns that "political economy" required non-intervention in free trade. Advocates for the poor, such as William Cobbett, responded that the "moral economy" required food prices that the poor could afford.

In the wake of this conflict between free markets and the poor, much larger enterprises emerged in the early nineteenth century to process and trade grain and other agricultural produce. The winners in the subsequent competitions remain the dominant actors in world food trade. They are also the main intermediaries between the decreasing numbers of farmers who produce food and the majority urban populations of the world who do not grow their own food. There were two main groups of these firms, although they came to overlap: the traders and the processors.

The most important of these first agribusinesses were the grain traders – Continental, Dreyfus, Bunge, and Cargill. They all began as small-scale local traders but had executives who used effective tactics and luck to take over competitors. A new development in the world agricultural economy was industrialized food processing. This sector derived from the technological and scientific breakthroughs and also from imperialism. The global export booms in cotton, edible oils, tropical products like coconuts and cacao, and livestock products all required extensive processing. Some of the enterprises that managed both shipping and processing became quite large. Lever Brothers, a soap-making firm, moved into the African export sector in the early twentieth century. This company dominated African exports of oil crops and other crops during the peak of imperialism, and later became one of the three largest food companies in the world.

Conclusion: world agriculture and history in the nineteenth century

Agriculture in the nineteenth century shook off its main medieval vestiges and rapidly acquired all the characteristics of the leading industrial sectors: mass production, world markets, extensive wide-ranging trade, and increasing concentration in trade and processing. Yet agriculture retained its two characteristic subordinations. Natural disasters, reflecting vast global patterns like the ENSO and warming, devastated several large regions in the later years of the century and several smaller regions chronically. The ups and downs of markets, both international and national, created booms and busts that ruined many farmers and peasants, and forced many to surrender their lands and become laborers and debt peons. These crises contributed to massive rebellions in which peasants took a significant part. In developed European countries, farmers and landlords saw their political power decline despite the emancipations. Even when farmers did win the policies they sought, their success reflected the interests of other stronger political groups, and agriculture had become one of several special interests.

The stage was set for major political–economic conflict and reforms. It was not in the interest of these industrial economies to have to rely on poor peasants and backward agricultural sectors, even in the United States. Peasants themselves wanted release from the new subordination that they had traded for the past slavery and serfdom. Public opinion criticized political leaders for famines. Reform was demanded and would be forthcoming but in unexpected ways.

The evolution of the agrarian world in the nineteenth century demonstrated the importance of agriculture in the world economy. Even though the development of industry in Britain and other countries soon outweighed agriculture in value terms, agriculture remained the basis of even the most industrialized societies. Britain, for example, became "the workshop of the world," an enormous industrial power. Yet politicians and industrialists structured the economy with free trade so that Britain needed that power to feed itself. Industry produced the cargo vessels, military vessels, coal, and communications that allowed Britain to run down its agriculture and depend on imports for most of its food. Thoughtful observers like Alexis de Tocqueville suspected that the future powers of the world would be the large land powers that could support themselves in agriculture first of all, the United States, Russia, and later Brazil.

Further reading

In addition to sources listed in the previous chapter, the following readings are useful for eighteenth–nineteenth-century topics. On Europe: B. H. Slicher van Bath, *The Agrarian History of Western Europe* (London: Edward Arnold, 1966); Mark Overton, *Agricultural Revolution in England* (Cambridge: Cambridge University Press, 1996); J. V. Beckett, *The Agricultural Revolution* (London: Blackwell Publishers, 1990), which has numerous primary source excerpts.

On the Americas, see Gilbert Fite, *American Farmers: The New Minority* (Bloomington, IN: Indiana University Press, 1981); Douglas Hurt, *American Agriculture: A Brief History* (Ames, IA: Iowa State University Press, 2002); James R. Scobie, *Revolution on the Pampas: A Social History of Argentine Wheat* (Austin, TX: University of Texas Press, 1964).

On South Asia, see Mike Davis, *Late Victorian Holocausts* (London: Verso, 2001), which however overstates its case somewhat; Blaire Kling, *The Blue Mutiny* (Philadelphia, PA: University of Pennsylvania Press, 1966); Tirthankar Roy, *Economic History of India, 1857–1947* (New Delhi: Oxford University Press, 2000).

Chapter 6

Agriculture and crisis
1900–40

In the twentieth century, agricultural modernization became a central goal of governments and societies all over the world. This orientation toward agriculture derived from two broad historical processes in the rural sector: the early-twentieth-century economic and political crises, and the later-twentieth-century competition for economic development. Never before in history have so many groups, within and outside of governments, made such consistent efforts to improve farming and farmers' lives. Yet never before had so many farmers abandoned farming to live and work in cities. The old dual subordination was mitigated and changed, but remained in effect.

In the early twentieth century, agriculture played a central role in a series of economic and political crises. These crises inspired often dramatic efforts by governments, businesses, and public organizations to transform agricultural practices and even whole agrarian societies. These agencies had the objective of solving problems of food supply and agrarian economy and life. In many cases, however, their objectives went beyond this pragmatism, as several countries attempted substantial reform and even revolutionary changes in agriculture and its relationships to those outside rural life.

The first section of this chapter provides the environmental context for the entire twentieth century, for this chapter and the next. This environmental history is better documented and understood than any previous period, and that understanding contributed to policies to aid farmers. The rest of the chapter examines the main agrarian trends and decisive turning points of twentieth-century agrarian life before the Second World War.

Environment and agriculture in the twentieth century

Agriculture since 1900 has had to contend with the global warming that began in the nineteenth century, causing the accelerated melting of glaciers and polar ice caps. Weather crises caused by warming often interacted with problematic actions by farmers to cause serious disasters. In North America, American and Canadian farmers responded to increased demand in the First World War and the fall in prices in the 1920s by intensive plowing and grain production in the Great Plains, which exhausted and dried the soil. An extremely severe "Great Southern Drought" in 1930 followed by droughts and hot summers from 1932 to 1934 resulted in the Dust Bowl. Windstorms stirred up massive clouds of dry soil over thousands of miles, making farming and sometimes even breathing impossible, and hundreds of thousands of people fled the region. Extensive scientific studies analyzed the causes of the Dust Bowl, and the U.S. and Canadian governments used the results of these studies to help farmers avert disaster during a similar drought in the 1950s.

Serious droughts affected many countries during the twentieth century and challenged the resources and capabilities of governments. Russia and the Soviet Union faced droughts and famines repeatedly; the government organized relief and imported food. China had 20 droughts during the century, including intense ones in 1921, 1928–30, and 1941 that caused crop failures, famines, and millions of deaths. India had serious droughts and famines in 1941–43, 1951, and 1965–66; governments undertook relief measures and significant food imports. Prolonged droughts struck the Sahel region between the African savannah and the Sahara desert in the 1970s–1980s. These resulted both from weather cycles and from cash crop production that pushed nomads to northern pastures. Many developed countries provided famine relief and development aid.

Some regions endured massive floods, as in China in 1931 and 1959, and cyclones, as in India in 1942 and in Bangladesh in the early 1970s. Yet the main pattern was warming and drying, the result of both long-term climate warming and human actions. Deforestation – half of the world's forests have been cut for farms or cities – eliminated the cooling effect of forests, and expanded farming to poor-quality lands. The soils of former tropical rainforests have little organic material and deteriorate rapidly. They require decades of intense work and much fertilizer and irrigation to be restored.

Plant and animal diseases played a large but overlooked role in shaping agrarian and world history in the twentieth century. Fungal diseases, such as rust, contributed to major crop failures, such as the Soviet famine of the early 1930s and the Bengal famine of 1942–43. A rust outbreak in Mexico in 1939–41 led Mexican officials to seek help from the United States. The result was the development of high-yielding varieties (HYVs) and the Green Revolution. Animal diseases were resolved without much publicity, until the most notorious animal illness in history, BSE or mad-cow disease, caused a prolonged international emergency.

The early-twentieth-century agrarian crises

The world's agrarian economies and societies went through a series of complex economic, social, and political crises during 1900–40. Governments responded with unprecedented policy initiatives, most of which are still in effect. The crises in Europe and North America had particular significance because of the dominant role of the U.S. economy and agriculture in the world, and because European countries and colonies controlled most of the rest of the world's farmland.

By 1914 much of Western Europe, especially Great Britain and Germany, depended on imports for most of their food. Europe imported from the United States, the rising agrarian powers of Canada, Argentina, and Australia, and relatively poor and backward economies and colonies like Russia, India, Southeast Asia, and Mexico.

Government officials and educated observers feared that this dependence would make England and Germany vulnerable to blockade in what appeared to be an approaching war. The exporters relied on elaborate systems of internal trade and distribution. The Punjab region produced a surplus on which much of India depended. The American Great Plains provided grain and meat for the cities of the United States and Canada. In Russia, Ukraine exported more of its produce because of its proximity to Black Sea ports. The large villages of the Volga Basin sent produce to the cities of Central Russia. China had a vast peasantry with limited food reserves, highly vulnerable to natural disaster.

In the early twentieth century, agriculture recovered from the depression of the late nineteenth century. Farm prices rose and trade expanded. Economists determined that U.S. farmers' income from sales of farm products in this period approximately equaled what an urban worker earned for a similar amount of work. This "parity" served as the basis for the price supports and other subsidies that the U.S. government would provide farmers during the Great Depression and afterwards.

Nonetheless, the agrarian sector began the twentieth century in Europe and the U.S. in decline, relative to the booming and modernizing industrial sector. In England, the landed elite declined in status while tenants gained unprecedented rights. Low-priced food imports left dairy production for the towns as the main profitable farming sector. In the U.S., in 1908 President Theodore Roosevelt appointed a Country Life Commission to modernize rural areas by extending urban standards of housing and education to farmers. The U.S. government also supported scientific and economic research in agriculture.

Peasants and farmers in Europe and many of the colonies became increasingly integrated into urban and world economies. Many French peasants bought (rather than grew and made) their bread and clothing. German peasants were included in the social welfare systems set up in the early twentieth century. Even African colonial farmers now produced cacao and coffee actively for urban and European markets. Ironically, as farmers in Europe became less traditional, scholars published works about disappearing folklore, and conservative politicians and writers glorified the peasant as the essence and core of the "nation." The basic works of "peasant studies" and agricultural economics, such as those by the Russian economist Alexander Chayanov, appeared in this period.

Agriculture and the First World War

The First World War, the largest war in history up to that time, had unprecedented agrarian consequences. Since all the major combatants had comparable militaries, food supplies played a crucial role in the war.

All the major powers in the war had food crises and established some degree of state control over food distribution and production. The German government miscalculated its food reserves, and potato blight created an unanticipated food shortage. The government imposed requisitions and forced cultivation on resistant German farmers, and rationed its dwindling food reserves, yet Germany had 750,000 more civilian deaths than normal during the Turnip Winter of 1916.

Britain, with German submarines blockading its food imports, by 1916 established rationing and production controls. The government ordered farmers to plant grain, and confiscated the farms of hundreds of farmers who refused to do so. The government set minimum prices, sent POWs to work on the farms, and the British pulled through with minimal losses. In France, the army mobilized some two-thirds of adult male farmers, leaving women, children, and elderly and disabled people in the villages. This caused a sharp decline in food production. As in Germany and England, the government imposed requisitions and government control over food distribution. It also made desperate efforts to obtain farm labor, from POWs and colonial Algeria, with limited success.

Both sides also tried to obtain food from abroad. Germany and Austria received a windfall when the Bolshevik revolution of November 1917 gave them the opportunity to occupy Ukraine and requisition food from the peasants there, but they obtained less than they had hoped. Britain, France, and Italy in 1916 began a policy of purchases in common on foreign markets, under administrations (called "executives") for cereals, meats, and other items. This Inter-Allied Food Council, with the U.S. as the key supplier, divided imports among the allies; this system greatly aided their victory.

Britain also obtained food from Egypt, which it had occupied in 1882. When the Ottoman Empire declared war on Britain in 1914, the British occupied Egypt and subsequently forced export of millions of bushels of grain in 1915–16. These exports depleted peasants' reserves. In 1918 the British purchased the entire Egyptian cotton crop, a source of edible oils and animal feed, and requisitioned more food from peasants. The British also forcibly recruited 500,000 peasants as laborers, with hundreds of police and peasants killed in the process. These and other abuses inspired a nationalist movement and a rebellion in 1919. Peasants tore up railroad lines and seized food and animals from large estates, and cut off food supplies for Cairo until British forces suppressed the unarmed rebels.

Canadian and U.S. farmers benefited from the First World War's increased demand, but U.S. farmers also faced a domestic crisis. The U.S. wheat harvest fell by a third in 1916–17, while the cereal executive (Britain, France, and Italy) purchased double the normal U.S. exports. U.S. grain prices tripled, leading to protests and proposals in Congress to embargo U.S. grain exports. President Woodrow Wilson and other Americans suspected grain traders and farmers of collusion to lower production and raise prices (in fact drought, plant disease, and other natural factors reduced harvests), but they opposed government intervention in markets.

Then in February 1917, while the U.S. had food riots, Britain introduced price supports for farmers. Progressive leaders advocated this for the U.S. to increase production and lower prices. Congress introduced a major price control bill, but U.S. farmers were suspicious and the Farm Bloc opposed the proposal. The Allies informed President Wilson that they faced famine without U.S. supplies. Wilson selected Herbert Hoover, a mining engineer who had managed food relief, to be the U.S. Food Administrator, and Congress passed a Food Control Act in 1917 that set minimum wheat prices. Farmers anticipated high prices and plowed millions of acres, often with new Fordson tractors, introduced in 1917. Hoover imposed price controls on food in fall 1917, and played the dominant role in world food trade during the war.

Grain traders profited regardless of government policies. The American company Cargill made such large profits trading grain that it was accused of war profiteering. Nonetheless, by 1918 the U.S. and Europe had developed reliable procedures for dealing with wartime food and agricultural emergencies by extensive government intervention in food production and marketing.

The failed restoration of the 1920s and the Great Depression of the 1930s

After the war America was the main country with the food reserves necessary to feed starving Europe. The U.S. used food as a weapon by withholding aid from Germany until its new leaders accepted the harsh Versailles treaty in 1919. U.S. exports to Europe in 1918–20 kept U.S. prices high. As Europe recovered from the war and revived domestic production, however, farm prices fell more than 50 percent from June 1920 through 1921, and stayed low throughout the decade. In the U.S., Europe, and most of the world, farmers in the 1920s faced chronic overproduction and persistent low prices. Farmers, farm politicians, and specialists proposed measures to alleviate the situation, but governments, guided by outdated economic theory and sometimes by farmers' fears of government interference, refused to intervene in the economy until the 1930s crisis.

In the U.S., George Peek, a farmer turned executive, proposed a plan in which the government would purchase farm products at parity prices, protect prices with tariffs, and dump surpluses on foreign markets. Congressmen from farm states formed a Farm Bloc and attempted to implement this and other reforms in several McNary–Haugen bills during 1924–28. None passed because the conservatives claimed they would increase production in swamped markets and keep inefficient farmers in business. Farmers tried to protect themselves against low prices by forming cooperatives, but only small groups of specialized growers succeeded, like orange growers in California who formed Sunkist or cranberry growers in New England who formed Ocean Spray. Grain farmers were much more numerous and more inclined to break from the coop.

In the U.S. South, impoverished tenants sometimes earned as little as 14 cents a day, while landowners, often descendants of the old planters, profited from the international demand for cotton. Yet the South faced a serious environmental and economic problem as the boll weevil devastated many cotton fields. These economic conditions and racist violence in the South, which state and federal governments made no effort to alleviate, persuaded tenants, who were mostly African-American, to begin the Great Migration to industrial jobs in the northern cities.

In the plains, farmers significantly increased mechanization. The 90,000 acre farm of Tom Campbell in southeast Montana grew grain on an entirely mechanized basis, employing only a few seasonal laborers. Campbell's farm was the forerunner of modern industrial farming. The Secretary of Agriculture made speeches urging that every farm become a factory, and increasingly farms applied mechanization and factory-inspired production approaches. In the west, especially California, farms relied on immigrant labor from Mexico in the booming fruit and vegetable sectors. In both of these cases, the government's efforts aimed to encourage farm efficiency and productivity rather than to help farmers hurt by falling prices.

Canada extended government control over marketing from 1917 to 1920, under an agency that was renamed the Canadian Wheat Board in 1919. In 1920 the government abolished this agency and restored market exchange, but farm prices collapsed. Farmers protested, demanded the abolition of private grain trade, and attacked the system of futures contracts in the Winnipeg Grain Exchange. In this system, as at the Chicago Board of Trade, traders purchased and sold farm commodities in advance of their production. Canadian farmers instead proposed the idea of a pool; farmers would sell their crops to a single large common fund, and receive distributions of net income after the crop was sold, rather than competing with each other and driving down prices. Only half of Canadian wheat went through the wheat pool in the 1920s before it collapsed in the Depression.

In Britain many farmers after the war returned their grain fields to grass. The Agriculture Act of 1920 extended price supports and minimum wages for farm workers, but farmers' protests persuaded the government to repeal it in 1921. Soon afterwards in Britain as elsewhere the prices collapsed: wheat fell from 80 shillings per hundredweight in 1920 to 47 shillings in 1922, and most other products fell similarly. French peasants became more literate and politically involved after the First World War, but their numbers fell from more than five million farms before the war to four million by 1929 due to wartime losses and migration to cities. Urban demand exceeded farm production, and France had to import one-fourth of its food needs. Many French farmers had to restore lands damaged by the war, and lacked the capital and incentives to introduce modern technologies. The French government provided little support in this period.

The World's Economic Conference in May 1927 under the League of Nations focused attention on agriculture's chronic crises. Conference reports interpreted agriculture's woes as the result of the disequilibrium between low prices for farm products and high prices for industrial products. Other observers blamed the crisis on falling farm prices, that farmers after the harvest could not repay credits from the previous spring and often lost their farms. Conventional economics did not have any solution that could resolve these problems. Only a major crisis forced leaders to resort to alternative approaches.

That crisis was the Great Depression that began in 1929. It had many causes, but a crucial one was the 1920s agricultural crisis. If some of the proposed policies to support farmers had been applied in the 1920s, the situation could have been quite different. Officials and most economists rejected such intervention as applicable only in wartime, and expected a return to "normalcy" that never came. While the U.S. stock market crash and bank collapses triggered the Depression, the economic circumstances of the agricultural sector, which employed about two-thirds of the world's economically active population, made a serious economic downturn almost inevitable. By 1929 countries that produced primary products had much larger surpluses, and lower prices, than ever before. During the peak of the crisis, 1929–33, prices declined despite crop failures because aggregate production swamped world markets.

While traders desperately tried to sell surpluses, governments tried to alleviate farm debt and farm abandonment while maintaining food supplies and low prices for both working and unemployed citizens. In August 1933 the League of Nations belatedly held an International Wheat Conference at which exporting countries agreed to limit exports, but several countries violated them when they saw an opportunity to produce and sell more.

Faced with this intractable crisis, governments had to determine the role that the agrarian sector would play in the foreseeable future. Decreased foreign investment forced many countries into economic self-sufficiency. Several formerly agricultural countries implemented policies to reduce farm production and to enlarge the importance of industry. As a result, after the Depression, many countries became less agrarian and had more balanced economies.

The global economic dominance of the United States makes its experience central for understanding the Depression. Farm prices, low and unstable through the 1920s, fell steadily after 1929. Because of America's role in propping up the European economy, declining American prices drove prices down all over Europe and ultimately the world. In many countries the U.S.–European influence reinforced pre-existing local factors.

President Herbert Hoover refused to repeat wartime market interventions, saying that the market would correct the temporary "slump." The few measures he applied were no help. He established the Federal Farm Board, which purchased eight million tons of surplus grain, yet prices continued to fall. His administration refused to use these reserves for starving southern sharecroppers during the Great Southern Drought of 1930, claiming aid would "demoralize" them and shrink the market, even though sharecroppers were too poor to buy most products. The Red Cross provided what it considered inadequate relief. After drought in Montana in 1931, Hoover provided monetary relief that reached only a fraction of needy farmers. Against the advice of economists and businessmen, Hoover imposed tariffs on thousands of imports. This prompted retaliatory tariffs against U.S. exports and further reduced trade, especially in agriculture.

Meanwhile farmers in the Midwest and Plains states faced plummeting prices, overdue loan payments, and foreclosures. In May 1932, long-term farm activist Milo Reno formed the Farmers' Holiday Association, to organize a farmers' boycott of national markets, and force the government to protect farm prices. In August the farm holiday began in Iowa and Wisconsin with attacks on banks, blocking of roads and trains, and violent conflicts with police, with deaths on both sides. Association members also went to foreclosure auctions and bid pennies, intimidating bankers into accepting these bids. They then returned the farm they bought for a dime back to the former owners. They also worked to have farmers and creditors meet and resolve debts without foreclosures. These, however, were not typical events, and hundreds of thousands of farmers lost their farms to foreclosures.

Growing discontent with Hoover's timidity in dealing with the economic crisis paved the way for the election of Democrat Franklin D. Roosevelt. FDR's agrarian reforms were basic parts of the New Deal. Roosevelt grew up on his family's rural estate in Hyde Park, and had a personal commitment to farming and rural life. His advisors included Secretary of Agriculture Henry A. Wallace, a top-level agricultural scientist who edited a farm newspaper that published numerous articles about the agricultural situation.

The FDR administration's farm policies derived from proposals circulating in the 1920s and earlier. The main categories were credit reform, acreage limitation, and price supports. The Farm Credit Association purchased mortgages of defaulting farmers from banks and arranged refinancing with farmers. The Agricultural Adjustment Act offered producers of the main farm products – grains (corn, wheat, rice), industrial crops (cotton, tobacco), and livestock (hogs, milk) – payments for agreeing to reduce their production. When these were first introduced, farmers were obliged to destroy large amounts of farm products and livestock, causing a huge scandal in a period of widespread hunger. The Commodity Credit Corporation advanced loans to farmers on the collateral of their crops valued at near-parity prices. If the prices rose above that, the farmer could sell the crop and repay the loan. If the price remained low, the farmer could keep the loan in exchange for turning the crop over to the CCC to sell abroad or use for other purposes. The administration's policies also imposed cooperative-type marketing that still controls much of the marketing of milk, fruit, and vegetables. The FDR administration also developed rural electrification, soil conservation projects, and relief measures.

These were the first large-scale farm subsidies in U.S. agriculture, and they remained the basis of farm policies for decades afterwards. These reforms derived first of all from proposals made by farmers, specialists, and commentators in the U.S., but they also derived in part from foreign models. Wallace conceived of the CCC as part of a system to regulate prices and food supplies, based on the model of the ancient Chinese "ever-normal granary." The increased role of government reflected policies in the Soviet Union and fascist countries. To some extent the U.S. and other democracies tried to avoid the potentially disastrous political consequences of the Depression by adapting elements of such economic policies to a democratic polity. The U.S. farm programs allowed a degree of abuse and corruption, and demanded substantial government spending, which ultimately led to efforts to reverse them after the Second World War. Their implementation also reflected a growing bias against African-American farmers, and toward large-scale farmers, which ultimately became legal and political issues.

The Great Depression affected Britain less harshly: prices fell but farmers had limited debts and farm bankruptcies increased only slightly. To address falling prices, in 1931 Parliament passed the Agricultural Marketing Act to allow farmers to establish organizations to control marketing. When prices for milk, the main product, fell in 1932 to one-quarter of the 1922 price, 100,000 dairy farmers voted to establish a Milk Marketing Board. Later boards were established for potatoes, pigs, and pork. The government also imposed import tariffs (partly in response to the U.S. tariff), and provided price-support subsidies.

In France in 1932–33, farmers produced the largest wheat and grape harvests in their history and drove prices down. The French government restricted foreign trade, fixed prices, and spent billions of francs, more than on defense, on subsidies and other aid programs. Yet by 1934 prices fell to one-fourth of their high in the 1920s. Peasants felt that no one in the Republic understood their concerns. In response to this crisis, a French journalist, who used the pseudonym Henri Dorgères, began a political campaign, like Milo Reno in the U.S., using boycotts, disrupting farm foreclosures, and advocating non-payment of taxes. He organized peasant youth into paramilitary Greenshirts, and invoked nationalism and anti-Semitism. Dorgères' movement and the agrarian crisis in France faded during 1936 because farm prices rose and most peasants preferred democracy.

Canadian farmers encountered collapsing prices, extraordinary heat that killed people, intermittent dust storms, vast grasshopper infestations, millions of gophers, and rust diseases that prevented wheat from developing. Crop production fell by at least one-third, and a quarter million farmers left for the towns. From 1931 provincial governments organized relief for farmers. In 1935 the Canadian government established the Prairie Farm Rehabilitation Administration to restore agriculture, planted the most arid regions with grass, and formed the Canadian Wheat Board to purchase surpluses and influence prices.

Australia developed into a major exporter of wheat, meat, and dairy products by 1900. In the First World War, central and state governments formed a wheat pool and an Australian Wheat Board to accommodate the large harvests, but closed the system in 1921 because it was too costly. The government tried to reintegrate rebellious demobilized soldiers by settling them in Western Australia as farmers, but despite large expenditures because of the region's arid climate, thousands of these new farmers ended up in debt and abandoned their farms. In the Depression, more farmers abandoned indebted farms for the towns, or declared bankruptcy. Provincial governments provided financial aid and postponed debt repayments, which helped some farmers. The central government organized farm support only when the Second World War began. It reestablished the Australian Wheat Board as a grain export monopoly called the "single desk." It guaranteed minimum prices for farmers, and though conceived as temporary, it lasted 60 years.

Argentina, the remaining major agrarian democracy, during 1900–13 tripled its cropland and became one of the top world grain exporters. Yet Argentine farmers were tenants, usually immigrants, who earned too little to buy land, and worked on short-term rentals, hiring *braceros* or landless laborers. In good seasons they could make a lot of money. In 1912, however, after an enormous harvest, prices collapsed, farmers could not pay rents, and landlords began evicting them. A large strike then began a decade of conflict between tenant farmers, landlords, and braceros. The central government, controlled by landlords like President Hipólito Yrigoyen, tried to suppress the strikes, sometimes deporting immigrant tenants. Only the improved prices during the 1920s stopped the strike movement.

During the late 1920s the Argentine government provided limited aid to farmers, chiefly education, and imported 15,000 tractors and 25,000 combine harvesters. The crash in 1929 combined with good harvests to drive prices down. Farmers switched from tractors back to horses, and by 1933 farmers were burning their crops or letting them rot in the fields. That year the government established agencies to purchase surpluses at prices that would meet farmers' needs without encouraging further production. The Wine Board destroyed the stocks it acquired, and the Grain Board exported their surpluses.

In the large democratic countries, scientific, technological, and economic improvements enabled farmers to produce large surpluses. Yet the large scale of relatively uniform crops meant that major environmental disasters or economic downturns could have similarly large-scale consequences. Governments, farmers, and other observers viewed the persistent surpluses and low prices of the 1920s as a temporary aberration that would correct itself. Very few people anticipated anything like the Great Depression that followed. Virtually all of these countries in the 1930s implemented support programs to help farmers that went beyond any previous government agrarian programs. Still none of these programs helped every farmer, and millions of farmers, such as African-American farmers in the U.S. South, left the countryside for work in cities.

Agriculture and the fascist states

Despite their non-democratic systems, the fascist states also took measures to help farmers. These regimes saw agriculture as central to their nationalist ideologies. They also came to power on the promise of improving food supplies or rescuing the country from depression.

Fascist Italy

Italy began the twentieth century with two broad agricultural regions. The north had large modern farms, scientific knowledge spread by universities and extension agents, land reclamation and irrigation. Landlords employed tenants with long leases, while small-scale tenants or sharecroppers often employed rural laborers who comprised more than half of the rural population. Production was high and growing, but Italy still imported a million tons of wheat every year. The south, called *Mezzogiorno*, had large estates still called latifundia, owned by absentee landlords and worked by impoverished tenants, smallholders, and laborers. Landlords held power from local levels to central government, while most peasants and laborers could not vote. Italian legislators introduced some measures to alleviate rural poverty, but agrarian policies mainly served landlords' interests. Government indifference led rural laborers to strike over wages and land. In north Italy large unions of farm laborers conducted 3,000 strikes in 1900–14 and won wage increases. Still rural income remained far below urban.

In the First World War, the Italian government focused on industrial production to meet military needs. By 1917 the country became short of food and resorted to rationing. Italy lost 2.5 million men during the war, mostly rural, and like France depended on women and children as farmers. Recognizing that farmers endured military service, requisitions, and price controls, Prime Minister Antonio Salandra promised "land for the peasants." Some farmers benefited from high prices and bought land, and some landowners sold plots to reduce the risk of rebellion. During the First World War about a million peasant families thus acquired some 800,000 hectares, but the number of smallholders grew. War profiteers and speculators also acquired large holdings and became a new landlord class.

Italy after the war fell into a major crisis with industrial bankruptcies and unemployment, labor militancy, high food prices, and food riots in 1919. During 1919–20 more than 1.5 million laborers and tenants went on strike, winning major concessions, while peasant leagues and cooperatives took over lands, and some southern latifundia disappeared. In the north, tenants protested high rents while laborers demanded wage increases. Marketing cooperatives now began cooperative farming on 100,000 hectares. Landlords felt threatened as the government sided with peasants and laborers.

In this complex context Mussolini and his fascist party came to power. Initially the fascists advocated socialist policies, including division of landed estates among the peasants. As prospects for the left declined in 1919–20, Mussolini revised fascism into a radical conservative movement to win support from businessmen and soldiers. In the countryside fascists now defended private property. In power after the "March on Rome" in 1922, Mussolini repealed laws and withdrew proposals for division of latifundia, restriction of evictions, and cooperatives. Yet he also appealed to peasants by describing them as the core of the nation and asserting he would "ruralize Italy." Many peasants and tenants feared socialist policies of land confiscation and labor unions, and supported the fascists. Fascists conducted "expeditions," financed by landlords, against rural cooperatives and labor unions, which lost members, and rural strikes ceased by 1923.

Mussolini revised his agricultural policies again in 1924, after Italy had a low harvest and imported two million tons of wheat. This emergency occurred at the same time as the Matteoti crisis, when a leading legislator and political opponent of Mussolini exposed fascist abuses and was found murdered shortly afterwards. For economic reasons and to distract attention from this crisis, Mussolini declared the "battle for wheat." This policy imposed import tariffs, subsidized inputs and transport, and spread propaganda to promote self-sufficiency. Farmers began growing wheat everywhere, inspired by high subsidized prices offered by government-run "wheat pools."

These policies increased production 50 percent, making Italy nearly self-sufficient in most years. The wheat campaign benefited big landlords and industrial sectors that produced tractors and other equipment. Yet ordinary townspeople and laborers had to pay more for bread and pasta because of tariff protection of wheat producers. The campaign diverted land from other crops and livestock. Italy had fewer cows in 1930 than in 1908, imported olive oil, and exported less fruits and vegetables. Had Italy focused on these products, it could have earned more than it saved by reduced grain imports, since world grain prices were so low.

Nazi Germany

In 1900, a quarter of the German Empire's population worked in farming. In eastern Germany a few thousand Prussian Junkers owned almost half the land and ran large estates employing peasant laborers, yet Germany remained a significant grain importer. In western and southern Germany, small peasant proprietors predominated and focused on livestock. These two main agrarian groups were at odds: Junker demands for tariffs conflicted with the small peasants' need for cheap forage. German industrial expansion deprived the agrarian interest of the political power they had held in the past.

Germany's food shortages and civilian mortality during the war provoked hostility between town and country. Farmers claimed they deprived themselves to feed the towns, and evaded fixed prices and requisitions through a black market that further alienated townspeople. Consequently, after the German collapse in November 1918, most peasants were indifferent to the workers' rebellions in 1918–19. Peasants in Weimar Germany sought not land but fertilizer, equipment, and improved housing. The financial crises of the 1920s drove them into debt and hindered their adoption of new technologies and techniques. By 1928 many disillusioned peasants joined the Landvolk movement which began violent and anti-Semitic protests in northern Germany. In 1929 the Junkers tried to form a Green Front with peasants, but peasants resented the landlords, many of whom received *Osthilfe*, state subsidies for debt relief that ordinary peasants did not receive.

By the late 1920s the Nazi party won peasant support by advocating their interests and glorifying them as the basis of the nation and the source of the future "master race." They also appealed to the large Junker landlords. In the elections of July and November 1932, peasants and landlords massively supported the Nazis and helped Hitler come to power.

The Nazis controlled German society and economy through a corporatist system, in which the government required all members of related groups to belong to a state-run organization that managed their work and labor relations. In September 1933, the Nazis established the National Food Estate, which encompassed farming, food processing, distribution, and sales. Everyone who worked in a field related to food production and distribution was required to be a member of this estate. It ultimately included three million farmers, 300,000 processors, and 500,000 stores and traders. This may have been the first government institution to conceive of agriculture as part of a large "food system." All of the other systems, even the contemporary Soviet communist system, managed farming separately from processing and distribution. In institutional terms, the National Food Estate anticipated the agribusiness structures that have dominated the world food system increasingly in the postwar period.

The National Food Estate employed 130,000 personnel, set prices and wages, and allocated resources and products. The Nazis even tried to establish their own agrarian aristocracy by identifying 600,000 mid-sized farms as *Erbhoeffe* or hereditary estates. The Nazis also attempted to improve the conditions of farm laborers by freeing them from taxes and regulating employment on farm estates, but rural unemployment remained high. On the other hand, in 1934 the Nazis tried to prohibit farm workers from leaving their jobs, but the gap between rural poverty and urban opportunities grew as the Nazis prepared for war. The period saw a growing flight from the land, as in the democracies.

Brazil

Brazil in 1900 was the largest coffee producer in the world. Most of it was grown in the southeastern state of São Paulo on a few thousand large plantations or *fazendas*. The planters employed immigrant *colonos*, like Argentine tenants, to produce the crop. They allotted colonos small subsistence plots to reduce the wages they had to pay them. The state Minas Gerais, north of São Paulo, had a large cattle and dairy economy, employing gauchos as in Argentina. These two states dominated Brazil in what was called at the time "coffee-and-milk politics." During the 1920s, one-fourth of the colonos migrated inland seasonally to farm independently, aided by government railroad construction. This new small farm sector produced one-third of São Paulo's coffee, as well as crops and livestock for the cities.

The strong ruling party relied on the cities and smaller farmers. Discontented planters turned to a rising politician, Getulio Vargas, a gaucho's son turned lawyer. He promised to defend the planters' interests and came to power in a coup in 1930. In 1937, after suppressing a communist coup attempt, Vargas declared the New State (Estado Novo) a dictatorship similar to European fascist regimes but less repressive. At the same time he instituted a series of unusual policies to keep the planters afloat.

Brazilian coffee exports collapsed dramatically in the 1930s, by 1939 down to 20 percent of their 1929 value. The government had dealt with surplus production in the past through "valorization," a policy of storing surpluses until prices recovered. The coffee planters persuaded the government in São Paulo to make this system permanent in 1924 by establishing a Coffee Institute to regulate sales. The crisis of 1929–30 was much more serious than any previous market collapse. Vargas replaced valorization with *autarquias*, government institutions to regulate trade and production.

The first autarquia was in coffee, a National Coffee Council (later Department), based on the São Paulo Coffee Institute, with the power to destroy excess coffee and to ban coffee planting. During 1931–43 this agency burned 77 million sacks of coffee. By 1937, however, the approach had decreased Brazil's share of world exports more than 50 percent. After an ineffective Pan-American Coffee Conference, Vargas cut back on valorization and urged producers to produce and compete on world markets, and Brazilian coffee exports increased. Similar autarquias were formed for cotton, manioc, and sugar, but not for basic food supplies which were traded within Brazil. The manioc and sugar autarquias produced alcohol as a gasoline additive, called motor-alcohol.

The fascist regimes promised land and higher social status to both peasants and landlords, but in practice extended often quite repressive state control over them. These regimes were much more conservative than the democracies in agrarian policies. They undertook no significant land reforms, and relied on the grudging support of old landed elites. They used their control over agriculture to subordinate it more fully to the government, in an effort to resolve the same basic problems faced by the democracies, which included assuring urban subsistence, keeping farmers afloat, and improving farm production. The fascist regimes' comprehensive control over agriculture and food distribution anticipated aspects of the postwar corporate agricultural system.

Agriculture and the capitalist colonies

In the early twentieth century the colonial empires of Europe, the U.S., and Japan included vast areas of Asia and Africa. Agriculture remained by far the main economic sector. Colonial regimes emphasized export production of 'cash crops,' such as tea, cocoa, coffee, peanuts, and cotton, and also staples like rice or corn. Colonial expenditure and investment, especially in railroads, stimulated the growth of towns and trade and expanded internal markets. In most colonies, European trading companies, such as Lever Brothers (now the multinational Unilever), monopolized export and processing of farm crops, which held back economic development in the colonies.

In settler colonies, European immigrants usually dominated cash crop production, appropriated the best lands, and reduced the native populations to laborers or small producers for local markets. Such practices often provoked conflicts over land and fueled the economic grievances of anti-colonial movements. In the colonies with few settlers, colonial authorities' emphasis on exports and taxation forced native peoples to divert so much land and time to cash crop production that they often could not maintain previous levels of food production. Yet some native farmers produced for markets so effectively that they managed to become a native elite who benefited from colonialism at the expense of most of the rest of the native populations.

Africa

European colonial expansion established settler colonies in parts of northern, eastern, and southern Africa, and non-settler colonies in central and western Africa. Kenya provides a case study of a settler colony in which European migration and land claims brought the marginalization of the indigenous peoples. British explorers made treaties with local leaders and then claimed their lands, most notably in a Crown Land Ordinance in 1902. The British government then invited Europeans to settle in Kenya. One British aristocrat, Lord Delamere, eventually acquired more than 100,000 acres and bred sheep, cattle, and rust-resistant wheat. Hundreds of settlers followed, employing subterfuges to acquire more land from Africans. By 1905 so many settlers demanded land that officials in London wanted to impose limits on them to avoid conflict. Settlers and officials in the colony wanted to claim the highlands for white Europeans, with access to African laborers. The settlers, led by Delamere, organized and soon achieved these objectives.

These Kenyan laws distinguished the white highlands, exclusively for whites, from the "reserves" where Africans were required to live. By 1929, at the peak of white cultivation, the 2,000 white landowners held 2.5 million hectares but cultivated only 300,000 hectares. The government and settlers allowed African "squatters" to live on white lands in the highlands as informal tenants. They paid rent with labor on the white farms while expanding cultivation on lands that the settlers lacked the capacity to cultivate. The government prohibited violence and coercion in recruiting and managing Africans, and required white farmers to provide basic food, housing, and medical care for squatters. The African reserves included much more land, but lower quality land, than the white highlands, in contrast to South Africa where white colonists held most of the lands.

White settlers in other colonies suppressed African resistance with harsher domination. In South Africa, in the nineteenth century, Afrikaners, of Dutch origin, defeated the African peoples and seized much of their land. Despite losing the Boer War with Britain in 1899–1900, Afrikaners passed laws that transferred most of the land to the minority white population. They confined the Africans into reserves, called *Bantustans*, which had limited and low-quality land. African men had to migrate to Afrikaner farms and other enterprises to earn the money necessary for taxes and their families' subsistence.

Algeria, an Ottoman territory, had good farming conditions and supplied food to France during the revolutionary wars. France conquered Algeria after a diplomatic conflict in 1830, and during 1830–80 suppressed rebellions while confiscating vast areas of land for French settlers, the *pieds-noirs*.

Their holdings grew from 765,000 hectares in 1870 to 2.3 million hectares in 1917, well over half the arable lands. The pieds-noir grew wheat and phylloxera-resistant grapevines. The Arabs and Berbers were reduced to sharecroppers or smallholders working on the pied-noirs' farms for subsistence.

The First World War had uneven effects on African agriculture. While British and German forces fought in part of eastern Africa, in Kenya the settlers rapidly increased crop production. Sisal and maize became the settlers' main cash crops and acquired even larger scale in the 1920s. The African farming sector suffered greatly during the First World War. Britain, France, and Germany recruited or forced nearly two million Africans to serve in the war, and requisitioned so much food and livestock that they depleted local surpluses, which along with drought caused famines in several regions.

After the war the colonies went through the same sudden drop in prices as the developed world. British policy statements after the war, such as the Devonshire Declaration at the Imperial Conference in 1923, committed the government to developing the colonies economically and preparing them for self rule. Yet Britain could not afford to spend significant amounts on colonial development. Colonial officials also implemented policies without fully anticipating local responses. In Kenya, during the 1930s and 1940s, officials encouraged African peasants to plant black wattle trees for dyes, promising large profits. When peasants realized that they could not expect that income for years, they cut down the trees and used them for other purposes.

Generally the policy emphasizing cash crops had ambivalent results. In some regions, Africans produced such large amounts of cash crops that they competed with settlers. In Kenya, white settlers persuaded the colonial government to issue laws to prevent Africans from growing coffee for this reason. In other cases cash crop cultivation shifted so much land away from subsistence cultivation that chronic malnutrition developed among Africans and escalated into famine when crops failed. The colonial authorities pressured Africans to grow subsistence crops, such as cassava, but their demands for taxes and labor, and incentives to produce cash crops, deterred food crop production. These demands also shifted more subsistence production to women, who were lower in status and usually remained at home while their husbands migrated to earn money for taxes. Even at home the men tended to grow the cash crops.

The Great Depression shifted the economic balance in British East Africa. The collapse of farm produce prices drove many settlers, already in debt, to abandon their farms, while others could not afford to pay African laborers as much as earlier. As settler agriculture declined, the British shifted their policies toward greater support for African agriculture. In 1935 the government issued laws to organize marketing of Africans' crops, encourage better farming methods and soil conservation. But they never gave up on the white settlers, issuing laws to restrict squatters' rights to land in the white highlands.

In South Africa, the government created one of the most expensive subsidy programs in the 1920s–1930s for the white farmers, including marketing boards, protective tariffs, and export bounties. South African farm prices rose well above world market prices, and the country's trading agencies accumulated so much wheat, sugar, and dairy products that the government imposed quotas to hold back production. Yet a 1937 law imposed greater restrictions on the African population. Meanwhile, investigations found a growing problem of soil erosion, caused by the crude farming methods of both white and black farmers, and indirectly by their low educational level and conservatism, problems that the government did not address until after the Second World War.

The French and British colonies in West Africa (and some colonies in East Africa) had few settlers. Native peasants grew cash crops quite successfully from 1900 to 1929. The French ran their colonies in West Africa through a centralized administration in Senegal, with a hierarchy of officials based on local village headmen. These agencies oversaw tax collection, which required the local population to grow at least some cash crops for sale. Africans soon understood the potential profits from cash crops, usually peanuts, palm kernels, bananas, or cacao, and rapidly adopted them. French colonies increased their exports from £11 million before the First World War to £200 million by 1951. Yet the French system was set up so that farmers earned relatively little of this income compared to the export companies as well as the government through taxation.

The British colonies employed a system of indirect rule through local chiefs. Yet here too cash crop sales dwarfed income from other exports. In 1951 the Gold Coast earned £27 million from gold, diamonds, manganese, and timber, but £60 million from cacao, even though many trees were infected with a plant disease. From the 1920s government marketing boards paid low prices to farmers while allowing the government to profit from world market prices, so only a small portion of this income reached farmers.

The European powers imposed on African colonies agricultural systems derived from their own farming systems. The emphasis on cash crops in Africa resembled the European farmers' pattern of producing for markets and purchasing food. The Kenyan white highland farmers' reliance on poor tenants and migratory labor resembled the reliance of Argentina's landlords on tenant farmers migrating from Spain and Italy. South Africa's racial–territorial segregation, and reliance of white farmers on labor from land-short African small farmers, resembled U.S. southern planters and sharecroppers.

Yet agrarian political relations differed greatly in the colonies from those in the home countries. While the colonial governments transmitted the Depression through tax systems, marketing boards, and trading companies, they rarely took measures to alleviate its economic and social consequences, and then for white settlers much more than Africans. The main attempt by colonial authorities to alleviate native farmers' conditions was Imperial

Preference, essentially the use of tariffs to favor trade within the British Empire. Political division prevented its implementation beyond a few minimal measures.

Colonial Asia

In Asia, agriculture was central to European colonial domination, but in extremely contrasting ways. The French dominated Vietnam based on an extremely harsh exploitation of peasants and agriculture, while in India the peasantry had much more autonomy and a large role in the independence movement.

Before the French conquest in the 1860s, Vietnam had a highly productive agriculture. While there were many peasant rebellions, some Vietnamese governments cared enough about peasants to force landlords to return illegally appropriated lands back to villagers. After conquering Indochina, the French colonial leaders eliminated most limits on land holding. French entrepreneurs took over almost half of village lands and left more than half the peasants landless by the end of French rule in the 1950s.

These expropriated peasants became tenants, sharecroppers, or laborers. Sharecroppers and tenants had to pay large rents and taxes, sometimes 50 percent of their crops or more, and even had to buy French wine every month. Many peasants ended up in debt to usurers who sometimes charged 100 percent interest per year or even per six months. Laborers in some cases endured much worse conditions. Many were forced to work on rubber plantations, where they had to cut in a very exacting way three hundred trees and gather the sap from them, and were beaten or tortured for the slightest infractions. One-fourth or more of these workers died on the plantations.

This harsh colonial regime produced substantial exports of rubber, rice, and other crops. Most Vietnamese obtained less food under the French than under their own rulers, and any crop failure would lead to starvation. The French violently suppressed peasant movements of protest, such as that of 1930–31.

Indian agriculture and the nationalist movement

After the great droughts and famines of the later nineteenth century, Indian farmers' conditions slowly improved. British colonial authorities managed relief efforts in the scarcities that did occur much better than earlier. They also made serious efforts to address agrarian problems. By 1900 they expanded irrigation until some 43,000 miles of irrigation canals provided water to almost 20 percent of crop land. Farm production in India in the first half of the twentieth century was inconsistent. While statistics are uncertain, cash crops rapidly increased, wheat production increased, but rice production fell behind the growth of population in northeastern India. The notorious crops of the nineteenth century, indigo and opium, declined after 1900. Opium was now grown legally only for medical use on a few small government farms.

Only a minority of peasants participated in the growing commercialization of Indian agriculture. A Royal Commission on Agriculture gathered testimony on agriculture and rural life all over the subcontinent in 1926–28, and found vast and serious social and economic problems. The colonial government established an Imperial Council of Agricultural Research, which employed many Indian scientists and laid the basis for future progress.

The problems and prospects of agriculture were crucial issues for the Indian independence movement. Many in the movement, such as Jawaharlal Nehru, supported modernization and industrial development. Mahatma Gandhi rejected these and advocated reliance on manual labor and the traditional peasant village to keep people employed and give their lives meaning. He proposed replacement of the zamindars with a system in which the village leaders would allot land to villagers in exchange for a rental payment in kind. Gandhi recommended land consolidation, cooperative farming, and other agronomic measures.

Gandhi's views, not widely shared in the independence movement, reflected Indian peasants' ideals. In the actual freedom struggle, the Indian National Congress early on recognized that they had to rely mostly on peasant support as by far the largest social group in the country, yet they also needed to win over many landlords both to finance the movement and to weaken support for the British, who favored landlords. Congress thus tended to be ambivalent in dealing with peasants.

Gandhi's earliest and most dramatic actions to realize his goals for peasant India were his *satyagraha* campaigns – non-violent protests – to benefit peasants. The first took place in Champaran in northern India, where landlords, mostly British, demanded high rents from poor peasants, beat and brutalized them, and committed many other abuses. In 1918 Gandhi organized a campaign with local lawyers and others to accumulate evidence of landlord abuses, poverty, and backwardness from peasant testimonies. The information acquired was so inflammatory that the local police arrested him, but a massive peaceful protest intimidated the local judge into releasing him. The testimonies persuaded the government to form a commission that validated the evidence against the landlords. In 1919 the government forced the landlords to make restitution to their tenants.

Gandhi and his associates organized several satyagraha protests in the following decades. Peasants called Gandhi *mahatma*, "great soul," because his satyagraha campaigns reflected, in their view, his concern for peasants. Gandhi and Congress saw these actions as small parts of a larger effort to discredit and weaken British colonial authority and gain *swaraj*, or self-rule. Therefore Congress often restrained peasants in their protests, sometimes told them to pay their taxes and rents, and tried to persuade them to join with landlords against the British government.

By the 1930s this difference in views divided the independence movement. Peasants began to form *Kisan Sabhas*, peasant associations, while a left-Congress faction advocated class struggle and revolution. In 1934 these two groups worked together to demand abolition of zamindar status and transfer of their lands to their numerous tenants. In the elections of 1937, for legislative councils recently established by the British, Congress won decisively, so the Left Congress-Kisan Sabha group radicalized their demands, and in a few places peasants began murdering zamindars, burning down their houses, and invading their lands. Landlords held meetings demanding that Congress support them against these threats. The Congress party tried to get the radicals to compromise, but they refused and held mass protests demanding zamindari abolition and denouncing non-violence; Congress resorted to British-style coercion to suppress them. Still these radical movements survived to play an important role in later Indian agrarian politics.

Agrarian revolutions

In certain important regions, the agrarian crises of the first half of the twentieth century exploded into agrarian revolutions. Revolutionary governments dramatically changed farming systems, often with considerable violence and disruption. These transformations set precedents that revolutionary leaders in the later twentieth century tried to emulate, and that non-revolutionary leaders tried to avert. The two revolutions examined below differed in significant ways, but both greatly increased government intervention in agriculture and rural life. Their actions went far beyond the capitalist support measures of this period and similar to the controls of the fascist regimes during the Depression.

Mexico

The first major agrarian revolution of the twentieth century began in Mexico during the revolution of 1910–20. The Mexican peasants or *campesinos*, the majority of the population, played a central role in this revolution. In the following it is necessary to distinguish between the *pueblo*, a general term for a peasant village, and *ejido*, which could mean either the common lands of the pueblo, or the pre-Columbian village, as a community that held at least part of its lands in common.

Mexico in 1910 had an extremely inequitable and exploitative agrarian system. A few hundred landlords, including several U.S. investors and corporations, owned half of the land. Peasant communities held only six percent of Mexico's land, and most peasant families owned no land at all.

Under President Porfirio Díaz (1876–1910), big landlords took land illegally from five million *campesino* households. Many peasants lived under conditions of near-slavery, poverty, and starvation. Landlords, including some wealthy U.S. investors, often literally purchased thousands of peons to work on their estates. They paid these peons very little or only in scrip for the store on the estate. Campesinos from the 1890s protested and filed lawsuits to regain these lands. Small-scale wars between peasants and landlords' "white guards" – and often the Mexican Army – convulsed the Mexican countryside. Officials, economists, and others warned that the peasants' oppression and poverty risked rebellion, but Díaz's government took no actions.

When a political revolution finally ousted Díaz in 1910–11, governmental control over Mexico began to disintegrate. As liberal reformers took over town governments, in villages peasants formed militias, invaded estates and seized their lands, destroyed debt records, and intimidated landlords into surrendering weapons and supplies. The main peasant leaders were Emiliano Zapata and Francisco "Pancho" Villa. Zapata (1879–1919) was a petty landholder and village mayor in the small south Mexican state of Morelos, where most peasants, descendents of the Aztecs, had lost their lands and worked as semi-slaves on sugar plantations. Villa (1878–1923) was a poor peasant from a hacienda in the northern state of Durango who became a soldier and a bandit.

The campesinos' resentment of the hacenderos' land seizures and their efforts to regain their former lands were the main popular forces behind the Mexican Revolution. Zapata and Villa formed armies in the south and the north respectively that seized plantations and haciendas and divided their lands among poor and landless peasants. When the liberal revolutionaries who overthrew Díaz refused to cooperate with Zapata's military forces, Zapata announced in November 1911 the Plan of Ayala. This document rejected the authority of the liberals for compromising with the hacenderos. It declared the goal of the revolution to be the restoration to the pueblos of the lands taken by the landlords, with additional lands to be nationalized and distributed among the needy or for other state purposes. Zapata's slogan was "tierra y libertad" – land and liberty. The Plan of Ayala was the most radical agrarian document of the revolution.

The fierce conflict between contenders for the Mexican presidency early in the revolution allowed Villa's and Zapata's armies to take over Mexico City in 1914–15. President Venustiano Carranza, who fled to Veracruz, opposed land reform, but his leading general Álvaro Obregón persuaded him to agree to a land reform proposal, in order to win support away from the peasant leaders. In January 1915 he issued a law that established procedures to restore to peasants their community lands, or *ejidos*, that had been taken from them illegally. It also granted land to communities that had lost lands legally or needed more. This law was incorporated into the 1917 Mexican constitution as Article 27, and became the basis for all subsequent Mexican land reforms.

This law aimed to satisfy peasant demands for lands only partially. They would still need to work on the haciendas but they would have their own lands for the seasons when the haciendas did not need them. Carranza also intended this law to delay the process with bureaucratic procedures, so during 1917–20 only 80,000 peasants obtained authorization for 400,000 hectares, and only about half of them actually received lands by 1920 when Carranza was ousted.

Meanwhile, peasants in many regions of Mexico, especially in the south which Zapata dominated, seized and distributed much hacienda and plantation land. Carranza's forces managed to trick Zapata into an ambush and kill him in 1919. The army also weakened Villa and in 1923 he too was assassinated. The Federal armies defeated Zapata's and Villa's armies, which had few weapons and insufficient supplies, and forced peasants to surrender the lands they had seized during the revolution.

Nonetheless, millions of peasants supported Zapata, Villa, and other peasant leaders, so the government could not afford to back down on its promises of land reforms. The revolution had also sharply decreased food production in Mexico; people were starving to death, and dying of typhus and other famine-related epidemics. Carranza's successor Obregón had been a farmer and attempted to conciliate peasants. He included Zapatista supporters in his government and accelerated land reforms, distributing 1.6 million hectares, and his successors from 1924 to 1934 continued the process.

The land reforms of 1920–34 explicitly aimed to return land to peasants and support collective land ownership. Laws in this period limited haciendas to 400 hectares, leaving the rest subject to confiscation and redistribution. The Law of Ejidos in 1920 specified that ejido lands should be divided into individual plots large enough to provide peasants with an income from production equal to twice the minimum wage of urban workers. This idea resembled the concept parity promoted by reformers in the United States. Later laws established the goal of forming a rural middle class, and gave ejido members, ejidatarios, deeds to their plots. These and other laws were compiled in the Agrarian Codex of 1934 that again emphasized restitution of lands to peasants. From 1917 to 1934 the government distributed some 11 million hectares among 6,000 ejidos.

This process involved considerable conflict. Many landowners fled, were killed, or lost their estates to military officers in the revolution. Yet most landowners survived, kept their lands, and remained a powerful group. They resisted land reforms, relying on white guards and other armed retainers to intimidate and even kill peasants and *agraristas* – the intellectuals, teachers, labor organizers, and activists who tried to help peasants. Henequen planters in 1924 murdered the Yucatan state governor who supported land redistribution. In Veracruz, peasants seized estates for land distribution and landowners retaliated by burning peasants' villages and crops. Landowners supported anti-government movements such as the Cristeros, rebels (including many peasants) against the government's anti-clerical policies from 1926 to the early 1930s. The government tended to support landlords or take a middle course in the many land disputes of the period. The government in the 1920s encouraged campesinos to form cooperatives to overcome their small-scale and backward methods, but provided too little support to make them successful.

Despite these reforms, by 1934 haciendas still dominated the Mexican countryside, kept many peasants in subservient status, and peasant protests continued. In this context, General Lázaro Cárdenas came to power in 1934–40 and intensified the land reform process, partly in response to a surge of landowner–peasant conflicts. Cárdenas, who grew up poor in a big city, was a remarkable progressive leader who reduced his own salary in the Great Depression and never needed bodyguards. He introduced reforms for peasants as part of broader nationalist reforms, including nationalization of U.S.-owned oil companies in Mexico and abolition of capital punishment. During his term he expropriated from haciendas and distributed some 20 million hectares to 11,000 peasant ejidos. By the end of his term, ejidos occupied half of Mexico's cultivated land and were a core part of the economy.

Cárdenas began his radical land reforms in mid-1936, in response to a year of violent strikes of rural workers against landowners in the Laguna region of the western states of Coahuila and Durango. Cárdenas went to the region and ordered confiscation of 448,000 hectares from hundreds of haciendas to be divided among peasant communities. During the next two years he extended the reform to many other districts where peasants had lost vast land areas and had been fighting with landlords for decades, including Yucatan and Morelos in the south, the Yaqui valley in the north, and elsewhere. In some cases landlords resisted Cárdenas' reforms, bullying peasants and refusing to surrender lands. Cárdenas established armed rural militias as part of the Federal army to resist landlords' aggression. For a few years conflicts killed thousands of peasants and landlords' bullies, but by 1940 peasant militias had 60,000 men and could defend their ejidos.

The government distributed lands to peasants as small farm plots, ejidos, or collective farms. The ejidos distributed lands allotments to peasant families, who could use the lands indefinitely but could not legally sell or rent the lands. In practice, ejidatarios often ignored these regulations, and the ejidos became highly stratified, with smallholders working for larger ejido landholders. As reformers had envisaged earlier, ejidatarios also worked on haciendas, most of which remained and retained often vast land holdings.

The government formed many collective farms from large estates that were consolidated farming units not amenable to division into ejido plots. These also reflected Cárdenas' almost utopian commitment to collective ejidos, in which peasants farmed collectively and distributed income according to work. At the strike in Laguna in 1936, Cárdenas distributed most of the confiscated lands into 300 collective farms. Foreign owners tried to frustrate this by destroying irrigation canals until the armed militia began guarding them. The government divided the henequen haciendas in Yucatan between hacienda owners and ejidos that farmed their henequen lands collectively. By 1940 about one-eighth of the ejidos in Mexico were collectives.

Cárdenas' intensive land reform provided nearly a million peasant families with lands at least at the subsistence level. The government backed up the reform with the Ejido Bank, a vast economic agency that issued loans, provided storage and marketing of crops, organized cooperatives for farmers, allotted agronomic aid to fight crop diseases and distribute better seed, and undertook basic planning for the ejido sector. This aid, a type of agricultural subsidy, played a crucial role in the success of these reforms. Ejidos operated democratically, with a general assembly that would meet once a month, an ejido commissariat, and a "vigilance committee." Local government remained under control of *caciques* or local strongmen, who managed the other social welfare aid that the government provided to the rural sector.

Cárdenas' reforms stopped most of the land conflicts that had plagued Mexico for decades, and in the process transformed Mexican society. They transferred half of Mexican croplands from planters and hacendores to peasants, driving many large landlords off the lands. The remaining landlords soon came under pressure from Cárdenas' successors to modernize their farming. The government supported them with irrigation construction and many advances in farming technology, eventually including the new high-yielding seeds of the Green Revolution. Cárdenas used his reforms to secure peasants' political support, through the National Peasant Confederation, a corporatist body similar to those he established for other groups.

The ejidos included a large minority of the peasants, but still had less than half of the total land, including ranch and other non-arable land as well as cropland. There were still 10,000 holdings larger than 1,000 hectares, which were 0.3 percent of all land holdings but held 60 percent of Mexican land. Three hundred owners each had more than 40,000 hectares, in total more than 32 million hectares, one-sixth of the land area. Two-thirds of these large holdings were in the arid north, while ejidos were the most numerous farms in central and southern Mexico. Still, while landholding remained highly concentrated, the land reforms and other measures brought great change. In 1910 almost all of the peasants were landless, by 1940 only one-third remained landless.

The Mexican agrarian revolution brought a large-scale land reform imposed by the government against resistance by domestic and foreign landowners. The revolution achieved its main goal of placating Mexican society, but it did not overcome Mexico's agricultural backwardness, and in 1940 Mexico remained a significant food importer. Still, Mexico was the first Latin American country to undertake significant land reform. The Mexican reforms remained the most far-reaching and successful until Cuba's revolution in the 1960s. Even though the ejido was an agrarian pattern specific to Mexican history, many advocates of land reform elsewhere have advocated the application of such a system for their own countries. Mexico's reform set a pattern of resolving rural discontent with periodical land confiscations and distributions for the next four decades, until new economic ideas and circumstances forced the Mexican government to change policies.

Eastern Europe and the Soviet agrarian revolution

Eastern European countries in the interwar years remained peasant societies dominated by large landlord classes. The character of their domination can be seen in the brief rule of the peasant Alexander Stambolisky, who rose up through education and political skill to be appointed Prime Minister of Bulgaria in 1919. He took the grain trade out of the hands of big business, and introduced land reforms against the interest of large landlords. A military coup overthrew and assassinated him in 1923. In Eastern Europe it appeared that only a revolution could break the power of the landlords.

That revolution took place in the Russian Empire, which despite rapid industrialization was still an agrarian society in which peasants comprised more than 80 percent of the population. While Russia was one of the top two world grain exporters by 1900, many observers considered the country to be in an agrarian crisis. They thought this because of the primitive farming methods of the country's peasants, low harvest yields, and chronic crop failures and famines. The crop failure and famine of 1890–91 killed perhaps half a million people. This "crisis" may have been overdrawn, but peasant discontent over local issues stimulated many protests. Peasants in the Russian Empire had the secure land holdings that Mexican peasants wanted. Villages in most cases held property rights over the land, however, and distributed allotments in medieval-style strips. Many peasants thought that the only solution to their farming problems would be to obtain more land by taking over landlords' estates.

The largest peasant protests before 1917 followed the political revolution of 1905, which forced the regime to form an elected parliament. Inspired by workers' protests, peasants attacked landlords and seized estates. The government responded to these rebellions with violent repression, but also with a large-scale land reform. The Stolypin reform, named after the Russian Prime Minister who introduced it, began the process of consolidating peasant lands that began in Europe in the nineteenth century. The reform also enabled about one-tenth of the peasant population to separate from the peasant village communes as independent farmers by 1914, and many others to leave for work in mines and factories.

During the First World War, requisitions for the military reduced food supplies for the capital Petrograd, which was swamped by war refugees.

Food shortages led provincial governors to restrict food movements, which disrupted supply and worsened shortages. Local governments and voluntary organizations could do little to alleviate the food supply difficulties. Food prices increased faster than town wages, and townspeople grew discontented with government and peasants. While some peasants made money, the collapse in industrial production decreased agricultural equipment and consumer goods in town markets. Many peasants lost interest in selling to the towns or working on landlords' estates, which produced most of the food for the towns.

The food crisis, worsened by the Tsarist government's incompetence, exploded in protest marches, strikes, and a mutiny in the garrison surrounding Petrograd in February 1917. This February Revolution overthrew the Tsarist regime and established a democratic provisional government, but it postponed action on agrarian issues. Vladimir Lenin and the Bolsheviks took advantage of this delay to seize power in a coup in October 1917. Lenin then withdrew Russia from the war, and issued the Decree on Land. This decree, based on peasant petitions to the provisional government, authorized peasants to take over landlord estates.

What followed was a violent three-year civil war between four groups. The Reds, Bolsheviks, fought to retain power and establish socialism. The Whites, former Tsarist officers, fought against the Bolsheviks without a clear commitment to another system. The Greens, peasant rebels, fought for peasant autonomy. The nationalists fought for the independence of the various regions from the Russian empire. All of these groups relied mostly on peasants for soldiers, which had several consequences.

Peasants would often desert, so the side that employed the most coercion to retain troops (the Reds) had the military advantage. Peasants would also support the side that promised them the most favorable outcome. The Whites, while they held Ukraine and Siberia, restored landlords to estates that peasants had confiscated from them. The Reds supported peasants' land seizures and arrested and executed landlords. The peasants thus on balance tended to support the Reds. Because of the collapse of market trade, all sides requisitioned food from the peasants. The Reds called this policy "food distribution," and rationalized it as necessary to support the revolution and the peasants' control over the land. The Whites and nationalists requisitioned without showing much concern for the peasants, which again led many peasants to support the Reds.

After defeating the Whites by 1920, however, the Bolsheviks continued the requisitioning system in order to create "communism," by which they meant systems of exchange without markets or money. Both peasants and townspeople opposed this. Peasants in several regions formed what were called Green armies and rebelled against the Bolsheviks. Like the Tsarist regime, the Bolsheviks responded with violent repression, carried out by the mostly peasant Red Army, and with concessions. In March 1921 Lenin announced the so-called New Economic Policy or NEP that officially ended requisitions and allowed free trade. During 1920–21, however, two serious droughts devastated most of the grain-growing regions and created a serious famine. The civil war had weakened agriculture and killed many peasants. Lenin requisitioned food from less affected regions to provide relief, and obtained food aid from the U.S. Nonetheless, the famine still claimed millions of lives.

During NEP the Soviet government soon faced two more crop failures and famines in 1924–25 and in 1928–29. In these cases the USSR also obtained food relief from abroad, and fortunately loss of life was much less. During the 1920s, even before Lenin died in 1924, a power struggle ensued in the USSR between his top officials – Joseph Stalin, Lev Trotsky, and Nikolai Bukharin. A central issue in this conflict was policy toward agriculture.

All the contenders agreed that sooner or later Soviet agriculture had to undergo collectivization. A collective farm, or *kolkhoz*, consolidated the individual peasant farms in a village into larger plots that would facilitate mechanization. Soviet leaders saw it as emulation of large-scale U.S. farming. The regime also established state farms, or *sovkhozy*. These were large-scale specialized farms, often based on old landlord estates, but again emulating U.S. industrialized farming. All contenders also thought that a small group of "rich" peasants or *kulaks* dominated the villages and opposed Soviet policies.

The contenders for leadership debated whether Soviet agriculture should develop gradually toward a more modern system while retaining its traditional village structure, the view of Bukharin and the "Right," or should be actively transformed by the government into a large-scale industrial farming system, the view of Trotsky and the "Left." They also debated whether to tolerate the kulaks, the view of the Right, or expel them from the villages as class enemies of the Soviet regime, the Left view.

Stalin initially sided with the Right. The three famines of the 1920s, and the decision to begin a five-year plan of forced industrialization, finally persuaded him to remodel Soviet agriculture, on the assumption that Soviet agricultural backwardness was at the root of these repeated famines the country faced.

Stalin and his associates imposed collectivization coercively starting in December 1929, accompanied by a policy of "dekulakization" to exile the kulaks out of the villages. By March 1930 a highly militarized campaign had forced nearly half of the peasants to reform their villages into kolkhozy, and hundreds of thousands of peasants had been exiled from their villages as kulaks. The process inspired thousands of local peasant rebellions that persuaded the regime to call off the campaign. Many peasants left kolkhozy, and several thousand "incorrectly dekulakized" peasants returned to their villages. The country managed to have a fair grain harvest, much of which the government exported to earn money to buy machinery for industrialization. In 1930–31 the government again initiated collectivization and dekulakization. By fall 1931 about 60 percent of peasants were in kolkhozy, and two million "dekulakized" peasants worked as forced laborers at factory sites, logging enterprises, and in labor camps of the Gulag.

During 1929–33, forced rapid industrialization and mass migrations, both involuntary (like dekulakization) and voluntary, disrupted the Soviet economy. The government expanded food rationing to encompass more than 40 million people by 1932, and established an internal passport system in 1933 to restrict movement into cities. In the midst of this strained situation, drought in 1931 and exceptionally wet weather in 1932 caused low harvests. These combined with large grain exports in 1930–31 to create another serious famine. This time the Soviet government, fearing attacks from Nazi Germany and imperial Japan, concealed the famine and imported very little food. It did, however, organize a large internal relief effort that enabled the peasants to produce a large harvest in 1933 and ended the famine. During the 1930s harvests varied, with droughts in 1934, 1936, and 1938, and the regime provided food and seed relief to villages almost every year. In 1937 the USSR had the largest harvest in its history.

While both Soviet and Mexican revolutions involved collective production, the Mexican revolution transferred lands to formerly landless peasants, while Soviet collectivization represented a kind of expropriation of peasants. The kolkhoz consolidated village lands under the control of the kolkhoz; ultimately the Soviet government, and the individual peasants, lost most of the individual authority they had over their own plots. Soviet kolkhozy gave peasants "private plots" that peasant families farmed on their own, and these were highly productive.

Both Mexican ejidos and Soviet kolkhozy and sovkhozy received and depended on government aid, and leaders in both countries saw their respective farms as means to help modernize their farming and assure a reliable harvest, while also maintaining the peasants at a basic level of subsistence. Mexico did not have the agricultural disaster and famines that the USSR had, although farm production plummeted during the 1910–20 revolution, causing many starvation deaths before farming recovered. Both systems enabled their countries to achieve food self-sufficiency after the war but then both became dependent on imports from the U.S. Both systems thus ambivalently helped protect farmers from environmental hazards, but both also kept farmers economically, socially, and politically subordinate.

Conclusion

In the first half of the twentieth century, world agriculture went from the prosperity of the prewar years to a series of crises: from war, overproduction, famine, and economic depression. Governments responded to these agrarian crises more rapidly and with more programs, reforms, spending, and responsiveness than in any previous period in human history. Democracies in the U.S., Europe, Australia, and Latin America established government programs of price supports and regulation of farm production and marketing. Democracy and scientific development in these countries had enabled farmers to overcome much of the former dual subordination that still prevailed in other countries.

Other regimes addressed their agrarian crises in more aggressive ways. The fascist states harnessed farmers to larger government goals that ultimately included war, but in the process set certain precedents for management of agriculture as part of a total food system. The Mexican revolution renewed peasant villages as ejidos with forced land transfers back to villages from the landed estates that had taken their lands in the past. The Soviet revolution transformed villages into kolkhozy, a type of land reform in reverse. In both of these cases, the revolutionary governments took on the responsibility of supplying the new farms with supplies, technology, and guidance, in the Soviet case also planning production directives. Yet in all of these cases, farmers remained socially and politically subordinated. The aid they received seemed tainted by the fact that it was in part oriented to encourage them to produce more for government objectives, even if those objectives included improving rural conditions.

In the vast areas of Africa and Asia under colonial rule, the presence or lack of white settlers shaped colonial policies. In settler colonies such as South Africa, Kenya, Algeria, and French Southeast Asia, Depression-era policies favored the European farmers, providing most of the benefits that European farmers received. Native farmers and laborers received little or no aid, but had to take low-paying menial jobs and often to live as semi-legal squatters in order to pay unremitting taxation and fulfill other state obligations. In non-settler colonies, ranging from the Gold Coast to India, native farmers had more freedom and opportunities, but often had to contend with abuses from their own bullying landlords and rapacious moneylenders. They often had to market their produce through government marketing boards or foreign trading companies, whose prices benefited those agencies more than the farmers.

In all of these cases, governments to some degree or other supported farmers with technical and material aid, but in return farmers had to conform to some degree or other to government procedures and priorities. This aid functioned in part as a safety net that protected farmers, and indirectly society, from the deleterious effects of the environment. This aid also, however, imposed constraints on farmers, sometimes quite serious ones. To varying degrees, this unprecedented government responsiveness also created an unprecedented subordination of farmers to government bureaucracies. Yet the farmers were being placed in this position to insure reliable production and food supplies to benefit masses of people. These trends continued during and after the Second World War, with the addition of another category of actors: large-scale corporations.

Further reading

Avner Offer, *The First World War: An Agrarian Interpretation* (Oxford: Clarendon Press, 1989) is a basic study. Ellis Goldberg, "Peasants in Revolt – Egypt 1919," *Journal of Middle Eastern Studies* 24 (1992), summarizes the rebellion. Gerald Friesen, *The Canadian Prairies: A History* (Lincoln, NE: University of Nebraska Press, 1984), is a comprehensive study. Deborah Fitzgerald, *Every Farm a Factory* (New Haven, CT: Yale University Press, 2003), documents the early industrialization of U.S. farming. Frank Clarke, *The History of Australia* (Westport, CT: Greenwood Press, 2002), has much on farming. Annie Moulin, *Peasantry and Society in France since 1789* (Cambridge: Cambridge University Press, 1991) and Robert Paxton, *French Peasant Fascism* (New York: Oxford University Press, 1998) are central works. G. E. Mingay, *Land and Society in England, 1750–1980* (London: Longman Group, 1994), is comprehensive. Martin Clark, *Modern Italy, 1871–1995* (London: Longman Group, 1996), has much on farming and farmers. Richard Grunberge, *The Twelve-Year Reich* (New York: Holt, Rinehart, and Winston, 1971), has a good discussion of Nazi agrarian policies.

Dana Markiewicz, *The Mexican Revolution and the Limits of Agrarian Reform, 1916–1946* (London: Lynne Rienner Publishers, 1993), presents a stimulating interpretation. On Argentina, see Carl Solberg, "Rural Unrest and Agrarian Policy in Argentina, 1912–30," *Journal of Interamerican Studies and World Affairs* 13:1 (1971), and Simon G. Hanson, "Argentine Experience with Farm Relief Measures," *Journal of Farm Economics* 18:3 (1936). On Brazil, see Fiona Gordon-Ashworth, "Agricultural Commodity Control under Vargas in Brazil, 1930–45," *Journal of Latin American Studies* 12:1 (1980), and Mauricio Font, "Coffee Planters, Politics, and Development in Brazil," *Latin American Research Review* 22:3 (1987), and an exchange about this article, *Ibid.* 24:3 (1989). On Russia and the USSR, see Mark B. Tauger, *Natural Disaster and Human Action in the Soviet Famine of 1931– 1933* (Pittsburgh: University of Pittsburgh, CREES, Carl Beck Papers, 2001). On the international grain trade, see Dan Morgan, *Merchants of Grain* (New York: Penguin, 1980).

On the colonies, see C. H. Lee, "The Effects of the Depression on Primary Producing Countries," *Journal of Contemporary History* 4(4) (1969). On Africa see Bill Rau, *From Feast to Famine* (London: Zed Books, 1991); W. E. F. Ward and L. W. White, *East Africa: A Century of Change, 1870–1970* (New York: Africana Publishing Corporation, 1972); E. A. Brett, *Colonialism and Underdevelopment in East Africa* (New York: NOK Publishers, 1973); and Robert Maxon, "Where did the Trees Go? The Wattle Bark Industry in Western Kenya, 1932–50," *The International Journal of African Historical Studies* 34(3) (2001). On South Africa, see Monica Thompson, Leonard Thompson, eds, *The Oxford History of South Africa* (New York: Oxford University Press, 1971). On Algeria, see V. B. Lutsky, *The Modern*

History of the Arab Countries (Moscow: Progress Publishers, 1969), and Kjell H. Halversen, "The Colonial Transformation of Agrarian Society in Algeria," *Journal of Peace Research* 15(4) (1978). On India see Shriman Narayan, *The Gandhian Plan of Economic Development for India* (Bombay: Padma Publications, 1944), and D. A. Low, *Congress and the Raj* (New Delhi: Oxford University Press, 2004).

Chapter 7

Boom and crisis

Agriculture from the Second World War to the twenty-first century

Between 1940 and 2000, world agriculture underwent two periods of transition to create the modern world agro-food system. During the Second World War and the following decades, the United States came to dominate world agriculture and shape the world food system. From the 1970s, many countries became major farm producers, competing successfully with the U.S., and destabilizing world markets. Transnational corporations used their wealth, market power, and technological expertise to control food consumption. This in turn made it difficult for farmers to escape the production requirements these firms impose on farm production, and the role of farmers in the global food system.

In the context of this transformation of world food regimes, five processes have shaped agrarian life. These included the rise and decline of communist agrarian systems, the Green Revolution and the increased food production it brought in many developing countries, the industrialization of farming and decline of farmers in the developed world, the emergence of Africa as a region of agrarian crisis, and the unanticipated repercussions of agrarian technological advancement. By the early twenty-first century, world agriculture produced vast amounts of food, but its dependence on fossil fuels, and environmental changes like global warming, threaten to undermine world food security.

These developments in contemporary farming have changed the old dual subordination. Governments, international organizations, and businesses all over the world have worked to support farmers, conduct research and shape policies in farmers' interests, and produce products that make farming more efficient. At no time in human history have there been such concerted efforts to weaken the dual subordination, to help farmers overcome environmental difficulties, and empower farmers politically. Yet many of these efforts have ironically relegated farmers to new and different forms of subordination. Consequently, in no previous period have so many farmers left farming, so that for the first time in history farmers are no longer the majority of the world's people.

The Second World War and the formation of the modern agrarian system

Before and during the Second World War, the U.S. and Europe established institutions that enabled them to meet the demands of the second "great war" more effectively than they met those of the first. In Britain the Agriculture Act of 1937 increased subsidies to encourage more grain production. During the war, the government induced farmers to shift 5.5 million acres of pasture to grain, nearly doubling grain production. It confiscated 1,500 farms from farmers who resisted these policies, but most cooperated. Their increased use of tractors set a pattern that intensified after the war. The mobilization of more than 20 million men depleted farm labor, but several countries organized women from cities to work in farms, and put POWs to work in farms.

In the United States, during the war, farm prices more than doubled, and total farm income more than tripled. The farm bloc also passed the Steagall Amendment in 1941, which substantially increased and expanded farm price supports. As with U.S. farm subsidies before and afterwards, these benefits went disproportionately to larger and better-off farmers, while government programs to benefit poor and minority farmers faded. The war showed U.S. farmers' enormous productive potential: they kept U.S. consumption at a relatively high level for wartime while providing food and other agricultural exports as part of the Lend-Lease program that provided aid to 38 countries.

Farmers and agriculture in the other exporting countries – Australia, New Zealand, and Canada – generally did well during the war, benefiting from increased demand and high prices. These countries also developed Lend-Lease programs, rationing food to their own populations to provide food supplies for Britain and other recipients. Latin American farms initially faced a collapse of demand from submarine warfare and a U.S. blockade. With U.S. support, they recovered by increasing their trade among themselves and with the U.S., by shifting production to meet wartime needs.

In the USSR, Africa, and Asia, agriculture went through more difficult circumstances. The Soviet regime mobilized more than 34 million people, mostly peasant men, out of a total population of about 170 million, and millions more from villages worked in war industries. Industry shifted almost entirely to military goods. The remaining farm workers – children, women, and old and disabled people – worked with deteriorating equipment and few horses. The regime imposed nearly confiscatory procurement quotas on the produce of the collective and state farms. Peasants survived the war on what they raised on their private plots and livestock. The regime temporarily ignored the peasants' expansion of their private plots, and some produced a small surplus to sell in towns. The limitations of this extremely deprived and strained agricultural system explain why the USSR needed millions of tons of U.S. Lend-Lease food aid.

African farmers had to contend with colonial demands as well as internal problems. France and Britain recruited more than 300,000 Africans as soldiers and many more for labor and transport, which removed many workers from farming. After Japan seized Southeast Asia, Europe turned to the Belgian Congo for desperately needed rubber. The colonial government increased farmers' obligations to work in rubber plantations, which provoked rebellions. Colonial powers increased demands for cash and food crops from peasant farmers, which reduced their subsistence production for their own needs. In these circumstances even partial crop failures could cause famines and loss of life, as in Tanganyika in 1943–44. In Kenya the colonial government had to set up a Food Shortage Commission in 1943 to secure town supplies and deal with famine from droughts. The colonial powers did persuade farmers to grow drought-resistant crops.

Nazi Germany's food production could meet only 85 percent of its agricultural needs. Peasants evaded government rationing systems, sold produce on black markets, and withheld produce in defiance of Nazi regulations. The Nazis compensated with mobilization tactics like other European countries, and also applied a "destruction policy" in occupied Eastern Europe and the USSR, to extract by force all the food supplies they needed, even if it would result in mass starvation of the local population. In practice, however, Nazi occupation authorities resisted this policy because it undermined the willingness of local farmers to produce anything at all. The immense strain and destruction that the war brought to the agrarian system by the end of the war reduced German food consumption below subsistence.

Agriculture, 1945–70s: separate paths, Cold War, development

During the three decades after the Second World War, world agriculture like the rest of the world economy fragmented into the capitalist agriculture of the first world, the second world of communist agriculture, and the third world that emerged from decolonizing states. The capitalist first world served as a model for the others, and established crucial links to the third through economic development, especially through the exchanges and policies of the Green Revolution. By the 1970s, several third world countries became substantial agricultural powers, while the backwardness of others caused substantial problems.

Agriculture in the capitalist world

The capitalist countries continued the government subsidy and protection policies from the Depression, supporting increasingly modernized, mechanized, and scientific farming systems. As a direct result, the farm sectors in these states drastically decreased in employment, and became integrated into an increasingly globalized world food system.

The war devastated agriculture in Europe and the USSR. A drought in 1946 sharply reduced harvests that in any case would have been low, in the USSR causing a widespread famine. In Europe the agro-food crises led many people to support communist parties in elections. In response, U.S. Secretary of State George Marshall proposed in June 1947 that the U.S. undertake a large program of aid, first of all food, to help Europe recover. This European Recovery Program, or "Marshall Plan," set the tone of U.S. economic and agricultural dominance in the world for the next 25 years.

Even before the Marshall Plan, the United States shaped the postwar economy through international meetings. The world economic conference of 44 powers at Bretton Woods, New Hampshire, in 1944, established the key postwar international financial institutions (IFIs): the International Bank for Reconstruction and Development, or World Bank, and the International Monetary Fund, or IMF. These provide countries with, respectively, long-term loans to support major projects, and short-term loans to deal with financial difficulties. Eighteen leading powers also signed in 1948 the General Agreement on Tariffs and Trade, which supported free trade except for agricultural commodities, on the insistence of the U.S. Almost all countries in the world eventually signed GATT.

The postwar powers also organized the United Nations (UN). A British nutritionist, Sir John Boyd Orr, worked with agriculture secretaries to establish the Food and Agricultural Organization of the UN in October 1945. Boyd Orr, elected the first director general of the FAO, tried to establish a world food board to distribute surpluses to famine regions. Britain, the United States, and other countries rejected this and similar proposals because they would have brought these countries' farmers under the control of a non-elected outside agency, and would never have gained any political support.

The U.S. farming system became the main supplier of food to postwar Europe and regions leaving colonialism. The government used U.S. dominance in world agriculture in the Cold War, to attract third world countries away from the USSR, and also to avoid policies to reduce U.S. overproduction. The government followed the Marshall Plan with a larger program, the 1954 Agricultural Trade Development and Assistance Act (issued as Public Law 480, and renamed in the 1960s the "Food for Peace" program), which has provided more than 100 million tons of food aid to 135 countries at low prices. The U.S. has other aid programs as well. Yet these programs, ironically, have harmed farmers in the aided countries.

New technologies allowed farmers to increase yields and productivity even more than these policies could accommodate. Even with acreage controls, price supports, and export subsidies from the Food for Peace program, millions of U.S. farmers could not cover costs and lost or abandoned their farms in the decades after the war. The number of farmers declined from seven million in 1940 to two million by 2000. In the U.S. South tenant farmers left for the cities, and cotton farmers tried to mechanize cotton production. They could not compete with cheaper cotton from the south-west, and had to diversify. Southern agriculture lost its uniqueness and came to resemble the rest of U.S. agriculture.

European agriculture also saw declining populations and rising productivity. After the war, European countries oriented agrarian policies toward moder-nization. Europe dramatically increased farm mechanization, introduced improved crop varieties, and expanded livestock breeding. Dependence on food imports from the U.S. after the war contributed to these changes. In the early 1950s Britain was still rationing and spending vast sums importing food. Investigations in the 1930s–1940s urged government reform of agri-cultural training and research to stimulate domestic food production. These investigations and political organizations of farmers and academics all rejected communalizing land holdings and instead urged technology and scientific research to improve farming. Other West European countries reached similar conclusions.

In Italy, from 1943 on, veterans returning to the impoverished south invaded estates and took over thousands of hectares. The government acquiesced and launched a land reform that redistributed 673,000 hectares from large estates to landless and small farmers in 1950–65. After Italy's long history of inequitable land holdings, this might even be seen as fulfill-ment of the Gracchi plan two thousand years late. The government provided advice, irrigation, and price supports, and many new farms were successful.

Spain moved in the opposite direction. General Francisco Franco won the Civil War of 1936–39 with promises to help peasants, but then revived the rural power of big landlords. After years of declining food production, in 1959 Franco opened up the Spanish economy to world markets. Spain in the 1960s boomed, and laborers and small farmers left villages for the towns. Larger farms, mechanization, and modern inputs dominated Spanish agriculture by the 1970s, although many small farms survived.

As Europe moved toward economic integration with the European Union (EU), European governments agreed in 1958 on the Common Agricultural Policy (CAP). The CAP created a unified market for farm products among its members, which by the 2000s included almost all the countries of Western and Eastern Europe. The CAP supported research and provided price and marketing support for EC farmers, taking up by far most of EC expenditures. The CAP also imposed limits on crop and livestock production, much like acreage allotments in U.S. farm laws, but these limits resulted more from lobbying than from comparative advantage. Spanish farmers produced milk more cheaply than farmers in the Netherlands and northern France, but northern European farmers persuaded the EU to prohibit Spanish farmers from producing and selling milk, and allow only northern Europeans to do so.

European farmers produced massive surpluses, yet often ended up in debt, and frequently protested, demanding more support.

U.S. and European agriculture after the war benefited from government supports, favorable market conditions, new technologies, and economic growth to expand or even leave farming. Overall the farm sector declined in numbers while growing in productivity. Many people became part-time farmers while working in industry or other urban jobs, or retiree farmers dependent on government pensions.

Communism and agriculture

The communist countries formed or expanded state farming sectors, in most cases involving collectivization of agriculture, and in all cases including a smaller sector of state farms that emulated large-scale capitalist farms. These countries tried to modernize their farming, using capitalist farming as the model. Yet because of their poverty and their ideology, their trade and technology contacts with the capitalist world were limited.

Agrarian policies in Eastern Europe were central to the Cold War. In almost all of these countries agriculture was the largest economic sector, and a small class of large landowners had considerable power. The communists usually began by installing a communist agriculture minister. He would introduce a land reform that confiscated landlord estates and divided them among the peasants. This weakened the landlords and won support from peasants, both essential steps to communist takeovers.

Once in power, the communist regimes began to collectivize agriculture. They approached it more cautiously than the USSR, but employed similar tactics, such as removal of the "kulaks" from the villages, and encountered varying levels of resistance. Bulgarian peasants, accustomed to communal villages, accepted collectivization and increased food production with government support. In Poland peasants and officials resisted collectivization until the 1956 crisis, and then abandoned it.

The Soviet Union after the Second World War was devastated, especially the farms. After more than 25 million deaths in the war, Soviet farms had a labor shortage, and lost many horses and tractors to military requisitions and Nazi scorched-earth tactics. By 1945 most farm workers were women, who often had to pull the plows themselves. The 1946 drought reduced an inevitably small harvest and brought a famine that caused two million deaths. The system recovered from this disaster, as in the 1930s, with food rationing and intensive farm work, but the retention of the high procurements quotas and low prices of the war era left peasants impoverished and hostile.

In a remarkable event in Soviet agriculture, from 1948 until the mid-1960s Soviet agricultural research came under the control of a pseudo-scientist who persuaded Stalin that Soviet farming did not need "Western" science. Trofim

Lysenko used political connections to become director of the All-Union Center for Agricultural Research by 1948. He and his cronies expelled many legitimate scientists from research institutions, and some were imprisoned or even executed.

Stalin's death in 1953 finally allowed reforms in Soviet agriculture. Stalin's successor Nikita Khrushchev raised state procurement prices, including grain prices, by a factor of ten, enlarged farms to multi-village scale, and provided more machinery, supplies, and inputs. Soviet agriculture became more modern – Lysenko's influence now declined and he was ousted in 1964 – but also more subsidized. In the 1960s and 1970s the government finally granted pensions and internal passports to collective and state farm peasants, making rural people for the first time in Russian history legally equal to urban workers.

Still, Soviet agriculture did not produce enough for the growing population. Khrushchev revived an earlier scheme to farm the "virgin lands" east of the Volga, a vast campaign to build large farms that assimilated more than 30 million acres. The Virgin Lands increased grain production, but in the long run these arid regions risked natural disaster. One took place in 1963, when a severe drought destroyed the region's harvests and created dust storms. Khrushchev had to import 17 million tons of grain in 1963–64 to avert hunger and livestock losses. In response to this crisis, his successor Leonid Brezhnev emphasized agricultural development and irrigation.

China began the twentieth century with natural disasters, military defeat, foreign domination, and peasant rebellion. In 1898 the Yellow River overflowed its banks and flooded 2,500 square miles, and along with drought and locusts produced millions of starving refugees. Some Chinese blamed foreigners allowed into China by the "unequal treaties" for these disasters, and revived a secret society, the Boxers, that violently attacked foreigners in 1899–1900, until suppressed by a multinational intervention.

Popular discontent then focused on the fading Qing dynasty propped up by the intervention, and peasants served in and supported the military forces that overthrew it in the 1911 revolution. The new republican China soon disintegrated into warlord states that could not cope with the drought and famine of 1918–21 in north China. Several countries and Chinese states formed the China International Famine Relief Committee, which worked for 17 years (until the Japanese invasion of 1937) to provide food relief and development aid to improve farming and living conditions and prevent famine.

In the interwar years, China exported silk and cotton, but farmers endured abusive taxation by warlord governments and armies, while landlords often took peasants' lands, made them tenants or landless laborers, and demanded high rents and other obligations. These conditions worsened in the 1930s with the Depression and the Japanese occupation.

During these years the new Chinese Communist Party followed the Soviet party line: that peasants as a backward "capitalist" class could not serve as the basis for revolution. In mid-1926, the Nationalists under General Jiang Jieshe (Chiang Kaishek) conquered several warlord states. Guided by educated organizers from towns, peasants formed peasant associations in the liberated provinces. They took over power from the landlords, clans, and religious leaders, banned opium, alcohol, and gambling, advanced women's rights and ran schools. They restricted rents and usury. A rising Communist leader, Mao Zedong, in 1927, wrote a long and glowing report about the peasant associations. With others in the Party, he came to see the peasants as the main revolutionary force.

In the wake of his military victories, however, Jiang Jieshe decided the Chinese Communists were a potential threat. In Shanghai in April 1927 he launched a bloody attempt to kill or expel as many of them as possible. His forces also organized landlords to carry out a "white terror" against the peasant associations. The Communists' flight from these attacks culminated in the Long March of 1934. During this retreat the Party shifted to support the peasants as the main revolutionary force, and Mao became head of the Party. The Communists ended up concealed in a remote province, Yenan, where they revived the peasant associations under their own leadership. The Communists won substantial peasant support, while the Nationalists could only count on the landlords.

When the Japanese began their war against China from 1937, Communists formed peasant armies and used guerilla tactics to resist Japanese search and destroy missions, with much more success than the Nationalists. After the Japanese defeat, the CCP's pro-peasant policies and the Nationalists' miscalculated wager on the landlords enabled the CCP to defeat them in a last civil war in 1949.

Mao Zedong, now ruling China as head of the CCP, extended forced land reforms begun in Yenan. In public sessions, peasants would express resentments that they had to suppress while the landlords were in power. Thousands ended up killed in this process. No sooner had the peasants settled down to their new lands than Mao decided that the time had come to begin his long-term project of collectivization. The process was less violent than under the Soviet regime because the peasants still retained loyalty to the Communist Party, but it involved four times the number of peasants as in the USSR in about the same length of time. By 1957 more than 90 percent of peasants had been persuaded or induced to join the cooperative farms.

Then concerns about food supplies, industrialization, and the future needs of farms led Mao and his followers to conclude that only collectivization encompassing whole districts of many villages, to form "people's communes," would overcome the tight food situation. Party organizers promised peasants free food, as much as one could eat, served in mess halls so women would not need to do housework, because the communes would be so much more productive. Peasants trusted the Party and believed these promises, and in the communal mess halls they ate freely after years of rationing and conserving for the next harvest. Then food supplies ran out. Local officials sometimes forced peasants in the communes to farm in irrational ways, and their large size and management problems, unprecedented in China, brought serious disorganization. Farm production collapsed, worsened by droughts and floods in some regions.

The result by 1959 was a huge famine that caused tens of millions of deaths. Some provincial leaders concealed the crisis, but others accurately described it. Mao dismissed these reports as temporary difficulties, but as more reached the center he was observed staring into the distance for long periods of time, and went into a kind of shock; ultimately he ordered food imports. In 1961 Mao reduced the power of the people's communes, and made the team, essentially the village, the main economic unit. Even during the famine, China began some basic reforms, including irrigation construction; these supported recovery from the disaster and slow increases in production, more or less at the rate of population growth. Nonetheless, the disaster turned many officials and party members against the Communist regime's policies.

The Chinese communists dedicated themselves to the peasants, won a major revolution with enormous peasant support, then shifted its orientation toward cities and industry, and subordinated peasants as much as any anti-peasant regime. Yet Mao's shocked reaction to the famine and his decisions to import food and partly reverse his communalization policies indicated that this regime retained some of its old concern for peasants.

Communist regimes thus came to power at least partly in the name of the peasants, but subordinated them to a government-run estate system in order to harness their work to the regime goals of industrial development. The communist systems aimed to increase production, but experienced some of the worst natural disasters, mismanagement, and famines up to this period. They did take steps to strengthen and increase farm production, and the status of farmers in certain ways improved over the previous systems. Still, many farmers and officials in these governments anticipated larger reforms.

Agriculture in the third world

The former colonies became independent through a long, complex, and often violent process of decolonization for most countries during the 1950s–1960s. The political and economic changes in the former colonies and other third world countries had important agrarian components. All of these countries' economies were greatly or mainly agricultural, and all of them set out to modernize and develop after the war.

To achieve these goals, these countries often had to restructure their agricultural systems to reduce landlessness, but land reform turned out to be a complex and often ambivalent process. They also sought policies that would help them develop into more modern and better-off societies, which required increased food production, and the key agrarian component of this effort was the Green Revolution. These two policy directions can be interpreted as policies oriented toward reducing or eliminating the dual subordination of farmers to society outside the farms and to the environment. Both the new decolonized states and their supporters in developed countries and IFIs had high hopes for improving living conditions and empowering the previously oppressed rural majorities.

The developing countries were sites of experimental application of conflicting economic theories. In the first decades after the war, the U.S. and the IFIs advanced programs based on modernization theory. This approach held that the development of the United States and Europe was a model that every country would inevitably follow. Some modernization projects were successful. The Gezira Scheme, an irrigation project in Sudan built from 1925 to the 1960s, diverts water from the Blue and White Nile Rivers to irrigate 8,800 square kilometers. This vast project produces cotton, wheat, and other crops and for years provided most of Sudan's foreign exchange.

Other large-scale development projects often failed because planners did not fully understand the needs and capabilities of the developing countries. In the "groundnut scheme" begun in 1946, British colonial authorities spent £49 million to organize mechanized farms in an arid region of colonial Tanganyika to grow peanuts for cooking oil. The scheme encountered obstacles ranging from funding cuts, machinery unsuited to local conditions, and hungry lions and elephants, to drought and labor strikes. It produced only 2,000 tons of peanuts before it was cancelled in 1951.

In Africa, some large projects were part of a last resurgence of colonial control after the war, often described as the second colonial occupation of Africa. Thousands of Europeans moved to African colonies hoping to set up new farms and businesses. In Asia, no such resurgence took place, as the Asian colonies gained or fought for independence from the end of the war.

Other developing countries followed communist-inspired policies that were similarly inappropriate. In Tanzania the idealistic but dictatorial president Julius Nyerere from 1968 to 1975 applied a socialist policy called *ujamaa*. It involved a villagization program in which peasants living on family homesteads in this arid country were to resettle together in villages with the ultimate goal of forming collective farms to produce more food. Tanzania had low harvests and was spending a great deal on food imports.

Villagization was practical from a government standpoint but ignored the environmental difficulties of large settlements in an arid region best suited to dispersed, shifting cultivation. Nyerere had soldiers beat up peasants and burn down their homes in order to force them to resettle in villages. Farming in the new villages rapidly exhausted soils, had small harvests, and many people simply fled. By 1975 the government tacitly suspended the policy, but other developing countries applied it with varying results.

Land reform during the U.S. food regime

The most important agrarian policy in developing countries was land reform: the appropriation by governments of landlord estates, plantations, or white settlers' farms, their subdivision into smallholdings and distribution to poor and landless peasants. Peasants and others who fought colonialism demanded land reform to eliminate the domination of white settlers and landed elites who had supported and benefited from colonialism. In Latin America the policy aimed to weaken landlords and corporations, and restore land and autonomy to the rural poor, with 1930s Mexico as a precedent.

Economists and other specialists recommended land reform to keep migrants out of cities, and to provide a market for industrial goods and a tax base for government. Land reform promised to keep labor in the farm sector where it could be productive, allowing governments to save capital investment for industry. The FAO held an international conference on land reform in 1960 to encourage interest in it as a means to decrease poverty in developing regions. Land reforms often had the political objective of undermining revolutionary movements. Land reforms were also among the most dramatic, violent, and politically significant developments in these countries' histories.

The first major land reform after the war took place in Japan. Tenant farm families, most of the rural population, paid high rents to a few wealthy landlords, who had supported the imperial government. In 1946 U.S. occupation authorities, supported by Congress, imposed an egalitarian land reform in which the government purchased tenant lands and large holdings, and sold them in small plots to tenants and landless laborers, at mortgage payments one-tenth of their previous rents. This reform, like similar ones implemented in South Korea and Taiwan, was accompanied by price supports, credits, and research. In all these cases, farm production rapidly increased and laid the basis for industrial growth. U.S. politics played the opposite role when the Philippines considered land reform in the mid-1950s, at the peak of McCarthyism. U.S. legislators feared being labeled "communist" for supporting a redistributive land reform, so big landowners in the Philippines remained in power.

The largest land reform in the free world took place in South Asia, as colonial India divided in 1947 into independent India and Pakistan. One of the main demands of peasant movements in the subcontinent had been the abolition of zamindaris and other large landlord estates and the elimination of their privileges. These landlords, however, had supported the Indian National Congress and the Muslim League. Consequently the independent governments were ambivalent about dealing with this issue.

Yet peasant movements in South Asia demanded reforms after the war. One of the largest began in 1946 in the Telangana region of Hyderabad. The Nizam, the leader of this princely state, attempted to maintain his kingdom separate from India, relying on local landlords who held peasants in debt bondage. In 1948, while India invaded Hyderabad and defeated the Nizam, peasant rebels led by the Indian Communist Party took over estates, freed the debt peons, killed or expelled landlords, and redistributed lands. Having defeated the Nizam, however, the Indian forces suppressed the peasant movement, even though it had helped weaken the Nizam's resistance.

The violence of the Telangana movement persuaded a follower of Gandhi, Vinobha Bhave, in 1951 to try to avert such rebellions with the Bhoodan or free gift movement. He and his followers walked from village to village and appealed to landlords to donate land to the poor. Landlords donated more than 2.7 million acres, but often gave their worst land, and the inequitable distribution in India's villages survived.

The Prime Minister of newly independent India, Jawaharlal Nehru, and his economic planners, sought increasing production more than equity and reform. They considered large farms more modern and productive. Still, Congress Party leaders had committed themselves to abolition of zamindars and other landlord groups. The central government left much of agrarian law to the Indian states, to accommodate local conditions, and they implemented reforms from the late 1940s. Some landholders tried to conceal their holdings, but peasant protests and land takeovers forced redistribution. Most zamindars had some or all of their lands taken and redistributed, but often they retained local political power. Kerala, a state with two strong communist parties and a Hindu–Christian population, conducted the most effective reform, eliminating absentee landlordism, serfdom, and tenancy, and transferring lands to the cultivators. Yet landlessness, debt bondage, and other exploitative agrarian relations survive in India.

The government of Pakistan faced similar peasant demands, but Pakistan's leaders were landlords themselves. At independence less than one percent of the farms held 25 percent of the farmland in large holdings, while 65 percent of the farmers held only 15 percent of the land in smallholdings, and there were many poor tenants and landless laborers. The regime declared two land reforms, in 1959 and 1972, reducing allowed holdings to 150 irrigated acres and 300 non-irrigated, with exemptions. The reformist president Zulfikar Ali Bhutto in 1977 tried to lower those limits, which may have been a factor in the coup by General Zia al-Haq that ousted and executed him. Despite the laws, Pakistani landowners surrendered only four million acres, or eight percent of farmland, for distribution to poor peasants. Subsequent governments have ignored these laws, and small farms are disappearing while middle and larger farms grow. In the southern province of Sindh landlords hold some 1.8 million peasants in debt-bondage.

In Bangladesh, where 85 percent of the people are rural, the government has introduced several land reforms, but all of them failed because of peasants' poverty and the tangled and corrupt government bureaucracy. Landlessness increased from less than ten percent of Bangladeshi peasants in

1947 to more than 60 percent in 2009. Overall, land reform in South Asia has only marginally improved the status of peasants and rural laborers, although more in India than in Pakistan or Bangladesh.

In Africa, dozens of colonies became independent after the war and others went through major political transitions; almost all of these political changes affected agriculture. All of the African countries with significant populations of European settlers had to deal with land reform issues, but their experiences varied greatly.

Kenya's land reforms benefited many Africans, after a last-ditch attempt by white settlers to stop them. The main issue was control over the fertile white highlands. British settlers there had large farms that depended on 250,000 squatters living on small allotments. After the war the settlers and colonial authorities attempted to expel squatters, replace them with mechanization, and employ them as forced laborers.

These and other abuses by 1952 provoked the Mau-Mau rebellion against British settlers and African loyalists. The British finally saw that they had to address African agrarian issues. They suppressed the rebellion by confiscating rebels' lands, detaining thousands of Africans in concentration camps, and resettling a million Africans to separate them from the rebels. In 1954 the Swynnerton Plan reoriented policy toward smallholding Africans. It redistributed seven million hectares to thousands of African farmers by the 1970s. It ended restrictions on African cultivation of cash crops, established research and extension programs, and provided aid to farmers. This reform tripled Africans' farm production by 1959. White settlers now began to leave. To aid rural squatters and landless people, the government in 1961 launched the "million acre scheme," which eventually allocated 1.2 million acres to 35,000 farms for landless Africans.

While wealthy African businessmen or government officials appropriated some of the farms abandoned by departing white settlers, more than two-thirds of the former whites' farms were transferred to 50,000 African farms. By the 1970s Kenya still had many poor and landless rural people, but it had a large and stable peasant farm sector. Land reforms were implemented in Egypt and other African countries, with varying results.

Latin American land reforms in the decades after the war varied in origin, character, and effects. The U.S. government's power in the Americas often determined the results. Two cases that show this contrast are Puerto Rico and Guatemala.

In Puerto Rico, a U.S. territory from 1900, the economy was dominated by U.S. corporate sugar farms that had appropriated land illegally, leaving most peasants landless and poor. In the late 1940s, simultaneously with the Japanese reform, U.S. and Puerto Rican authorities expropriated the five big sugar companies with compensation. Rather than dividing them into small farms, they turned them into "proportional profit farms," which remained large scale but in which workers and managers shared profits, almost a commercial collective farm. They were a political success and raised living standards.

Guatemala had long been under indirect U.S. domination because the United Fruit Company owned and ran vast banana plantations, but the company used only a small portion of the land it held. In 1952–54, the newly elected president, Captain Jacopo Arbenz, working secretly with the Guatemalan Communist Party among other groups, appropriated some 400,000 acres from the company, paying compensation based on the company's own estimate of the land's value. United Fruit persuaded CIA director Allen Dulles that Arbenz was a Communist. The CIA and dissident army officers overthrew Arbenz in 1954 and reversed the reform. Subsequent governments violently suppressed protests by the mostly indigenous peasants, killing almost 250,000 of them. Ironically by 1958 the U.S. government found United Fruit guilty of antitrust violations in the banana business and forced the company to divest itself of its banana farms in Guatemala.

Other Latin American countries had unique experiences in land reform. In Venezuela, income from oil sales enabled the government to offer attractive compensation to landowners in a land reform in the early 1960s. Landlords even organized tenants to demand land reform so they could sell their estates at high prices and move to cities. Peru in the 1960s still had plantations and servile laborers. The dictator General Velasco Alvarado, from a peasant family, in 1968–75 appropriated most of the big estates and distributed them to peasants. Food shortages caused by his policies led to a coup that overthrew him in 1975, but Peru now had family farms instead of exploitative estates.

Two Latin American countries applied land reforms under socialist governments with generally positive results. In Chile, two percent of the population held 80 percent of the land in large estates, with peasants in debt peonage into the 1960s. The labor movement, leftist parties, and family farmers demanded land reform. In 1964–70, President Eduardo Frei, a Christian Democrat elected with CIA support, expropriated three million hectares from poorly run estates, to distribute to 20,000 workers and peasants. Communist Salvador Allende, elected in 1970, completed Frei's land reform but some of his radical followers seized 2,000 farms illegally. General Augusto Pinochet, with U.S. support, overthrew Allende in 1973, returned the illegally seized farms to their owners, but left the legally reformed farms unchanged. Despite dramatic political conflicts over other issues, Chile's agriculture changed from large estates and landless laborers into one of small and medium entrepreneurial farms.

In Cuba in 1959–63, Fidel Castro, who led the communist takeover of Cuba and became Prime Minister, nationalized the sugar estates and made them peasant cooperatives, reducing the maximum holding to 67 hectares. These reforms brought the main export sector of the Cuban economy under state control and tripled the number of small farm owners, creating a substantial peasantry from a landless laboring class. Yet Castro did not force Cuban peasants to join collective farms. Voluntary collectivization began only in 1977 and grew until state funding for the collectives fell. Most peasants stayed independent peasants in communist Cuba with the active support of the regime.

Certain countries did not apply land reforms: Brazil and Argentina maintained large landed estates. Other countries did not implement land reforms because they were never settler colonies and have few if any large plantations or settler estates. These include such countries as Ivory Coast, Ghana, and Malawi.

The record of land reform reflects each country's pattern of political and economic development. Japan and Taiwan, for example, were economic and political successes, and their land reforms were similarly successful. In Guatemala, by contrast, the dominance of United Fruit frustrated land reform just as it frustrated Guatemalan democracy. In between such extremes, land reforms in Kenya, Chile, and Cuba significantly improved many peasants' lives but involved compromises and constraints that reflected other aspects of those regimes. This era of land reform resembled and to a degree continued the era of emancipations, and in places like Italy it partially fulfilled poor and landless peasants' long-held desires for land. The reforms reduced and sometimes eliminated the peasants' social subordination to those outside agriculture, at least temporarily.

Technological revolution in agriculture: the Green Revolution

The Green Revolution refers to the large increase in grain production in many developing countries in the 1950s–1970s that resulted from farmers' use of high-yielding varieties (HYVs) of rice and wheat. This increased production resulted from an international research effort sponsored by private endowments, government agencies, and universities, which formed a network of research agencies around the world who work to increase food production.

The Green Revolution emerged from Japanese and U.S. innovations in plant breeding. Japanese farmers in the nineteenth century developed dwarf varieties of rice and wheat with thick stems and high yields. These *rono* or veteran farmer varieties became the basis for government efforts to increase food production to support industrial growth after the Meiji Restoration of 1868. The new government supported *Meiji Noho*, or Meiji agricultural methods, which gave rise to a high-yielding "fertilizer-consuming rice culture." One Japanese farmer discovered an extremely high-yielding rice, *Shinriki* or "power of the gods," in 1877, and by 1920 it was Japan's leading variety. During the First World War shortages and high prices led to the Rice Riots of 1918. To overcome these shortages, the government enlisted scientists to breed varieties suited to Japanese-controlled Taiwan and Korea, which soon produced surpluses.

In the U.S. in this period, agronomists discovered how to breed high-yielding corn plants by cross-breeding pure strains to produce *hybrids* or plants with *hybrid vigor*, extremely high yields. One breeder, Henry A. Wallace, a farmer, farm journalist, and son of a USDA secretary, started a seed company in 1926, Pioneer Hi-Bred, that by 1944 had sales of $70 million. By then most corn grown in the U.S. was hybrid.

In the midst of these developments, during the Second World War Mexico had three successive failures of its wheat crop caused by rust, a fungal plant disease, and in 1943 the Mexican government appealed to the U.S. government for aid. The U.S. government referred the Mexicans to the Rockefeller Foundation, which turned to the University of Minnesota, where one of the top specialists on rust, Elvin Stakman, was based. Stakman organized a team of specialists to go to Mexico to deal with this problem. One member of his team was Norman E. Borlaug, who completed a PhD under Stakman in 1942.

This team set up a plant breeding program that also trained Mexican scientists. In a few years they developed wheat varieties resistant to rust, suited to Mexican conditions and higher yielding. Borlaug, however, saw the potential to achieve something better. The U.S. in 1945–46 had obtained a dwarf wheat from Japan, Norin-10, which produced a short thick-stemmed plant with a large head. It was a descendant of the Rono varieties developed in the nineteenth century but with admixtures from American and Russian varieties. Borlaug and his team crossed Norin with the new rust-resistant varieties for seven years until they finally developed varieties with the genetic characteristics they sought.

By the 1950s his program was breeding dwarf wheats that responded to heavy doses of fertilizers by growing much more grain on a sturdy stem that would not lodge – collapse – from the weight of the head full of grain. The breeders called these high-yielding varieties, or HYV. The program organized Mexican landlords to produce seed, distributed this to farmers widely, and by 1956 Mexico became self-sufficient in wheat. The key to this success was a "package": the seed, fertilizers, and adequate irrigation, and the researchers insisted that it would work on any scale of farm with those inputs. Borlaug's research center was renamed the Maize and Wheat Improvement Center, or based on the Spanish version, CIMMYT.

Borlaug then set out to proselytize in Asia for adoption of these varieties. He met with Pakistani and Indian leaders and specialists in the 1960s, persuading them to try the new varieties. In India, in the mid-1960s, Borlaug met with officials against the backdrop of the 1965–66 crop failures, which made it relatively easy to persuade them to try something new. These countries adopted the new seeds, their food production increased dramatically, and the number of people starving or malnourished began to decline.

On the basis of this work, Borlaug was awarded the 1970 Nobel Peace Prize. The increased production of the HYVs gave farmers a weapon against the first subordination, to nature. They could accumulate reserves that would enable them to withstand crop failures and grow another crop the next year. In his acceptance speech, however, Borlaug described his success as merely postponing the inevitable expansion of the "population monster" that would overwhelm increased food production unless some action was taken.

The development of high-yielding rice similarly focused on dwarf varieties with high yields. Another American, Henry Beachell, chief rice breeder for the International Rice Research Institute (IRRI) in the Philippines, another Green Revolution research center, identified a sturdy dwarf variety that would not lodge, matured rapidly, and produced with fertilizer ten times the normal rice yield. This variety, called IR8, helped make the Philippines self-sufficient in rice. Farmers complained, however, about IR8's cooking qualities, taste, and vulnerability to diseases. Beachell and IRRI developed another variety, IR36, that matured even faster, was disease-resistant and better-tasting, and IRRI distributed this to millions of farmers around the world.

India provides an important example of the Green Revolution in one country. Indian planners emulated Soviet industrialization with five-year plans, but India became dependent on food imports in the 1950s. A report by U.S. specialists in 1959 projected vast food shortages by 1970, and Nehru shifted policy toward agricultural development.

Nehru's successors Lal Shastri in 1964 and Indira Gandhi in 1966 both recognized India's need for rapid agricultural development. They relied on the energetic Agriculture Minister Chidambaram Subramanian, who implemented many programs to modernize Indian farming, including importing new high-yielding varieties. After two years of serious crop failures, India had to import ten million tons of grain in 1965–66. Indian scientists worked with U.S. and other scientists in the mid-1960s to adapt the new varieties to India. The result was a massive increase in crop production. The first harvest with a large share of HYVs in 1968 produced so much wheat that schools had to be closed and used for storage.

The Green Revolution brought a long-term increase in agricultural productivity and food supplies. The area planted in high-yielding rice and wheat in developing countries increased from 41,000 hectares in 1965–66 to 50.5 million hectares by 1970–71. Perhaps two billion people in the world by 2000 could not have been kept alive without these HYVs. This success was also in part the result of increased fertilizer production. The work of CIMMYT and IRRI convinced the IFIs and the foundations to create a network of international agricultural research agencies, in order to improve many aspects of farming for specific regions. The CGIAR, the Consultative Group on International Agricultural Research, founded by the World Bank in 1971, today includes 15 centers.

Borlaug and others involved in the Green Revolution argued that the innovations would work on any size farm and would not lead to the division of peasants into rich and poor. Many small farmers in Asia did adopt the HYV package, but many others could not afford the whole package. Big landlords realized that the HYV package offered an opportunity to produce large amounts for domestic and international markets. They expelled tenants from their lands and bought tractors to rely less on laborers. Pakistan imported more than 100,000 large tractors in the decade after the introduction of the Green Revolution. While these farmers have become capitalist entrepreneurs focusing on exports, many villagers have become impoverished from declining work opportunities, and often leave for the towns. In Mexico, the HYV wheat package was too expensive for many poor farmers, while a group of some 200 wealthy entrepreneurs soon dominated Mexican farming even as the country became temporarily self-sufficient.

Costs to individual farmers were only part of the problem. The Green Revolution depended also on a long-term government commitment to infrastructure and research. Governments in Kenya, Zimbabwe, and Nigeria all financed indigenous research during the 1970s–1980s, developing HYVs of maize, cassava, and other crops suited to local conditions, and produced large harvests. Yet these programs benefited the small class of better-off farmers who produced for export. These and many other African countries had to import food aid despite having the potential to produce large harvests.

Globalization of world agriculture and its discontents: 1970s to 2000s

The success of the Green Revolution in increasing food supplies, despite its inequities, and the agricultural improvements in both developed and developing countries, seemed to promise the end of famine and beginning of steady agricultural growth. Instead, unanticipated events disrupted the relatively stable postwar world in agriculture. Crop failures turned out to be very difficult and disruptive to deal with. Events outside agriculture stimulated borrowing in the U.S. and by third world countries, which in the 1980s led to a vast international debt crisis connected in several ways to farming. "New Agricultural Countries" competed with the U.S. and Europe. Technological and environmental issues emerged from the highly industrialized agriculture that has developed around the world to threaten human livelihood.

The agricultural crises of 1970–86

A chain of events in the early 1970s began to fragment the world food regime. The Nixon administration changed U.S. grain trade policies by eliminating restrictions on transport, and requirements for licenses and for informing the U.S. government in advance. The administration also allowed the dollar to float against other world currencies, which decreased its value and made U.S. exports cheaper.

Then in 1971–75 the Soviet Union had a series of crop failures, just when they had raised large herds of livestock to increase meat consumption. President Richard Nixon and his advisor Henry Kissinger seized on this as a means to entangle the USSR in agreements, and move them toward greater arms controls. Nixon and Kissinger also hoped to use U.S. grain sales to improve the U.S. balance of payments.

The Soviets took advantage of Nixon's policy changes to purchase 23 million tons of grain in 1972 rapidly for low prices. When world commodities exchanges found out, grain prices skyrocketed. Developing countries found it hard to buy the food their people needed. U.S. farmers and the USDA viewed the Soviets as a giant market for the foreseeable future. USDA Secretary Earl Butz told farmers to plant "fencerow to fencerow." Counting on foreign grain purchases and U.S. export subsidies, many farmers borrowed heavily to modernize and expand their farms, engaging in a type of large-scale speculation, "betting the farm." U.S. farmers brought 40 million acres into production. Interest rates on loans began to increase but land prices more than doubled and farm prices were high, so farmers were confident they could cover their debts. Canadian farmers also participated in this debt-based expansion.

In a separate development, the OPEC oil cartel raised oil prices in 1973 to retaliate against the U.S. for its support of Israel in the 1973 war. Oil companies made a lot of money quickly, and deposited it in commercial banks that sought to loan as much as they could, especially to third world countries. Many countries took on this debt, partly for corrupt reasons, but also partly to support new projects or cash crop production.

Meanwhile, several other regions had droughts and crop failures, including India and China. The Sahel region along the southern border of the Sahara Desert in Africa has been plagued by severe droughts, but the 1950s was a relatively wet period, and the governments of the new post-colonial countries there did not anticipate a turn-around. Then in 1968–74 drought struck the Sahel. In Ethiopia, the government of Haile Selassie neglected the crisis, which threatened food supplies for the army and led to a military coup in 1974 that established a communist military regime. In the western Sahel, many farmers grew cash crops or peanuts for export, competing for land with pastoral herders who tended to stay near wells that development workers built for them. By the 1960s, cultivation and grazing, combined with the early stages of the drought, caused serious soil depletion which governments made little effort to alleviate.

In the early 1970s the drought became so severe it turned Lake Chad into a group of ponds. Millions of people faced starvation, whole families died, hundreds of thousands fled from the region, often to refugee camps, from which the world media broadcast images of children with emaciated legs and swollen bellies. The foreign relief providers began late, in some cases sent inedible and contaminated food, and did not send enough relief to stop the famine. Deaths from starvation and disease reached into the hundreds of thousands. Yet during the drought the region continued to produce and export cotton, peanuts, and other crops. In response to this crisis, the World Bank under the leadership of Robert McNamera refocused its development loans from large industrial projects to poverty alleviation, and participated in the lending spree along with the private banks.

The world agrarian debt crisis

The combination of crop failures, high food prices, and the spread of the Green Revolution and improved technologies had results that farmers did not anticipate. By the mid-1970s many countries began selling farm produce on world markets and prices fell. The USSR began to overcome its crop failures. The U.S. Federal Reserve Board responded to inflation with higher interest rates, which reduced land prices and increased the value of the dollar, in turn weakening farm crop sales. In response to the Soviet invasion of Afghanistan, President Jimmy Carter embargoed U.S. grain exports to the USSR, which left the field to other trading countries and made potential buyers look for other, more reliable sellers.

By the 1980s, the U.S.-based food regime had been undermined by the success of U.S. and other countries' efforts to help developing countries improve food production. Thanks to the Green Revolution, India became a grain exporter with a farm export surplus of a billion dollars in 1985, and provided famine relief to Ethiopia. Indonesia, previously a massive rice importer, now became self-sufficient. Japan and other small East Asian countries periodically had rice surpluses. Brazil, Argentina, Australia, and Canada added 40 million acres to the world's cropland. The European Union changed from large importers to large exporters. Fewer and fewer countries wanted or needed to buy many U.S. products, while U.S. farm production was growing because of new technologies and improved inputs.

The increased supplies drove world farm prices down from 71 percent of parity to 50 percent. Interest rates rose. Big farmers, with incomes above $500,000, withstood this, but the core group of middle-level family farms often could not cover their debts. Only 60 percent of total U.S. farm production met virtually all U.S. consumption needs, and another 25 percent of farm produce was exported, so about 15 percent of produce, or approximately that percentage of farms, were basically farming without a market, living off government credits and private loans.

U.S. farmers acted individually toward government farm credit offerings in the 1970s the way developing countries acted toward credit offers from banks trying to lend out oil money in the same period. Private banks pushed loans on farmers, just as large lenders and IFIs such as the World Bank offered loans to developing countries at low rates. In both cases lenders assured debtors that repayment would be easy. Latin American countries' debts grew from $35 billion in 1973 to $350 billion in 1983, with similar increases in Africa and Asia. Most of these loans had variable interest rates. During the late 1970s, all of this lending increased money supplies, which in turn led to inflation and rising interest rates, without simultaneous economic growth, a pattern labeled "stagflation." As farmers responded to the big grain sales of the 1970s by expanding their cropland and taking on debt, they grew increasingly dependent on foreign markets and the big grain trading companies.

American farmers had experienced volatile foreign markets repeatedly, especially in the 1880s and 1930s. For three decades since the war, the U.S. had been exporting food aid to developing countries at subsidized prices. This drove prices down in those countries so much that local small farmers could not compete, fell into debt, and often had to leave their villages for the shantytowns to try to survive. In the 1980s, farm produce from other countries drove prices down for U.S. farmers, who then could not pay their debts; thousands of them ended up losing their farm to foreclosure.

During the peak of the farm debt crisis in the U.S., in the mid-1980s, thousands of farm families lost their farms to foreclosure every week. In some instances farmers responded by killing bank officials. More common were suicides. Farmers committed suicide at about double the average rate for the U.S. population. Various agencies established hotlines for farmers to call if they were contemplating such violence.

Some farmers resorted to political activism. In 1978, when the crisis was only beginning, a group of farmers formed the American Agriculture Movement and drove their tractors to Washington D.C. in a "tractorcade." Congress allotted a small increase in farm aid, which disappointed many farmers. In a more aggressive tractorcade the next year they blocked traffic and fought with police. This public relations disaster split the movement into a lobbying group and fringe groups who blamed scapegoats for the crisis.

The Reagan administration came into office with a philosophical opposition to "big government," and prepared new farm legislation to reduce subsidies. The farm crisis created such strong public demand for action, supported by popular movies such as *Country* and media events like the "Farm Aid" concerts, that the administration was forced to act. The Reagan administration abandoned its attempts to eliminate price supports and spent in 1983 a record $51 billion on various farm subsidies.

Meanwhile, dozens of developing countries that had taken on large debts had great difficulties during the 1980s maintaining their payments schedule. Since most of these countries were agrarian and depended on farm produce exports to obtain hard currency to repay loans, the international commodities glut and the low prices it caused made it increasingly difficult for these countries to obtain the money they needed. This vast third world debt crisis thus had some of the same causes as the U.S. farm debt crisis. Developing countries took on these debts mostly to cover current expenses, including the rising cost of oil, just as U.S. farmers borrowed in spring to cover operating expenses, hoping to repay after the harvest.

Faced with this vast crisis, the IFIs decided that their previous loan policy of poverty alleviation had failed, but they could not resort to a bailout of the sort that the Reagan administration applied to help American farmers. Instead, the IFIs implemented the type of policy that the administration wanted to use domestically: structural adjustment. In order for a developing country to obtain a new loan to help pay off the old one, leaders had to commit to following market- and export-oriented policies. These included cutting back domestic government spending, including on healthcare, education, and farm subsidies, and orienting their economies toward exports at all costs. If the priority of exports sacrificed domestic food security, the IFIs held that the developed world produced staple crops so efficently and cheaply that developing countries should simply import them with the money they earned from their exports.

Most of the countries faced with structural adjustment programs (SAPs) were in Africa, but a few were in Latin America and Asia. Even when they agreed to these terms, they did not always implement them as harshly as the terms required. Some countries continued to subsidize agriculture while opening their markets. Still in most cases the SAP imposed obligations on agriculture in these countries that were very difficult to fulfill. One key reason was that many developing countries competed in selling basically similar products to wealthy countries, especially the U.S., Europe, and Japan, while those countries had protectionist farm support policies that gave them unfair advantages over developing countries in farm trade.

Thus farmers in many, perhaps most, developing countries benefited from land reforms and new crop varieties, but ended up in a new type of social subordination. They were now trapped by their countries' debts in a struggle to produce for extremely low prices and to compete with the subsidized farmers of the first world. Two sets of farmers, in the developing world and in the developed world, competed for sales with each other on the edge of insolvency, in order to pay off their country's or their own bank debts.

The socialist systems' turn to the market

During the late 1970s to 1990s, economic lags and inefficiencies and political discontent built up to menacing levels in the communist regimes and other countries which had significant socialist sectors, while the political leadership weakened or reformers came to power. In the end these regimes fell and new democracies privatized and marketized their agricultural systems. These changes were in line with the policies of the IFIs, and the World Bank intervened in many of these cases to guide and encourage market reforms, sometimes against the wishes of the farmers involved.

In the Eastern Bloc and USSR, these changes resulted from the reforms of Soviet leader Mikhail Gorbachev: *perestroika* or restructuring, and *glasnost* or accountability and openness. These reforms led in 1988–89 to the overthrow of all the Eastern European communist governments. Soon after establishing democracies, all of the new governments privatized their remaining collective and state farms, and invited Western advisors to help them bring their farms to European standards. By the 2000s these countries had begun integrating their agricultural systems into the CAP. This often required new members to cut back or eliminate some of their main farming sectors that would have competed with those of older CAP members.

The former Soviet states, including Russia, Ukraine, and the Central Asian states, have had more difficulty transitioning to a market economy. They introduced privatization, sometimes, as in Russia, after a long public debate. Yet most of the old collective and state farms transformed themselves and survived. In Russia and Ukraine the large farms became joint stock companies, with members holding shares in the farm and retaining the right to leave and set up as private farmers. As of 2005, 80 percent of farm land in Russia remained held by the successors to the large farms, and private farmers of various sizes, including household plots, control only 20 percent of the land. The transition brought a big drop in farm production during the 1990s, but by the end of the decade they began to recover. The main problems have become access to credit and other financial support, the same problem faced by all capitalist farmers.

In Kazakhstan, the former collective and state farms, many of which were established in Khrushchev's Virgin Lands Program, have become "agricultural enterprises," and still produce about two-thirds of the country's grain. Some 200,000 private farmers produce about one-third of the country's grain, often with outdated equipment, and numerous tiny household farms hold most of the country's livestock. Above all of these are "agro-holding companies" that provide capital and marketing for the enterprises and control huge areas and numerous farm enterprises. Behind the whole system the government owns all of the land. Post-Soviet Kazakhstan agriculture thus has become freer and semi-privatized, but retains many features reminiscent of the Soviet system. The CGIAR and other agencies have carried out aid programs in the region.

The most important communist agricultural region, and the one that underwent the most dramatic transformation, was China. Between the end of the famine in 1962 and Mao's death in 1976, the government tried to make collective farming work without the abuses of the Great Leap Forward. The government encouraged collective farming by bringing millions of peasants to observe the village of Dazhai in northern China after Mao wrote "learn from Dazhai" in 1964. The Dazhai People's Commune organized collective work that restored soils to high fertility, diversified production, and built local industry. Its leader, Chen Yonggui, became Vice-Premier of China under Premier Chou En-Lai.

Beneath the surface, however, peasants and many officials wanted to return to family farming. Communist China did have this as an option, called *baochan daohu* or family contracting. Peasants tried to persuade officials to allow it, and a few localities did allow it, concealing it from official investigating teams. The communal system organized infrastructure improvements, such as irrigation systems, but grain production lagged behind population growth, reaching a 10 million ton deficit.

Mao's death in 1976 changed the whole context. While reformers around Deng Xiaoping openly criticized collective farming, peasants took advantage of weakening administrative control and dismantled the collective system from below. They offered local officials higher production in exchange for allowing family contracting. In Anhui province, where the 1960 famine had been particularly severe, a drought in 1978 devastated crops, and the provincial Party committee decided to "lend" the crop failure land to individual households. Peasants enthusiastically planted more than 300,000 acres and raised the harvest by 50 percent over the previous year.

By fall 1978 the government had clear proof that areas using contracting, in defiance of central government directives, had much larger harvests. The press endorsed baochan daohu, and Wan Li, the Party chief of Anhui province, became Vice-Premier (in place of the former chief of Dazhai). Meetings of Party members and specialists in 1981 shifted agrarian policy to the "family responsibility system." By this time, most communes had divided village lands among the "teams," the official term for the family-size group. As they put it, "the rice was cooked." Now even Dazhai had to divide up its lands. This last land reform involved no violence and very little resistance. Communist Vietnam implemented a similar reform.

Algeria also went through a transition from socialist agriculture to privatization. The French colonists' abusive treatment of Algerian peasants and townspeople provoked a bloody rebellion in 1954 that forced out the French by 1962. The new socialist Algerian government turned the 2.3 million hectares of large farms into state farms, while emphasizing heavy industry. Yet Algerian farmers, even on state farms, employed traditional methods, and production lagged behind population growth, leaving Algeria dependent on grain imports. A socialist "reform" did not improve the situation in the 1970s. In the 1980s the new president Chaddi Benjedid reversed most socialist policies, privatized agriculture, expanded agricultural extension services, and eliminated price controls. Prices rose in the towns (there were food riots in 1988) but food production increased so much that the country was self-sufficient in most crops.

In Mexico, market reforms ended the revolutionary era of land reform in 1991. After Cárdenas, government policy alternated between support for collective ejidos and for division of lands into individual plots and privatization. Peasants demanded more land. In 1967 a peasant "party of the poor" occupied haciendas in southern Mexico and fought with big owners. The government suppressed this rebellion by 1974, but President Luis Echeverría allowed a last land reform, even calling on peasants to seize landlords' lands.

Mexico had some 30,000 ejidos on 103 million hectares, half of the total arable lands, and 3.5 million heads of households had become ejidatarios. The reform aimed to prevent land concentration that had dispossessed peasants in the nineteenth century by prohibiting sale of ejido lands. Local officials and other powerful people, however, had appropriated ejido lands for personal use. Available lands could no longer accommodate growing ejido populations. Usually only one son would inherit the land holding. Landless day laborers and neighbors of ejidatarios lived on the ejidos like landless cotters on the old English commons. Ejidatarios became a kind of rural elite, and the other groups, including ejidatarios' landless relatives, became a kind of subordinate class.

In the economic crisis of the 1980s Mexico defaulted on its large foreign debts. The IFIs demanded that Mexico implement structural adjustment. A new, American-educated group of Mexican leaders began to dismantle the semi-socialist land reform policies. The reform of the 1990s, based on a World Bank study, changed the constitution to allow ejidos and members to make ejido lands private property and use them for most purposes. The reform also eliminated the state's obligation to conduct land reform of large estates. By the 2000s most ejidos had undergone part of the process, but some provinces with large native populations including Chiapas and Oaxaca have resisted it. As a result of this privatizing reform, a small group of ejidatarios acquired larger holdings than others, and outsiders from local bosses to businessmen and state officials have begun concentrating large land holdings in ways reminiscent of the nineteenth century.

Industrial agriculture and global limits at the turn of the millennium

Most studies, economic theories, and state policies have long viewed agriculture and industry as different sectors and often attributed to agriculture the role of supporting industrial development. Since the war, agriculture and industry have steadily grown more interdependent. Most of agricultural production employs machinery, fossil fuels, and advanced technology as much as industry. Large corporations increasingly manage farm production. By the 2000s world agriculture has become for the most part one sector of a global industrial economy.

Yet agriculture has certain features that differ from all other industries, and makes the recent dependence of food on industry extremely risky for the world. Food takes precedence over all other products. Life forms are much more complex and less fully understood than most raw materials used in industrial production. The magnitudes of world population and agricultural production mean that changes in it can have serious and unanticipated effects on the environment and subsistence. This section will discuss some of the main components of industrial farming, their consequences, and responses to them.

Dependency on oil

Perhaps the most industrial aspect of modern farming is its dependence on fossil fuels for inputs, mechanization, and transport. Once American farmers began to use internal combustion engine tractors during the First World War, mechanization spread rapidly. Tractors, combine harvesters, and other mechanized equipment were much easier to use and more productive than horses or oxen, and allowed farmers to eliminate crops grown to feed their draft animals and produce crops exclusively to sell. U.S. farmers provided the model that most other countries adopted sooner or later. The Soviet Union's leaders saw mechanization as modernization and introduced tractors as fast as they could. By the 1980s they had more tractors than the U.S. (to use for spare parts). Farmers in Europe, Asia, and Latin America extensively adopted mechanized farm equipment after the war. Meanwhile industries developed many new types of mechanization, such as cow milking machines and harvesters of cotton, vegetables, and tree crops.

Food processors, which also relied on considerable amounts of energy, applied mechanization even earlier and more extensively. The needs of processors were among the main forces that drove farmers toward mechanization and many other modern techniques. The separation of processing from farming, which began in the nineteenth century, was a crucial part of the industrialization of agriculture, because it made farmers into narrow specialists who had to produce to meet processors' requirements.

Transport of farm products is another important aspect of agriculture's dependency on fossil fuels. Most of the food consumed in the developed and even in the developing world is transported, even food that farmers consume. Iowa in the nineteenth century produced its own apples, but now apples in Iowa come from Washington or New York. One Swedish study of an ordinary breakfast found that the various components of it had been transported a distance equal to the circumference of the earth. Regional agricultural specialization requires farm produce to be marketed far away, which requires transport costs and reduces the farmers' share of the price.

Farm inputs also depend on fossil fuels, especially fertilizer. Declining soil fertility is an ancient problem, and remains a chronic problem today. American farms lose millions of tons of topsoil every year, and in much of Africa soils are extremely depleted. In China farmers restore soils with wet-rice cultivation and use natural waste and composts. In the U.S., Europe, and many other countries, farmers struggled to obtain effective fertilizers.

Then in 1908–14 two German chemists, Fritz Haber and Carl Bosch, devised a complex process to extract nitrogen from the atmosphere and transform it into ammonia on an industrial scale. The process required natural gas as the source of hydrogen and extremely high temperatures and pressures, which required fossil fuel-powered machinery. Both scientists won Nobel prizes for this work, which was also used to produce explosives for weapons. After the Second World War, the U.S. and other countries used military Haber–Bosch processors to produce fertilizers. These fertilizers made possible substantial increases in crop yields, particularly when used in the Green Revolution package. The yield increases this fertilizer made possible allowed perhaps two billion more people to survive than would have been possible otherwise. Most people in the world have nitrogen in their bodies produced by the Haber–Bosch process.

Pesticides are crucial inputs also produced from fossil fuels. The most important pesticides until recently were organochlorides such as DDT. Paul Müller, a Swiss chemist, found in the 1930s that DDT killed insects very effectively. He won a Nobel Prize for this work. The U.S. produced massive amounts in the war to kill lice and malaria mosquitoes. After the war even larger amounts were used in agriculture, an average of 40,000 tons per year from the 1950s to the 1970s. Soon more pesticides were developed from the same base, including dieldren, 2.4,-D, and others.

Yet in the 1950s target pests evolved resistance to these chemicals. They killed good insects as well as bad, creating new insect problems. They killed birds through the insects they ate. They sometimes poisoned and even killed users, and users' cancer rates increased. Finally in 1962 a respected naturalist, Rachel Carson, published *Silent Spring*, a book that drew together research on these and other problems of the pesticides. Despite controversy, her findings were vindicated and persuaded Congress to ban DDT in the 1970s. Chemical companies developed new pesticides that degrade in the environment. Still many farmers have become trapped in a "pesticide treadmill," periodically needing new pesticides to deal with the bounce-back resistance from the first one they used.

Thus perhaps most people in the world live on foods produced, processed, and transported with fossil fuels. While certain foods have been transported increasingly since the sixteenth century, no major population has ever been this dependent for food on another non-food resource before.

The livestock boom

An important example of the problems caused by industrial agriculture has been the enormous increase in livestock production. American farmers had seen livestock as a way to "process" surpluses in the eighteenth century. By the late twentieth century, world agriculture has increasingly focused on livestock products. Most cropland in the U.S. and certain other countries is used for raising corn and soybeans to feed to livestock, ranging from cattle to fish, or to sell to other countries for their livestock.

Livestock production since the war has become remarkably industrialized. Cattle and pigs are raised and fed in vast feedlots holding thousands of animals, confined in stalls barely large enough for them to stand, and slaughtered in a mechanized assembly line that moves extremely rapidly, frequently injuring the poorly paid workers who kill, eviscerate, and section the animal. Henry Ford came up with the assembly line after watching a cattle-processing factory. Poultry are raised in similarly large buildings, holding tens of thousands of birds in extremely filthy surroundings, and often ten percent of them or more die before maturity from those conditions. Such large concentrations of animals spread diseases, and the animals have to be fed antibiotics to prevent large-scale deaths, which exposes people to trace elements of these drugs later on and creates conditions for development of resistant bacteria.

This industrial livestock system has serious implications for the environment and human health. Livestock contributes an estimated 18 percent of all greenhouse gases, including 80 percent of these emissions from agriculture. They cause one-third to one-half of agricultural water pollution, especially from concentrated feedlots. Land clearance for livestock is a major cause of habitat destruction and loss of biodiversity.

Perhaps the most notorious threat from the livestock boom has been the "mad cow" crisis, which resulted from the use of offal, or waste from livestock processing, for feed. The massive production of livestock created an enormous problem of offal and other by-products. Eventually processors utilized some of the waste by *rendering*: heating it at high temperatures to produce bone meal, tallow, or "tankage." In 1912 the firm of Swift and Company fed rendered feed to pigs that won first prize at an International Livestock Show in 1914. After the Second World War, rapidly growing demand for meat produced much more offal, and processors rendered it into feed for livestock, fish farms, and even pets.

From the mid-1960s, livestock spent less time outdoors grazing and more time indoors eating scientifically blended rations until they reached the prescribed weight. By the 1970s, renderers processed blood, hooves, feathers, sawdust, newspapers and cardboard, cement dust, waste water from power plants and nuclear plants, as well as the remains of diseased animals, and food products contaminated by insects and rodents, into feed. By the 1980s most commercial livestock were fed on the rendered remains of other animals.

Mad cow had its origins in scrapie, a poorly understood sheep disease: the animal would continually scrape itself against a tree or post, walk unstably, and eventually collapse. The mad cow epidemic began in spring 1985 when one cow in England developed scrapie-like symptoms and died. Within months, dozens of cases appeared, and research showed that the cattle had the same spongy brains as sheep with scrapie. Research in 1987 connected the cow disease to the feeding of the animals with rendered sheep offal.

Meanwhile, research on a similar human disease, Creutzfeld-Jakob Disease (CJD), isolated the causal agent, a protein compound called a prion that could not be destroyed by high heat or antiseptic chemicals. Then in 1993 a British teenage girl who regularly ate hamburgers died with symptoms resembling CJD. Numerous other cases soon followed. The British government at first minimized the threat, and delayed taking action. Public outcry and other countries' refusal to purchase British food products forced the government to destroy millions of ill or potentially ill animals.

The U.S. livestock and rendering industries, and some government agencies, denied the possibility of mad cow developing in the U.S. Companies have used lawsuits to stop people from questioning the quality of U.S. food, and propagandistic publications to reassure people that meat is safe. Yet mad cow has been found in some U.S. livestock.

Genetically modified agriculture

Genetically modified organisms are agriculture's counterpart to high-tech industry. In much the same way as high technology in industry, the development of this branch of technology raised the issue of the dominance of technology capitalists over the agriculture sector, especially in poorer countries.

Japanese cultivation of dwarf varieties, hybrid corn in the U.S., and the Green Revolution, all involved human efforts to alter the genetics of farm crops. None of these went beyond the genetic potential of the plants themselves, and sought only to intensify a plant's own characteristics. The GMO developers attempted to introduce significant changes in the plants with genetic and other characteristics from other organisms that plants could never acquire naturally. The approach began in 1983 with the use of a bacterium to transfer genetic material from one cell to another. Soon researchers began to move many genes between organisms. By 1990 there were several businesses working on a variety of genetic projects, and the first key issue came up: government regulation.

Genetic companies, most of all Monsanto, competed with opponents of biotech, led by science writer Jeremy Rifkin and including environmental and farmer groups, for influence over public opinion. The Reagan and Bush administrations supported the technology, and the Food and Drug Administration could find no risk in them. U.S. policy in 1992 held that GMOs would be considered safe if they were "substantially equivalent" to non-GMO versions. The OECD and the Clinton administration endorsed this standard. Environmental, pure food, and farmers' groups then began international campaigns to criticize GM crops. They depicted them as dangerous and repulsive, and tried to deter research by digging up plants on experimental plots at night.

GMOs also revived the issue of legal rights to new varieties and patenting life. The American breeder Luther Burbank early in the twentieth century had complained to Congress that breeders might not even have their name associated with a variety that helped many people. Subsequent laws in the U.S. and Europe gave breeders certain rights, but the key step took place in 1972 when a microbiologist at General Electric, Ananda Charkabarty, applied for a patent for a bacterium he had bred that digested oil. The U.S. Patent Office rejected the application because he was trying to patent a living organism, but a Supreme Court decision in 1980 reversed that and declared that anything could be patented.

Chakrabarty had only recognized the result of a natural exchange of genes between bacteria. Companies soon took advantage of the court decision, trying to patent everything they could, including varieties that people had used for thousands of years. One Texas company tried to patent Indian basmati rice with a slight alteration, but the Indian government took the issue to court and in 2001 the Patent Office rejected the patent because the new variety was "substantially identical" to the old one. Critics from the third world, like Indian Vandana Shiva, called such attempts "biopiracy."

Monsanto was the biggest company in the GMO craze of the 1980s and 1990s. Originally a chemical company that had produced notorious chemical weapons, like Agent Orange, in the 1980s Monsanto began to focus on GMOs. In 1995 a new president, lawyer Robert Shapiro, sold off the company's chemical branches and bought seed companies, making Monsanto the largest seed company in the world. He hoped the company could sell new genetically modified crops and other products to benefit humanity.

Monsanto and a few other companies produced two main products. The first was corn, soy, and canola seeds with a gene from a bacterium (*bacilium thuringiensis*, or Bt) that produces a chemical, which acts like an insecticide against these plants' main insect threats. The second was a cotton variety with a gene that allows it to resist the effects of the powerful weedkiller Roundup, produced by Monsanto, which allows farmers to replace weeding with spraying. The Bt crops came to be used widely in the U.S., Canada, and certain other countries. When the company tried to ship Bt soy to European buyers, opponents from organic farmers to environmentalists fiercely resisted. They blocked shipments and distribution, dug up plants, and demanded that food companies indicate on packaging whether the contents included GMOs. European parliaments unanimously endorsed that demand. By this point even Monsanto employees disagreed about these products, and about Monsanto's arrogant attitude toward Europeans' demands. Ultimately Shapiro had to issue a public apology for Monsanto's actions.

The GMO producers also made mistakes. A study found that Monarch butterfly caterpillars died after eating pollen from Bt corn. Another found Starlink Bt corn, authorized only for animal feed, in tacos. In Oaxaca, Mexico, a Vavilov center for old varieties of corn studies, found Bt corn genes. It turned out that local farmers had violated Mexican law and used GMO corn, and the modified gene had passed into non-modified varieties. In the U.S., farmers using Monsanto seed had to sign a contract guaranteeing that they would not use the seed they grew. Monsanto conducted surveillance of farmers' fields, and found one Canadian farmer whose fields had the modified genes, but he denied he used them. The case became a major scandal for Monsanto. Other farmers have complained of their intrusive and bullying style.

So far the benefits of GMO crops have been limited. They reduce the need for pesticides somewhat but they often have lower yields than non-GMO varieties. Monsanto did develop sweet potatoes resistant to a destructive virus, and have provided the variety free to African farmers. GMOs have potential but also have risks, and their producers need to be more sensitive to public concerns and the rights of farmers to traditional varieties in the U.S. and abroad.

Corporations and farmers

The industrialization of agriculture and the livestock boom have both made farmers increasingly dependent on large corporations. A common term used for the modern corporate structure of agriculture is "agribusiness," a broad concept that encompasses all the enterprises involved in commercial farming. The livestock boom makes it most profitable for farmers in many regions to grow corn and soybeans, both used almost entirely to feed animals directly and indirectly as fertilizers for forage crops. Large corporations like Cargill try to make it as convenient as possible for farmers to obtain inputs from and sell their crops to them. Cargill spent billions of dollars dredging the Mississippi and Parana rivers to enable their boats to buy soybeans for export.

Yet the vast sums of sales benefit U.S. corporations much more than the farmers. The farmers have become the only relatively small-scale independent operation in the world food system, bearing the main risks with limited protection and responsible both to input and purchasing agreements. The large multinational enterprises like Cargill, Tyson Foods, and others, dominate storage and marketing of crops and increasingly livestock. In order to market with these firms farmers must produce crops and livestock that meet certain standards, which usually requires them to purchase the seed, small animals, and other inputs from similar and sometimes the same large corporations.

Under these circumstances it is easy for farmers to fall behind in loans and go out of business. The 1980s farm crisis had now become an almost permanent condition. Successful farmers usually manage large enterprises and substantial amounts of money, and some regions like California rely on low-paid labor and tenants. Yet a farmer whose farm brings in $250,000 may end up with less than $20,000 after paying all the expenses. These people in some ways are the modern counterparts to the British nineteenth-century "high farmers" or the Roman latifundium. They are much better educated, however, and have access to much more information and ideas to deal with difficulties.

On the other hand, many farmers, even large ones, work essentially as tenants on farms that are owned by large corporations or wealthy investors. Ted Turner, the founder of the CNN cable network, may be the largest individual landowner in the United States, with two million acres of ranches.

Other corporations own large farms and hire farmers on a contract basis to operate them. Such farms are completely integrated into the corporate structure of inputs, processing, and marketing.

In poorer countries, of course, there are many more small farmers, and there are still large holders who exploit laborers. Yet both groups, like American farmers, increasingly work as processors of inputs into crops and livestock for agribusiness. For example, the avian flu pandemic of 2005–6 was at first blamed on small family chicken farmers, but was later traced to Charoen Pokphand, a Thai company and Asia's largest poultry producer. Like Tyson Foods and other firms, Charoen Pokphand raises chicks in large chicken hatcheries, but then distributes them among small farmers to raise on contract.

Not all farmers acquiesce in this corporate domination. The Mexican privatization of the 1990s was part of a process that led to the North American Free Trade Agreement, which opened up Mexican markets to foreign investment and trade. NAFTA allowed imports of subsidized American farm products that have driven millions of Mexican farmers out of business, brought many Mexican farms under the control of U.S. corporations, and supported the formation of Mexican corporations on the U.S. model. While many peasants resorted to illegal immigration to the U.S. or migration to towns, one group of peasants and others formed the Zapatista Army of National Liberation in Chiapas. The new Zapatistas demand the abolition of NAFTA, and measures to protect Mexican peasants and agriculture. They have engaged in a prolonged political and sometimes military conflict with the government and have won some concessions.

Besides debt, or what debt demonstrates to these farmers, farmers recognize that as competent and independent as they can be or wish to be, and whatever their income is, they are still basically outworkers in a global corporate food-producing system. Even when farmers in the U.S, Europe, or Japan receive subsidies, they are still subordinate, although less than before.

Contemporary issues

Regional issues

Certain countries and regions by the twenty-first century have developed unique characteristics that will influence world agriculture and the world economy.

Brazil is fast becoming an agricultural powerhouse second only to the United States. It never had any significant land reform. In 1950 0.6 percent of farmers, the rich landlords, owned 50 percent of the land, and 80 percent of the farmers, the poorer peasants, owned three percent of the land, with vast numbers landless. After a military coup in 1964, the military leaders began industrialization and modernization of agriculture. They established agricultural research institutions, revived the biofuels program that President Vargas had begun, and reduced the country's use of oil. When Brazil had to accept structural adjustment in the 1980s, its modernized farm sector adapted easily. It became the number two soybean producer in the world after the U.S., produces 80 percent of world orange juice exports, and has more cattle than any other country. Its beef exports have 30 percent of the world market and it plans to double that share.

The beneficiaries of these advances are the landlords and the decreasing numbers of laborers who work for them. In the 1980s a new Movement of Landless Workers, MST, demanded land reform and invaded abandoned lands. By 1995 President Fernando Cardoso implemented a small land reform, but more land reform is unlikely. Brazil and certain other countries have ceased to be mainly peasant societies and compete both in agriculture and in other sectors with first world countries. By analogy to the Newly Industrialized Countries (NICs) such as Taiwan and Thailand, some scholars call Brazil and certain others the New Agricultural Countries (NACs).

All of this agricultural expansion and ambition comes at the cost of Brazil's crucial environmental resource, the Amazon rainforest. The forest was protected into the 1960s, but then the government changed its policies to open the forest for agriculture. Small farmers were encouraged to settle in the forest, and cattle ranchers have burned down an area the size of Portugal in the Amazon rainforest to graze their herds and accommodate huge slaughterhouses to process the animals for sale.

Africa, by contrast, is a region of great potential that is in agricultural decline and has to import food. The "African agrarian crisis" emerged with the 1980s drought, and environmental factors are important causes of Africa's agricultural problems. Postwar development aid and generally the inheritance of colonialism made every problem worse. Aid providers focused on larger export-oriented farms, which benefited the small wealthy and official elites. The much larger numbers of subsistence farmers would have benefited much more from small amounts of targeted aid. Food aid, distributed to alleviate hunger, came from subsidized U.S. or European farmers and was sold at low prices. This undercut local African food producers and benefited townspeople at the expense of rural people.

This bias in aid toward towns and wealth resulted in millions of peasants abandoning their lands for town slums. Often the men went to towns while the women remained in the villages farming, which reduced farm production. Large areas of land, sometimes abandoned by peasants and appropriated by wealthy African businessmen or foreign agribusiness, are planted with monoculture cash crops, and after harvesting are left uncovered to be damaged by drought or heavy rainfall that leaches its nutrients.

Land also remains a vexed issue in Africa. In Zimbabwe, after winning the seven-year war of independence in 1980, President Mugabe began a moderate land reform, but many white farmers refused to surrender their farms. Africans living in reserves grew increasingly discontented. In 2000 Mugabe instituted the Fast-Track Land Reform Program and authorized Africans to take over white settlers' farms. Yet many of these farms went to political officials, as had many former white estates in Kenya. In South Africa, the new post-apartheid governments made promises of land reforms. Yet 60,000 white farmers, only five percent of the white population, own 87 percent of the arable land and produce more than 80 percent of agricultural produce. Meanwhile half a million Africans produce only five percent of farm produce, living with other Africans on 15 percent of the land. By the 2000s Africans disillusioned with government promises began occupations of white estates.

Behind many of these African agricultural problems is the spreading HIV pandemic, which is killing many farmers, who still have traditional knowledge of African crops, and complex production skills that could help depleted African lands recover.

China by virtue of its vast population and growing wealth could have a determining effect on the future of world agriculture. Chinese farm production increased perhaps by 50 percent from the reforms of the 1970s to the mid-1980s, but this was partly the result of the introduction of HYV rice and wheat. Production has slowed as some new varieties have reached their yield limit. The terms of family contracting hold back grain production because contracting families have to produce a certain quota of grain and sell it to a state agency at a fixed low price.

China has also developed a vast urban industrial sector. The government has tried to cover its expenses in infrastructure development and personnel through higher taxes and reduced expenditures for rural areas, often by paying for state grain procurements with IOU documents rather than money. These factors have angered many peasants, driven thousands of them to protest, attack local officials, withhold payment of grain quotas and taxes, and leave for the towns, while the remaining farmers take over their lands.

Behind these issues is the basic problem that China has only seven percent of the world's farmland but more than 20 percent of the population. China's urban growth comes at the expense of farmers and farmland. In a recent book, *Who Will Feed China?*, the economist Lester Brown warned that China's wealth and need for food could enable it to purchase most of the world's food exports and seriously disrupt the world food economy. The Chinese solution has been to send hundreds of thousands of Chinese to construct large farms abroad to produce for China's needs. More than 750,000 Chinese have been sent to Africa and leased millions of acres to produce oil palms, cotton, and other crops for export to China. In some cases, such as Zimbabwe, the African country has relinquished land in exchange for Chinese military supplies.

Many other countries, including third world countries that were once colonized themselves, are extending corporate control into Africa. Some of these investments can benefit these countries, but if they are implemented inflexibly they can have unexpected results. In 2008 the South Korean company Daewoo made a deal with the ostensibly democratic government of Madagascar and leased 1.3 million hectares, almost half the country's cropland, to grow corn and oil palms, ignoring the local farmers' land use and traditions. Massive protests followed, and the Madagascar army overthrew the government and cancelled the deal. Daewoo is still holding more than 200,000 hectares.

The decline of farming and the farm population

During the twentieth century the numbers of farmers and their share of the population in most countries in the world drastically declined. In the United States the share of the employed workforce in agriculture declined from 41 percent in 1900 to 1.9 percent in 2000. Even in China, the classic example of a peasant society, as of 2003 only 44 percent of the working population worked in farming, although 60 percent lived in rural areas. Many villages have shifted their focus to manufacturing, and others have become bedroom communities for migrant workers. Despite its internal passport system, the USSR became majority non-farmer and non-rural in the 1960s, and most Eastern European countries followed suit in that period. Mexico, Argentina, Chile, Cuba, and all other Latin American countries have similarly become by far mostly urban.

In most of the world, "urban" means a core city, with paved streets and well-constructed buildings, surrounded by shantytowns, slums, favelas, and other settlements built with whatever local materials people can come up with. Many residents continue to farm in open areas in the shantytowns, a practice called urbaculture or urban agriculture. This sector employs increasing numbers of townspeople – in Dar es Salaam in Tanzania, two-thirds of the townspeople were farmers. Town farmers, mostly women, raise many crops and livestock, provide subsistence, and bring in income for their families.

This urbanization, however, has resulted from and intensified the collapse of rural communities. In the United States, as more farmers fail, banks and businesses follow suit, and soon the only people left are those who cannot leave: old people on pensions, recipients of welfare who came to buy a house, and farmers still trying to hold on. Rural areas are becoming a new type of ghetto. These conditions have revived farm movements and radical right-wing groups in these areas. Similar rural decline is evident in Europe, Japan, and many developing countries. Farmers in developing countries who attempt to produce with modern inputs often fall into debt like U.S. farmers, but their governments often do not have the resources or the political will to help them when debt threatens their livelihood. Such farmers often resort to violence.

Yet farmers' direct violence is most often against themselves. The UN has recognized an international farmer suicide crisis caused primarily by financial stress and loss of independence from competition in international markets. In India, which opened its markets to international trade in 1991, more than 200,000 farmers have committed suicide. Small farmers have to borrow from usurious moneylenders because the Indian government and private sector have not backed up market reforms with sufficient small-scale credit and insurance programs. Similar problems and suicides take place in many developing countries. In Britain farmers commit suicide much more commonly than the rest of the population. U.S. farmers' suicides have significantly increased since the farm crisis began in the 1980s, and telephone hotlines still exist to deter them.

Even aside from such extreme cases, farming seems to be a disappearing profession. The average age of farmers in the United States, according to various estimates, is in the late 50s or even early 60s, very close to retirement age. Farmers in many other countries are similarly older than those workers in most other jobs. Even in China, the average age of farmers ranges by region from the 40s to 50s. Chinese officials report that in many rural areas the young people have left for cities and only "grandpa" or "grandma" farmers remain to grow crops. Farmers the world over suffer more than most workers from many illnesses and physical problems, including cancers from exposure to sun and chemicals, "farmer's lung" from exposure to crop and chemical dust, lost limbs from accidents, and psychological illnesses from the stresses of farming as a career. When a farmer retires, abandons the farm, dies, or commits suicide, it is not only a personal tragedy but a loss of valuable knowledge and experience for the world.

Global warming and agriculture

While there is some dispute about whether global warming has resulted from a natural cycle of the earth's climate or from greenhouse gases released by human energy use, it seems certain that the warming will continue and worsen for many decades at least. Warming began to affect world agriculture in the late nineteenth century, and its increasing intensity could be more devastating to agriculture than any previous events in human history. The most serious effect will result from the process that is the clearest evidence of warming: the melting of the world's glaciers, possible only because of climate change.

The most important glaciers for agriculture are located in the Himalaya Mountains and the Tibetan plateau, because they feed the Ganges, Yellow, and Yangtze rivers. The Ganges River and watershed provides water for more than 400 million people and irrigation for much of India's crops; the Yangtze River and watershed for some 500 million people, and irrigation for half of China's rice harvest. Both of these countries produce more wheat and rice than the U.S., as well as massive quantities of many other crops, most of which depend on irrigation. The Ganges and Yangtze flows have already begun to decrease, which has also lowered the water table, requiring irrigation pumps and wells to reach deeper for declining water supplies.

Global warming will also raise temperatures in the temperate regions, including the U.S., Canada, and Russia. These higher temperatures could increase grain production, but could also cause more intense and prolonged droughts. During a three-week heat wave of temperatures above 100 degrees in California's central valley in 2006, thousands of cattle dropped dead despite the fact that farmers set up fans to cool them. One county alone had losses of $85 million because of the heat. The U.S. also has rivers that run dry in summer, such as the Columbia, because of irrigation and urban needs.

Other regions could face serious difficulties. Central Africa, especially the Sahel region, will have much hotter growing seasons than ever before by 2050, hotter than farmers can adapt to with any crops available now. In South America, glaciers in the Andes that are the sources for many rivers are shrinking and disappearing.

Peak oil and agriculture

As discussed above, modern farming depends on fossil fuels. In the 1950s, an oil geologist, M. King Hubbert, showed that all oil wells follow the same pattern of rapid growth to a peak (now called Hubbert's Peak) and then decline. He argued that the same pattern applied to total global oil production. The very likely prospect of declining oil production will require more pervasive and rapid changes in farming than in any previous period in agrarian history. Two countries in the 1990s–2000s have experienced this kind of a collapse of oil supplies because of the collapse of the USSR, and present alternative images of global futures.

North Korea emulated the USSR and collectivized its agriculture on an industrial model, with extensive reliance on fuel-powered machinery. The USSR fell in 1991, and Russia and China now require payment for oil in hard currency, which North Korea did not have. Factories closed, farms returned to manual and horse labor, and three years of widespread flooding, 1994–96, devastated North Korean farming. Western news reports described the situation as a famine, and there was significant starvation, but the crisis was at root a nightmare-come-true of the collapse of an industrial farming system.

Cuba was another communist system devastated by the fall of the USSR. The new Russian government stopped providing cheap oil to Cuba, and stopped buying its sugar at five times the world market price. Food production and consumption declined, Cubans were consuming less than the minimum standard of the U.S., and on average lost 75 lbs. Castro consulted with agronomists, and the government actively introduced a series of reforms in agriculture. These included intensive, nearly organic farming to produce for domestic needs. Specialists devised local solutions to farm problems, including natural pest control techniques and composting fertilizer.

The arrival of Hubbert's Peak on anything like a global scale would entail vast changes difficult to imagine. Some writers argue that the world would ultimately return to medieval or even ancient styles of farm production, possibly even with a new slavery.

Sustainability

Even before the world would reach that level, however, existing farming systems have many characteristics that are unsustainable, in other words they cannot be continued without extremely serious environmental consequences or without losing their effectiveness. The examples that Rachel Carson identified in *Silent Spring*, of pesticides that cease to work as insects evolve resistance, is one example of a wider problem. Fertilizers and pesticides seep into groundwater or runoff into rivers, lakes, and oceans. They kill fish outright or cause algae blooms that deoxygenate the water, and making it impossible for other aquatic life to survive and the water dangerous for human use. Large-scale livestock feedlots or chicken houses produce millions of gallons of waste, often contained in lagoons that in some cases leak or overflow into local waters and fields, and create problems of smell and illnesses for the local population. Researchers are devising ways to deal with many of these problems, but some are much easier to solve than others.

The increasing corporate control of the world food system also threatens the genetic basis of agriculture by reducing biodiversity, the survival of different types of plants and animals. The expansion of farming by deforestation in the Amazon and elsewhere, the standardization of foods that requires farmers to raise uniform corn, bananas, or chickens, all reduce the number and varieties of crops and livestock. Such uniformity has had serious consequences. The Irish potato famine resulted from both a virulent plant disease and the uniformity of potatoes grown in Ireland. From the late nineteenth to the early twentieth centuries, commercial bananas were of the Gros Michel variety. A destructive fungal disease, Panama disease, spread despite farmers' desperate efforts to escape it, until by 1960 the Gros Michel could no longer be used. Fortunately scientists found a resistant variety, the Cavendish, and farmers and businesses shifted en masse to that variety at the cost of billions of dollars. Yet another plant disease is now threatening the Cavendish, which is again a genetically uniform variety.

Agricultural scientists are making concerted efforts to preserve the diversity we have left. Researchers in countries with Vavilov centers – geographical regions where the world's main food and livestock types originated – work to preserve these regions as key genetic resources. Most of the CGIAR and many other research centers maintain seed and semen collections. They use these to develop new varieties in response to chronic environmental threats, such as a recent rust disease from Uganda, Ug99, which threatens world wheat production. The largest and most important reserve is the "Doomsday Vault," a 500-foot-long building buried in an abandoned mine on one of the Svalbard Islands between Norway and the North Pole. Opened in 2008, it will preserve at least three million different varieties at a temperature of −4° F for at least 1,500 years.

Two related movements have developed among farmers and specialists to provide an alternative to unsustainable farming and uniformity: organic farming and sustainable agriculture. Organic farming as a concept was developed in the interwar years by British and American agricultural scientists, writers, and farmers who worried about the increasing use of artificial fertilizers and other chemicals in farming. One of the main propagators of these ideas was the Rodale Press, set up by the author J. I. Rodale to encourage farming without chemicals.

For most of human history all farmers were organic farmers, since artificial fertilizers did not exist until the nineteenth century and pesticides until the twentieth, on any significant scale. During the 1940s to 1960s, farmers and agricultural scientists dismissed organic farming as a fad and its arguments for non-use of chemicals as backward and unnecessary. After Rachel Carson's *Silent Spring*, the vindication of the dangers she identified, and the growing popular concern reflected in laws prohibiting certain pesticides, farmers and specialists took organic farming more seriously. By the 2000s, the USDA and agricultural agencies in many countries had established standards for organic farming, and many retailers carried organic produce or even specialized in such products. With the hazards to the environment, and to people, from agricultural runoff and vast factory farms, organic farming on an even larger scale may become necessary for public health.

Sustainable agriculture, a growing movement among agricultural scientists, farmers, and consumers, is the most comprehensive approach to address the problems of industrial farming. This approach includes not only farming in ways that can be continued indefinitely without harming the environment, but also farming that supports farmers and farm communities, and the urban societies that depend on them. One classic problem that sustainable agriculture seeks to address is farming in the American Great Plains. The region is so arid that farmers now rely on center-pivot irrigation systems to pump irrigation water from the large Ogallala aquifer. They have pumped up so much water that the aquifer has fallen to half of its original level and pumping is becoming very difficult. Before long it will be impossible to pump water from the aquifer, and not only will farming in that region become almost impossible but whole communities will become ghost towns and many people's lives will be disrupted. Meanwhile farming and cattle raising in the region have destroyed most of the grasslands, making the plains more subject to erosion, dust storms, and topsoil loss than earlier.

Sustainable agriculture urges people to approach farming in a more adaptable, flexible, and understanding manner that selects crops, livestock, and production methods compatible with the environment. This approach differs from most modern farming methods, which tend to see the soil as a sponge to hold crops and fertilizers. Sustainable farming involves in part an educated return to traditional farming methods that for most of the twentieth century were seen as backward and unproductive, but which did not cause anything like the vast and sometimes irreversible damage to environments and communities that modern farming has caused, and which supported people for thousands of years, albeit with serious interruptions. If the warnings of "peak oil" end up coming true, however, sustainable farming may be the only viable option for human survival.

Conclusion

The period from the Second World War to the twenty-first century saw remarkable changes in world farming. The central new factor was an almost unprecedented concern for farmers and agriculture, reflected in the establishment of the first truly global organizations to aid farmers, the Food and Agricultural Organization of the UN and the CGIAR. In addition, government agricultural agencies, agricultural research programs at universities and other educational and research institutions, and non-governmental organizations and farmers' groups all proliferated in almost every country in the world.

This new global concern for farming had substantial results. It led to a nearly unprecedented array of reforms to benefit farmers. Governments and businesses have provided more support for farmers and their work than ever before, from subsidy programs and pure and applied research to flexible loans and even counseling and suicide prevention lines. The technological improvements provided by new machinery, fertilizers and pesticides, and especially the genetic developments of the Green Revolution and GMOs allow farmers to produce more with less effort and worry than ever before. Land reforms implemented by many governments have provided more opportunities for individuals to farm than ever before, and have resolved some very old inequities. The payoff for the world has been unprecedented levels of food production, supporting more than six billion people in most countries with more than enough food, even if distribution remains a major problem. All of these changes have reduced the farmers' old dual subordination, at least as it prevailed in past societies.

Yet these improvements are not the whole story. First, they have not been distributed equally. Africa emerged from colonialism, but after a brief period of expansion farmers and agriculture in most of the continent fell into decline. A combination of vast environmental disasters, inept foreign aid programs, and flawed and corrupt governance has left African farmers impoverished and victimized by state policies, and Africa dependent on imports. Environmental problems of global warming, pollution, water shortage, and declining biodiversity threaten both farmers and urban societies. Agriculture's dependence on fossil fuels makes agriculture and world food supplies vulnerable to economic fluctuations, as well as the probable future decline in oil production. Farming in this period became globalized, and subject to both global opportunities and global risks.

Further reading

On Europe, see S. H. Franklin, *European Peasantry: The Final Phase* (London: Methuen, 1969). On communist agriculture, see Mieke Meurs, ed., *Many Shades of Red: State Policy and Collective Agriculture* (Lanham, MD: Rowman and Littlefield, 1999); Jean Chesneaux, *Peasant Revolts in China, 1840–1949* (New York: Norton, 1973); Dali Yang, *Calamity and Reform in China* (Stanford, CA: Stanford University Press, 1996); Kate Zhou, *How the Farmers Changed China* (Boulder, CO: Westview, 1996).

On the Green Revolution and biodiversity, see Lennard Bickel, *Facing Starvation: Norman Borlaug and the Fight against Hunger* (New York: Dutton, 1974); John H. Perkins, *Geopolitics and the Green Revolution* (New York: Oxford University Press, 1997); and Susan Dworkin, *The Viking in the Wheatfield* (New York: Walker and Company, 2009).

On the United States, see David Danbom, *Born in the Country: A History of Rural America* (Baltimore, MD: Johns Hopkins University Press, 1996); Bill Winders, *The Politics of Food Supply: U.S. Agricultural Policy in the World Economy* (New Haven, CA: Yale University Press, 2009).

On land reform, see Sidney Klein, *The Pattern of Land Tenure Reform in East Asia after World War II* (New York: Bookman Associates, 1958); Roy L. Prosterman and Jeffrey M. Riedinger, *Land Reform and Democratic Development* (Baltimore, MD: Johns Hopkins University Press, 1987).

On Latin America, see Tom Barry, *Zapata's Revenge: Free Trade and the Farm Crisis in Mexico* (Boston, MA: South End Press, 1999); Francisco Vidal Luna and Herbert S. Klein, *Brazil Since 1980* (Cambridge: Cambridge University Press, 2006); Gerardo Otero, ed., *Food for the Few: Neoliberal Globalism and Biotechnology in Latin America* (Austin, TX: University of Texas Press, 2008).

On Africa, see Göran Djurfeldt, *The African Food Crisis: Lessons from the Asian Green Revolution* (Cambridge, MA: CABI Publishers, 2005); Dahram Ghai and Samir Radwan, *Agrarian Policies and Rural Poverty in Africa* (Geneva: ILO, 1983); Lungesile Ntsebeza and Ruth Hall, *The Land Question in South Africa* (Cape Town: HSRC Press, 2007). On South Asia, see F. T. Jannuzi, *India's Persistent Dilemma* (Boulder, CO: Westview, 1994); Ashok Gulati and Shenggen Fan, eds., *The Dragon and the Elephant: Agricultural and Rural Reforms in China and India* (Baltimore, MD: Johns Hopkins University Press, 2007).

On globalization, see Raj Patel, *Stuffed and Starved: The Hidden Battle for the World Food System* (New York: Melville House Publishers, 2007); Geoff Tansey and Tony Worsley, *The Food System: A Guide* (London: Earthscan, 1995); Dale Allen Pfeiffer, *Eating Fossil Fuels: Oil, Food, and the Coming Crisis in Agriculture* (Gabriola Island, BC: New Society Publishers, 2006); Peter Pringle, *Food, Inc, Mendel to Monsanto* (New York: Simon and Schuster, 2005); Food and Agricultural Organization of the UN, *Livestock's Long Shadow: Environmental Issues and Options* (Rome: FAO, 2006).

Chapter 8

Conclusion

From the beginning of history, farmers appear as subject to both environmental disasters and dominance by empires and landlords. The earliest substantial records, from Ancient Greece, Rome, and China, show another side of farmers' conditions. Some leaders and other people outside agriculture recognized the oppression of farmers and tried to introduce the first reforms. At this phase the reforms were either limited in effect, or threatened powerful landlords, and were averted or reversed by violence.

A long cycle followed the collapse of the ancient civilizations: the medieval rise of servile systems and the early modern to modern emancipations. Again these changes reflected the emergence of leaders and groups outside agriculture willing to understand and sympathize with farmers' conditions and act on that understanding. Their actions also reflected, at least in part, the outsiders' recognition of the need for reform and modernization for their countries as a whole, in which farmers played an important but still subordinate part.

In the twentieth and twenty-first centuries, four developments outside of agriculture have raised the importance of agriculture and farming in new ways. First, the rapid advances of science and technology have been applied to farming since the late eighteenth century. These advances have resulted in nearly miraculous improvements but also made farming dependent on technology and energy supplies from outside agriculture. Second, environmental changes, especially global warming, have benefited some farmers but threatened to undermine farming in other regions. Third, rapid population growth expanded farming and markets, but also transferred land from farms to cities. Fourth, the expansion of corporations and their growing control over the world economy brought farmers, like workers in many other fields, into an intensely competitive market, and drove many, perhaps a majority of them, out of farming.

These developments have created a serious impending crisis by the early twenty-first century. Agriculture is now reaching global limits. Fresh water supplies are in decline as people drain aquifers and draw from rivers, so that rivers that in the past caused vast floods now run dry. Pollution from crop production and livestock raising now contaminates regional and international environments. Urban growth destroys not only farmland but also forests and other reserves of biodiversity. The dependence of farming on fossil fuels risks sudden price increases that can disrupt entire economies without warning.

The world agricultural system feeds, reasonably well, most of the world's six-plus billion people, with fewer farmers every year farming, with more advanced technologies and fossil fuels. In many countries farms also produce these supplies with poor laborers working under harsh conditions, while farmers grow older and retire every year. Farmers in many countries work under constraints imposed by governments for farm-support payments, or by corporations that provide seed or livestock and purchase produce to meet their standards. Some farmers work vast land areas under deadlines imposed by crops, weather, and contracts, while others work tiny subsistence plots which can also impose significant pressures. Many in the developed world stay in business on the basis of large government subsidies, which have to be confirmed every year and have been reduced in the past.

These descriptions indicate that world agriculture is functioning under significant strain, and with substantial vulnerability. Many industries, for example, have introduced the "just in time" system, in which, for example, automobile part suppliers ship parts to the assembly factory to arrive the day the factory needs them, to avoid storage costs. Whole countries and societies seem to be operating on an agricultural "just in time system," with food reserves sufficient for less than a year of consumption. In agriculture, such a system has unique risks. If auto parts are late, a factory can postpone production, but if food supplies are disrupted in any significant way, people can starve and a whole society could be disrupted. The cases of North Korea and Cuba could also anticipate future trends.

These considerations suggest that the old dual subordination is still operating, but in different, more global and more complex ways. Civilization still depends on agriculture, but agriculture now also depends on civilization. This interdependence seems unprecedented. Farmers in older societies, such as Ancient Greece, Tang China, or Mughal India, were relatively self-sufficient. They were certainly happy to trade their produce for manufactured goods from towns, and in crises they benefited from government relief, as in the Chinese "ever-normal granary" system. Still, when really necessary, farmers in these societies could survive on their own. Peasants had their own seed, their own livestock, and they could depend on their villages to an extent in emergencies. They were following practices that their ancestors had developed before civilization.

In the nineteenth century in the West and the twentieth century elsewhere, this situation changed. Civilization incorporated the farmers into itself, creating a relationship of interdependence. Somehow societies have to address this interdependence, the vulnerability of society and agriculture to dependence on oil, environmental threats, and socio-economic injustice. This rethinking is necessary because in the end, no matter how much these two sectors are interdependent, farmers are the ultimate source and resource for the continuation of civilization.

In this context, the first civilized farmers, the peasants, have certain lessons for the modern world. The peasants were low-energy producers, they recycled most of their waste, and they adapted to the environment and to markets, especially when the cities were somewhat considerate of them, as in certain periods in China, Vietnam, and the U.S. Jared Diamond blamed agriculture for the evils of civilization, but perhaps he misinterpreted the problem: it was not a situation of farming causing the evils of civilization, but of civilization ignorantly, but fortunately less and less as time went on, imposing harsh treatment on the farmers. The situation could be quite different if civilizations could learn from their unhappy pasts and treat farmers without exploitation and subordination, in a manner that respects the real dependence of civilization on agriculture.

Glossary

Assart a plot of land that has been cleared of brush and forest and planted with crops for the first time.

Autarquia Brazil, twentieth-century institution that regulated trade and production of particular farm products.

Bauchan daohu communist China, family responsibility system, euphemism term for family farming system that replaced Chinese collective farms after Mao Zedong's death.

Champa rice medieval China, rice variety from Vietnam that matured much faster than earlier Chinese varieties.

Chicago Board of Trade U.S., the oldest exchange for agricultural futures, founded in 1848, now part of the Chicago Mercantile Exchange.

Colonus/coloni a servile laborer, used in the late Roman Empire and early European Middle Ages.

Commons medieval and early modern England, section of village lands not included in regular rotations, open for poor and landless to use for residence and farming.

Demesne portion of land of medieval estate not allocated to peasants but farmed by the peasants under the direction of the noblility or church authorities.

Ejido Mexico, traditional peasant village, or common lands portion of a village.

El Niño/ENSO El Niño Southern Oscillation, warming of the eastern Pacific Ocean near Ecuador, associated with disruption of the monsoon rains in Asia, eastern Africa, and northeast South America.

Enclosure medieval and early modern England, a plot of land excluded from the peasants' village lands, surrounded by a fence, wall, or bushes.

Fayyum fertile irrigated district in Egypt, west of the Nile and south of the Nile Delta.

Hacienda colonial and independent Latin America, a landlord's estate, sometimes primarily oriented toward livestock, like a ranch.

Hectare 2.4 acres.

Hektemor   ancient Athens, a tenant farmer.

Helots   ancient Sparta, a servile farm laborer.

Hybrid   twentieth century, human-bred plant variety, initially corn plants bred by crossing pure lines.

HYV   twentieth century, high-yielding variety, specially selected varieties of wheat, rice, and other grains developed during the Green Revolution.

Inquilini   ancient Rome, tenant farmer.

Kolkhoz   Soviet Union, collective farm.

Latifundium, pl. latifundia   ancient Rome, a large farm.

Lex frumentaria   ancient Rome, law regulating grain prices.

Manor   European self-sufficient estate in the Middle Ages, usually populated by a lord and serfs.

Manse   European medieval agriculture, the large house of the lord.

Pampas   prairie region of Argentina.

Pastoralism   raising and moving livestock as a job or lifestyle.

Peasant   complex term, usually a farmer in an ancient, medieval, or developing country, who is usually not educated, lives in a village and farms by its rules, and is obliged to pay some sort of dues to an overlord.

Peon   mostly early modern or modern Latin America, a landless and usually indebted laborer who works on a hacienda or plantation to pay off the debt.

Quilombo   colonial Latin America, a settlement of escaped slaves.

Satyagraha   twentieth-century India, non-violent protest, initiated by Gandhi, took various forms.

Seisachtheia   ancient Athens, the document of Solon's reforms.

Serf   medieval Europe (though often applied more broadly), a servile farmer who works the lands of a manor in exchange for housing and a small land plot.

Servile   in many societies, unfree, restrained by custom, law, and power from independent activity, to degrees varying by time and place.

Slave   many societies, a worker considered to be the full property of an owner.

Sovkhoz   Soviet Union, state farm.

Three-field system   medieval Europe, crop rotation system alternating a spring crop, winter crop, and fallow. Early attempt to combat soil exhaustion.

Transhumance   pastoral practice of moving livestock, usually sheep, to pastures at higher altitudes in summer and lower altitudes in winter.

Tsing tien   ancient China, idealized "well-field system" in which fields are arrayed in a tic-tac-toe pattern around a well.

Zamindar   early modern and modern India, general term for a landlord, with a variety of regional meanings.

Index